Chips in a Bag, Classy Mr Murray

by Margaret Kelleher

ISBN 978-0-9933539-8-7

Copyright © 2017 Margaret Kelleher

Revised edition. All rights reserved. No parts of this publication may be reproduced, stored in a retrieval system or transmitted in any form or by any means, without the prior written permission of the author, nor be otherwise circulated in any form of binding or cover other than that in which it is published and without a similar condition being imposed by the purchaser.

This book is intended for your personal enjoyment only. All characters in this publication are fictitious and any resemblance to any person living or dead is purely coincidental. Published in Ireland by Orla Kelly Publishing Services. Proofread by Red Pen Edits.

Acknowledgements

I would like to begin by thanking everyone who have helped me on my first venture into the world of novel writing.

To my friends who waded through the first and second drafts, especially Jean O Sullivan, who was honest and astute and who should seriously consider editing as a career.

To Vanessa O Loughlin and Mary Stanley of The Inkwell Group for their invaluable advice.

Thank you Orla Kelly for helping me to finally push this baby from the nest!

Most importantly I would like to thank my family for believing in me. To my son Chris for designing the perfect book cover. It is good to know that all that money spent on his education was worth it!

Cover design by Chris Kelleher.

About the Author

Margaret Kelleher attended Mary Immaculate College of Education and spent the next thirty five years as a Primary School teacher.

Now retired, she is beginning the journey into her new career as a writer.

She lives in Cork with her husband and family.

Chips in a bag…Classy Mr. Murray is her first novel.

Contents

Prologue	vi
Chapter One	1
Chapter Two	11
Chapter Three	21
Chapter Four	39
Chapter Five	56
Chapter Six	72
Chapter Seven	92
Chapter Eight	109
Chapter Nine	129
Chapter Ten	142
Chapter Eleven	157
Chapter Twelve	164
Chapter Thirteen	183
Chapter Fourteen	201
Chapter Fifteen	216
Chapter Sixteen	226
Chapter Seventeen	239
Chapter Eighteen	249
Chapter Nineteen	254
Chapter Twenty	277
Chapter Twenty-One	289
Chapter Twenty-Two	302

Prologue

Brandon Lodge

Cascading red curls caressed the wood panelling behind her as she moved her head to the music. He wanted to stand there and stare at her profile all night, but he had to approach her.

"You've been stood up, pretty girl!"

Clodagh Kenny turned around. What the hell! He was drop dead gorgeous. From his coal black hair curling sexily on the collar of his jacket all the way down his long, long legs. She flicked her curls and eyeballed him, grateful for once for her height.

"Are you talking to me?"

"Indeed I am! Clodagh Kenny, I believe? James Murray at your service."

"Is this some sort of joke? Has my sister put you up to this? Come to think of it, I haven't seen her in a while. She's probably hiding somewhere nearby, laughing at me." Clodagh looked down at the spacious hall, convinced that Claire had planned this whole scenario. "I hope you've been well paid. You're not going to strip – I hope! I'll kill that sister of mine. She knows how much I hate surprises."

"Relax, no shedding of clothes, I promise. I haven't been hired by anyone, but maybe I should consider it as a side-line. The security business can be unreliable at the best of times!"

"I don't think so and if that is your idea of a chat up line… Anyway, I have a date tonight and Richard will be arriving soon." Clodagh looked down over the side of the spiral staircase again, hoping to see her boyfriend.

James came and stood beside her.

"Actually you've said the magic word… Richard is the reason that I know so much about you. He told me to look for the tallest, most beautiful stunning girl with long, long red curly hair and a smile that would light up the darkest night… so you were very easy to find."

"He said all that about me? How sweet!" Clodagh blushed and James had the grace to look guilty.

"Well, most of it. I added in the bit about your hair... stunning... tall. I'm sure he would agree with me but he is a man of few words. He gave me this."

He produced a photo from his inside pocket.

"I hate that dress. It makes me look like a blade of grass!" Clodagh was horrified. "Oh my God! I'll throttle him. Why do you have this?" she asked.

"I'm afraid Richard won't be coming tonight. He really wanted to but he was needed at home. One of the cows was due to calve or something. You know how much work he does on the farm since his Dad died and his mother depends on him so much. She is also very, very devout so I suspect that she didn't want him to go out during Holy Week. He is too nice to upset her, so he asked me to keep you company. He knew I was coming here and he didn't want you to be alone on your birthday. Maybe we can sit down over here and get to know one another a little better." He spotted an empty couch under the huge gilt mirror.

"Imagine being stood up for a cow on my birthday! That has to be a first," Clodagh burst out laughing.

"It was a very valuable cow! Anyway, it's your birthday so why don't we do as he wanted and celebrate it. Happy seventeenth birthday Clodagh Kenny." he said and then kissed her on the cheek.

"You know my name, you have my photo, and you know that it's my birthday, and my age. I'm wondering how much more you have been told. I wouldn't be surprised if you knew my shoe size as well!" said Clodagh.

"Ah, now you are expecting too much! Give me a chance. I'm only an innocent Kerryman! What do you call those things anyway?" he asked, glancing at her footwear.

"You really need to update your shoe knowledge. They are called platforms. It is the late seventies. You need to move with the times! These are the latest." Clodagh cocked her foot up so he could have a closer look.

"Those things are so high, you would need a stepladder to climb into them. It's no wonder you are as tall as I am."

"You sound just like my father. What age are you anyway?"

"Well, what age would you like me to be?" he asked.

"Well twenty would be nice, but I'm guessing that the last time you saw that number was printed on a door."

"The lady bites! Nasty, but true." he laughed.

"Just as well I'm thick-skinned, and like girls with attitude. I'm only twenty-four but that must seem ancient to a young one of seventeen. Hopefully my charming personality will compensate for you having to spend the evening with an older man. You can tell your parents that I was only standing in for Richard. I wouldn't want your father chasing me with a shotgun." James declared.

"Actually my mother would welcome you with open arms and a large slab of apple tart. My Dad is ten years older than her and she is determined to ensure that my sister Claire and I end up as happy as they are. I'm not sure what the age thing has to do with it."

"Well in that case Miss Kenny we should hit the dance floor. I'm pretty good so please try not to step on my toes with those ladders." he smiled and held out his hand.

"You really are full of yourself, Mr Murray!"

"I'll give you that one as a birthday present. Ready?"

They walked to the top of the spiral staircase and were about to walk down when James spotted his friends heading up towards them.

"These are the noisy lot that I came here with tonight. Let me introduce you to them. They will vouch for the fact that I am not an axe murderer and that you are quite safe in my company."

"Hi James! Looks like you are glad you came after all. Who is your new friend?" She turned to Clodagh. "I'm this fellow's sister, Mary, and these are Conor, Kate, Jimmy, Angela, Mark, Paddy and lots more. You are?" Mary smiled.

"This is Clodagh and you lot are drunk." James retorted.

"Ah brother, don't be such a killjoy. How often does a sensible married woman get a chance to let her hair down? You are the baby in the family so act like it. Conor will be going away tomorrow so let's have fun. I'm heading for the bar. Who's coming with me? Nice to meet you Clodagh." Mary waved and headed off, followed by all but one of the girls.

"You not going with them Kate?" James asked

She shrugged and sat down on one of the chairs by the wall.

"I'll stay here for a while with you. You did promise me a dance once you had completed your good deed for the night and spent some time with Richards's young one." She turned to Clodagh. "I presume you're the object of his Act of Mercy. Hope you don't mind if I steal him away. I'm sure you have some young friends around here somewhere! James and I have some catching up to do." She slipped her hand through his arm.

Clodagh stepped back. "I'm not anyone's Act of Mercy and have plenty of friends here. Enjoy your night. Thank you James for passing on the message." She skipped down the stairs and disappeared into the crowded dance floor.

"What did you do that for? It was rude and totally uncalled for. I haven't seen you since Mary's wedding and didn't even know you were coming tonight. We definitely didn't have any arrangement to dance." James fumed.

"Ah relax. I could see that you wanted to be rescued. Mary told me about Richard. That poor eejit is so scared of his mother that he couldn't even take his girlfriend out on her birthday. Why would you want to spend the evening with a teenager when you could be with a real woman!" she caressed his arm.

"I think you have had too much to drink, Kate. Your boyfriend would thump me if he thought that I was within half a mile of you, not to mind what your old man would do. Thanks for the thought but I liked her company and now I'm going to see if I can find her and apologise to her. You sit here for a while and I'll find Mary to keep you company. Good night Kate." James followed Clodagh into the crowd.

Clodagh was furious. That cheeky bitch Kate. Even if she was his girlfriend, she had no right to be so rude. James was nice and she had enjoyed his company. She couldn't find Claire anywhere. The music was lovely and she was itching to dance.

"I'm sorry Clodagh." James appeared beside her.

"You startled me. Where's the girlfriend? I wouldn't want to get on the wrong side of her again." She looked over his shoulder.

"She's not my girlfriend. She never was. She works with my sister and I haven't seen her for ages. She decided I needed rescuing but she was wrong. I promised you a dance so I hope you will agree. I will be gutted if I have to go home without having danced with the most beautiful girl in this ballroom, even if I am just standing in for one of the luckiest boyfriends in the country."

She smiled and held out her hand.

"I take that as a yes then, Miss Kenny. Just for one evening let's become part of the magic of this beautiful hotel. Shall we have our first dance together? We might even get as far as having a bag of chips later just to celebrate your birthday." They moved onto the floor.

She looked him in the eye. "Chips in a bag! Very classy, Mr Murray."

Chapter One

Clodagh & David
The hauntingly beautiful Brandon Lodge had guarded the village of Keele for nearly two centuries. Beneath rolling hills and surrounded by acres of fields dotted with tiny manmade lakes, it had undergone many changes. The solid stone walls had absorbed the laughter and joy of life and the sadness of death. Now all that seeped through was the dampness of silence and decay. The windows that once gleamed in the sunshine were now cracked and smeared with the handprints of those who thought that the sound of breaking glass was a modern sport to be proud of.

"It is so desolate looking. I can't believe it's been thirty years since I danced here." Clodagh looked at David.

He peered in the windows but all he could see was a dust laden staircase.

"If that is the stairs that you glided up and down on, then you had better not come any closer or all your illusions will be shattered," he said gently.

"This must be the auctioneer now." They watched as the black Mercedes raced up the avenue and braked suddenly scattering stones and dust. The flustered thirty-something occupant grabbed his jacket and a set of keys before presenting himself to Clodagh and David.

"Mr McGovern, Miss Kenny. I'm John Carey. I'm so sorry that I'm late. I had a problem locating some of the keys." He ran up the five steps and unlocked the faded blue door to the house which creaked before admitting the visitors into the dusty hallway.

"We cannot use the main staircase to access the upstairs rooms as it has been vandalised but we can use the other which is at the end of this corridor. You particularly wanted to see the ballroom. It is this way." He pointed towards a large room visible through an open archway."

"I'm afraid that the chandelier has been taken down as the house has been broken into on a few occasions. It is in storage, as is the one from the upstairs landing. I will give you a quick tour of the house before showing you the outside units which, I believe, you plan to develop and let out," he paused to draw breath.

"If we decide to purchase this house and lands, then we have plans to open Brandon Lodge as a type of Enterprise Park. I believe that steps have been taken to safeguard the house from further vandalism." David checked his notes.

"Yes, of course. A local company has been employed to watch the place, but to be honest, the owners have limited resources and this place is so vast, that it is difficult to implement a long-term plan before the future of the property has been secured," John Carey answered.

"I understand there is over two hundred acres here, as well as the main house and buildings. Maybe we will come back to the house in a while. If we could see the courtyard and the other buildings first. What do you think, Clodagh?" David was worried by the fact that the usually chatty woman hadn't spoken since they had entered the house.

"Sorry, I was miles away. This room used to be so beautiful." She shook the heavy brocade curtains and was rewarded with a cloud of dust. "Sorry."

She coughed and followed the men back out into narrow corridor that led out into what used to be the main kitchen. The fireplace took up one wall, opposite which a huge semi-circular window allowed the shafts of sunlight to dance on the grey flagstones.

"This would make a lovely little restaurant. What do you think David?" Clodagh walked across the flagstones and stood by the huge fireplace.

"Yes, I can see the attraction and it is a natural meeting point." David stood in the middle of the room and looked out onto the courtyard. The stables and outhouses were sitting in a straight line facing the kitchen.

"Let's have a look at the outside units. We can come back to the house later," David said.

"As you wish." John Carey walked ahead.

"We will follow you in a moment." David looked back to where Clodagh was standing trance-like in the middle of the floor.

"Are you feeling alright, Clodagh?" He gently touched her shoulder.

"I'm fine, David. It has been so long since I was here. The picture that I carried is nothing like the reality. Coming back here has been… strange. Still, onwards and upwards. I want to show you the cute little cottage that I have earmarked for my shop." She tucked her arm into David's and they walked outside into the blinding July sunshine.

Clodagh immediately led David over to the stone cottage and asked for the door to be unlocked.

Stepping inside, she opened the shutters and sunlight immediately flooded the large room.

"See what I mean? It is just perfect. I can have the main shop in here and my workshop in one of the smaller rooms. This cottage is connected to the kitchen by a corridor so my customers can walk between here and the restaurant. This used to be where all the laundry and repairs were done and my grandmother worked in this very room for over forty years. It's in the genes!" She twirled around the room.

"Well, you have all that worked out!" David was delighted at her sudden show of enthusiasm.

"Why don't we look at the other units? We can come back in here again afterwards," David said.

John Carey observed the couple and wondered at their relationship. She was a very attractive forty-something redhead and he was a flamboyant English gentleman, probably in his sixties. Neither wore a wedding ring and were very comfortable in each other's company. Her hair fell to her shoulders and she wore skinny jeans and a purple sweater that oozed luxury. David McGovern wore a silver grey pinstriped suit and red waistcoat. A red and grey spotted bow tie completed the outfit. The fact that they were interested in buying this sprawling estate marked them out as having money, as much as the gleaming BMW parked in the driveway did. The property had been on the market for over two years and the whole village waited and hoped for a positive outcome.

"Sorry for keeping you waiting, John. I think we are ready to continue the inspection now," David smiled.

"Take your time. There is a lot to take in. This place is very beautiful," John told them.

"What can you tell us about these outhouses?" David pointed to the group of six stone buildings which faced onto the courtyard.

"These were used as stables until recently so they are structurally sound." He unlocked and opened the solid door.

"Wow. It's magical in here." Clodagh walked to the centre of the rectangular space and stood in the path of sunlight that streamed through the three windows high up on the back wall.

"It is larger than I had expected. Are the other units of similar size?" David asked.

"Four of the other five are the same size but the last in the row is slightly smaller. I believe it was used to store the animal foodstuff." The two men walked back outside.

"Would it be possible for David and I to wander around on our own for a while? We could give you a call when we are finished. There would be quite a lot of work to be done – if we decided to go ahead with the project." Clodagh said as she re-joined them in the courtyard.

"No problem. I will be available for as long as you need me. If you would like to discuss your plans over lunch, I can recommend The Horseshoe Arms on the main street. It is within walking distance, just through the archway behind the main house." He pointed out the pathway.

"Thank you, John. We will see you later so." They shook hands.

As they watched him drive away, David turned to Clodagh.

"You seem very distracted. Are you having second thoughts?"

"No. I still want to come back here and open my shop. It is just that it seems different and yet the same..."

"Do you want to take another look around and then we can get some lunch. We can take as long as we like deciding about this. The asking price is reasonable and the other backers are happy to let me make the final decision. The place is perfect for a golf course and the house could be restored and rented out for corporate events. The plans also show some cottages by the back wall. Those could be converted into holiday homes. The management of the retail units would be your department," David said.

"It would be great to see this place alive again. The fact that it already has planning permission is a bonus. The grounds are huge. Do you fancy a walk? I want to show you something special, though you had better leave your jacket in the car. It's really hot."

"Why not! A walk would be lovely. Give me a minute." David grabbed his bag from the boot of the car and headed in the direction of the stone cottage that Clodagh had earmarked for her shop.

"Well, I never would have guessed!" Clodagh laughed as David reappeared.

"I come prepared. I even have the footwear," David indicated the runners he wore under his denim jeans and casual Armani t-shirt.

"Where to, my lady?"

"Follow me, sir."

They walked back passed the main house and followed the path over the wooden bridge and headed towards the small lake.

"As far back as I can remember swans have lived on that lake. I wonder if they are the same ones." She pointed at the two swans gliding gently on the still water.

"They might be but I am not an expert on swans. Where exactly are you taking me? This place is huge. All I can see are green fields." David stopped and looked around him.

"Just a little further on. It will be worth it." Clodagh linked him by the arm.

"Here we are." A few minutes later Clodagh led David through a small opening almost hidden by overhanging branches.

"There should be a gate here somewhere." She looked to her left and spotted the rusted gate. "I think we might have to climb over it."

"Maybe not. It looks like it might fall down easily enough. We may not be the only people who have visited recently." David pointed to the empty bottles and cans next to the burned out grass. He pushed at the gate and it moved easily enough.

"Oh God, it is wrecked!" Clodagh was devastated by the graffiti covered wishing chair.

David put his arm around her shoulders.

"Just close your eyes and imagine it is as it used to be. It can be restored to its former glory. Do you want to tell me about it?"

"It used to be so beautiful. There were flowers all along the back wall there." She pointed to the crumbling stone wall that was littered with cans and other rubbish.

"The chair was meant to be special… if you sat on it with the person you loved, then all your dreams would come true," she said sadly.

"Let's go and get something to eat." He took her hand.

The whole village had waited over seven months to find out exactly what was to happen in Brandon Lodge ever since the news had been filtered through the grapevine that it had been sold. Construction work had begun in August and was still ongoing. Now a meeting was due to take place and not even the dreary January weather was going to stop any of the residents from attending.

Ann

Ann Sheehan had arrived early so as not to miss out on any of the proceedings. She had her heart set on recreating an old-style Tearoom complete with whitewashed stone walls, lots of gingham tablecloths and china teapots! She twirled her long plait between her fingers as she watched the other people arriving. She pulled at her denim miniskirt and tried to stretch it down over her thick, black tights. Maybe she should have worn something more fashionable than ankle high boots which probably looked more suited to mountain climbing than being a business woman. Well, she was twenty-eight so she was entitled to look a little different to the gaggle of middle-aged men and women that were beginning to take their seats clutching the cups of coffee and tea that were being provided at the back of the hall.

She noticed that a few of the customers from the local bakery where she worked were chatting by the marble fireplace. She wondered what their interest in the place might be. She knew that Robert Munroe was a widower and was retired. He definitely would not be competition for a Tearoom. He had often bought cakes from her and she had given him simple recipes for healthy meals that she had devised herself. He had lovely manners and thanked her by giving her plants from his garden for her mother.

He was chatting to John Carey. The more Ann thought about what a big undertaking this would be, the more stressed she became and the more she twisted her hair between her fingers. She was so preoccupied that she hadn't noticed Robert crossing the room until he sat in the chair next to her.

"Hi Ann, I'm so glad to see you here. Hope this thing kicks off soon. Are you still interested in opening your own restaurant?" Robert smiled at her.

"Hopefully. I just hope I can afford the lease. Some of this crowd look more like business success stories than me!" she shrugged.

"Don't put yourself down. You are an excellent business woman. You practically run that bakery by yourself. You have a great manner with the customers and I am certain that you would make a success of any challenge. I have first-hand knowledge of how delicious your recipes are. As for your scones and cakes, they are second to none. Don't you dare underestimate yourself!" he scolded her.

Ann laughed out loud.

"Yes, sir. Do you mind me asking why you are here? You didn't mention being interested before," she looked at him curiously.

"I had a good talking to from my daughter Greta. She told me that I needed to get an outside interest. I even surprised myself when I said that I was thinking of opening a bookshop in Brandon Lodge."

Gary

Gary Maguire arrived just as the meeting was about to begin. He stood at the side of the room as all the chairs seemed to be occupied. He had just returned from Australia with a slightly dented heart and a pile of qualifications and he hadn't a clue what to do with them. He was good with his hands and could roll pastry as effectively as he could paint a sign. He was hoping to get some sign painting work as he had heard that the units were about to be allocated. He stroked his goatee beard and scanned the room.

A few rows from the back, he spotted long, thin fingers furiously twirling the longest plait that he hadn't seen in years.

'Ah, Rapunzel is here,' he thought to himself. 'I must have a chat with her before I leave.'

The Meeting

Several people took their places on the podium, all men except for two women. They looked like mother and daughter. The young woman was in her late twenties. She was smartly dressed in expensive jeans and a beautifully cut black jacket over a white silk shirt. Her black hair was interspersed with blood red streaks. It was poker straight and almost to her waist. The older woman was of similar height but her auburn hair fell in waves to just below her shoulders. Between them sat a short, stocky man. He wore a pink shirt over jeans, topped off with a wine-coloured jacket.

David McGovern stood up and addressed the room.

"Good evening. I am David McGovern and I would like to welcome you here on this very cold January night. I'm very glad to see that so many of you have braved the elements to venture out in such inclement weather. As you are aware my partners and

I have recently purchased Brandon Lodge and its grounds, which includes the beautiful hotel building and the cluster of cottages and stables. I hope, with the help of local entrepreneurs, to make it into a very successful venture. I would like to hear from anyone interested in renting units."

He paused to look around the room.

"I have brought a number of advisors together in order to help anyone with a viable idea. There are a number of grants available, so if you think you have a good plan then feel free to discuss it with the people seated around the room. I would like to introduce you to the woman who will be overseeing the running of the units." He pointed to Clodagh who had risen to her feet just behind him. The black wrap-around dress clung to her like a second skin. She oozed sexuality and confidence. She tossed her shoulder length hair as she approached the microphone.

"This is Clodagh Kenny and she will be opening a yarn shop which will not only sell exclusive yarns but will also feature her own collection of felted bags and cashmere shawls. I'm not an expert on all things associated with the world of yarn, so I will leave it to her to explain more clearly. Though I am reliably informed that no introduction is necessary. Ladies and gentlemen, I give you Clodagh Kenny." David moved to one side.

Clodagh smiled at David before turning to the crowded hall.

"Good evening. I still find it hard to believe that I am back in Ireland and opening a shop in Brandon Lodge. Even though I have spent over thirty years in London, I have always wanted to return home. Brandon Lodge has always held a special place in my heart.

As David has already mentioned, I will be opening Beth's Knits in the cottage to the left of the main house. I hope to make lots of new friends and sincerely hope that this venture takes off. Good luck to all of you. If I can be of any assistance, please feel free to ask me any questions. I look forward to getting to know each and every one of you. I'll hand you back to David and will talk to you soon." She gestured to David.

"What do you think of her?" Robert turned to Ann.

"She is very elegant. I love the dress and that purple wrap is to die for. My mother used to know her sister Claire years ago. They hung around together. She didn't know Clodagh well but said that they were a lovely family. Clodagh was almost engaged to some fellow but something happened and she went to London. She lived with her aunt who was a well-known knitwear designer. I guess it was hereditary. Clodagh is famous in London. That girl with her could be her daughter." Ann looked at Robert who was staring at Clodagh.

"She is very attractive, isn't she?"

Robert looked at the young woman beside him.

"Yes, she is but that's not why we are here. Why don't we mingle and get as much information as we can? After all, your restaurant and my bookshop will not open themselves. We can compare notes afterwards. Let's start with getting a coffee, though it's not a patch on yours. See you in a while. Good luck." He stood up and began to make his way across the room.

Ann's eyes followed his progress and alighted on a face that was a blast from the past.

"Gary Maguire! I thought you and Amy were in Australia. When did you get back?"

"Hi Rapunzel, you haven't changed a bit. Why are you here?"

"I'm hoping to rent one of the units as a Tearoom. What's your interest in the place?" She twirled her hair between her fingers.

"I'm hoping to get some painting work, but I would be prepared to roll some pastry if necessary. How about a coffee and we can catch up on the last few years? You can tell me what you have been up to." Gary led the way to the back of the room.

Chapter Two

James
James Murray picked up the file that Conor had left on his desk.

"Brandon Lodge. Now that's a blast from the past."

"You okay, James? It's a bad sign when you start talking to yourself!" Conor unwound his scarf and closed the door behind him.

"Oh, hi Conor. Don't mind me. Just thinking out loud. How long have we been involved with this place?"

Conor moved some papers around on his desk. "We moved in there last August. You have a bit of catching up to do now that you have decided to work back here permanently."

"All the travelling gets boring after a while. The younger generation can have that gig from now on." James sat on the edge of his desk. "Tell me about Brandon Lodge. I used to know the place – even danced there, back in the day," he continued.

"It closed about ten years ago and lately has become a target for vandals, which is where we come in. The new owners are reopening it. It has many outhouses, which have been leased out. A lot of work has been completed and all the units are due to be allocated. There's a problem with the hotel itself so the official opening won't be able to go ahead until that's sorted out." Conor moved to the kitchenette to put the kettle on.

"One of us will have to meet this David McGovern tomorrow afternoon. He will only be in Ireland for a few days. He's visiting friends, attending some birthday celebration." Conor handed James a coffee.

"I would like to see the place again, so I will go." James opened the file and looked through the photographs.

"Fair enough. We have a lot of projects on, so that suits me. It is a lovely place. I have been there a few times." Conor told him. "Come to think about it, wasn't that the place we went to when you were chasing some girl in a photo? Didn't she become your girlfriend for a while? Caroline or Caoimhe or something like that. It was while I was in London so I only met her the once," Conor asked.

"Clodagh, her name was Clodagh."

"That's it, Clodagh. You might bump into her again. You could certainly do with cheering up. I worry about you sometimes. I missed a lot when I was in England. I was only supposed to stay for a few months but that turned into five years. By the time I came home you were with Kate and had the twins – I didn't see that one coming at all. You and Kate barely knew one another. And now you have been on your own too long. Why don't you join one of those online dating sites? Find yourself a nice woman. You're not getting any younger brother." Conor sipped his coffee.

"You certainly know how to make someone feel old. Just because you are happily married. As for meeting Clodagh in Brandon Lodge, that's not a possibility. She went to London years ago. You'd have more of a chance of bumping into her on one of your frequent trips over there," James answered sharply.

"You okay? I didn't mean to open up any old wounds. I know that there was more to the story than I knew. If you don't mind me asking. Who broke up with who?" Conor looked at his brother.

"That's too long a story to go into now. We have more important things to discuss, like earning a living. I'll study the file and keep you in the picture. You will be busy with that new job in Listowel, so I'll take charge of this one," James said and checked his watch.

"That suits me. You know more about the place anyway. Let me know how it goes. I might not see you before the weekend. I've a few meetings arranged and I have to check on the factory in Fossa. Will catch up with you soon." Conor put his cup on the desk and left the office.

"I'll wash your cup, shall I?" James addressed the empty office.

James parked the jeep in the grounds of The Horseshoe Arms and hoped that he would be able to get a table.

Chips in a Bag, Classy Mr Murray

The bar was crowded. He spotted a high stool that had just been vacated. Soon his order had been taken. He liked to watch people and looked around him while he waited for his food.

Snippets of conversations sailed over his head until the words Brandon Lodge grabbed his attention. Glancing around him he saw two young women with their heads stuck inside a very large carrier bag.

"I couldn't resist showing it off, it's absolutely gorgeous. You have to be able to handle them in order to see the intricate little details that make each one unique. Imagine she is opening a shop a mile away from my house. How cool is that. You can practically see Brandon Lodge from my bedroom window."

James was so curious to know what item was lurking in the bag that he was almost tempted to ask. He waited for the unveiling. Eventually both women straightened up.

A handbag dangled from one arm.

"Wow Angela, it's to die for. That's one of the latest ones. I saw the collection online. I didn't think that you could get them yet. Tell me how you met her?"

"As you know we are opening a crèche in the new Brandon Lodge. It's almost directly opposite her new place. I was there last week helping to set up the new furniture when a delivery came for her. Her place was closed so I signed for it and stored it in the crèche overnight. She was delighted because if it had been taken away, she would have to wait days for it to be redelivered. She actually gave me the bag. I still can't bear to take it out of the carrier bag. I knew that you of all people would appreciate such beauty so I brought it to show you." Angela gave it a twirl before handing it to her friend.

Lunch arrived for the two girls so the bag was reverently placed back into the carrier bag which had the logo "Beth's Knits" printed on the front in vibrant reds and purples.

"Here you are, sir. Can I get you anything else?" The waitress placed the plate in front of him.

"That's great, thanks," he smiled at her.

James noted that the bar had been extended and modernised since he and Clodagh used to drink there. Well, it had been thirty years so changes were inevitable! Gone were the bare tiles and wooden barrels which had doubled as tables…replaced by wooden floors and tables.

He couldn't get Clodagh out of his mind. Each time he tried to push the memories away, they kept fighting their way back. It only seemed like yesterday since they had met, yet he knew that she had turned fifty the previous day.

She was probably married and living happily in London with her doting husband and two point four children. It was too late for regrets. That knitted handbag was just another reminder of her. When they were together she had been forever designing and making scarves and handbags.

Poor Richard was still living at home with his mother. It hadn't worked out between him and Clodagh. She and James had become a couple a few months after that, yet they had always considered her birthday to be the date that they celebrated their anniversary on.

By four o'clock he was pulling off the main road and driving into Brandon Lodge. It had been transformed since he had last seen it. The hotel itself looked empty and sad. It was cordoned off but the surrounding buildings were hives of activity. Painters, sign makers, and delivery trucks littered the courtyard. In the midst of the chaos stood a very dapper gentleman whom James presumed to be David McGovern.

He parked in front of the hotel.

"James Murray. Delighted to meet you, Mr McGovern." They shook hands.

"Please call me David. This is a beautiful place. I'll give you the grand tour. We will just about have time before darkness starts to fall. March can still be so cold and dark. Everything is progressing well but unfortunately the hotel won't be ready to be opened until November. After much discussion, we decided to go ahead with opening the units as soon as possible. You ready?" David asked.

"Lead the way. I understand that you want security on all the units, as well as on the hotel itself. You will receive a detailed breakdown in the next few days," James said taking out a notebook.

"We can start over here with the restaurant. As you can see it was originally built onto the front of the house as an L-shaped kitchen. It is now a Tearoom. The courtyard section beside it will be used for outdoor seating. The stables have all been converted into units suitable for any business. Some are good to go and the others will be moving in soon. As you can see, they are numbered one to six, one being the largest one to the left as we look at them. That one is a crèche. Next to it is a gym. Number three and number four are being opened as a vintage inspired shop and a milliner. Five and six are still free. By the gate is a bookshop and of course, behind us is Beth's Knits. The names are being painted as we speak. We have tried to employ as many local people as possible. We are also investing in the locality and are looking at ways of doing that. Maybe a park, or computers for the school? We are still considering it," David said.

"I can show you the inside of the hotel. We can pick up the hard hats over here," he said indicating a supply shed to their left.

"I already know this place pretty well. I used to frequent it when it was a dance venue. Mind you, that was back in the seventies and eighties so I suppose my memories may not coincide with today's reality. It was really popular back then. All the best show bands were delighted to play here. The bar was very quaint. Is it still standing?" James asked.

"It is indeed. I have it on good authority that even some of the décor is the same," he added with a smile.

"I didn't realise that you had connections to the place," James looked at him curiously.

"Not me personally. My interest is purely business. I'm always on the lookout for a good business opportunity and Brandon Lodge ticked all the boxes. I will be over and back from London on a regular basis, so for now you will be dealing directly with me. I do have a man who keeps an eye on the nuts and bolts, so to speak. Here Eamonn is now." David finished.

Both men turned as Eamonn approached.

"Pleased to meet you, Mr Murray. I have already met with your brother, Conor," Eamonn extended his hand.

"Likewise, Eamonn," James shook the other man's hand.

Eamonn turned to David.

"I will be in the site office in about fifteen minutes. That will give you time to see the inside of the hotel. You will only be able to go into certain rooms. The staircase is partly dismantled, so use the backstairs if you wish to see the first floor. I'll see you both soon." His mobile rang as he turned to go.

The two men walked into the hotel through the glass doors that opened into the old kitchen. James was amazed at the obvious transformation.

The huge open fireplace which dominated the back wall was flagged on one side by a glass cabinet which housed various cakes and desserts, and on the other by a sideboard which was tastefully set with willow patterned sets of china cups, saucers and side plates.

"This reminds me of my grandmother's kitchen. That sideboard is just like the one that she had. I thought sets of china were obsolete. It's usually mugs these days," James said.

"Well you can't get better than tea from a proper china cup and the young woman who has leased this kitchen fully intends to retain all the old traditions. She is even considering baking bread in that pot in the fireplace!" David added.

"Is it ready for business? I wouldn't mind trying some of that apple tart. It is a favourite of mine," James asked.

"Indeed it is. Some of the units are already up and running, though they officially open for business tomorrow. Ann has been feeding the workforce here for the past few weeks, hence the food. She is probably delivering sandwiches at the moment. You can drop back in before you leave. We had better move on. We can go through here and along the corridor to where the staircase is located." David led the way.

After walking through as much of the hotel as they could, David led James to the site cabin which was parked to the front of the hotel. Eamonn had the plans laid out on the table.

"About two years ago the hotel was targeted by thieves. Some antique furniture and valuable paintings were taken. The owner then decided to put it on the market as his insurance company were going to withdraw cover unless twenty-four-hour security was put on the place. It took a while to sell, so it was targeted again. This time machinery was taken. Now that some of the units have been outfitted we need to finalise security as quickly as possible. Some of the businesses will be open quite late in the evening, so people need to see that security is top priority. We need alarms, regular patrols, cameras, fencing and twenty-four-hour surveillance." Eamonn pointed to the plans on the table.

David and James pored over the map.

"You have seen the units that are ready to open for business. I will let you have a list of businesses and owners as soon as possible."

"What about the hotel? Do you have a long-term goal for it?" James asked.

"That's a tricky one at the moment. It is not a huge building. It has only twenty rooms, plus the bar, ballroom and restaurant. I will have to wait until the staircase is put back in. The people I work with would like to see it used for corporate weekends and maybe have a spa included," David said.

When the meeting was over, the men walked back out to the courtyard.

"I think that we have covered everything. I must get back to my hotel. I will forward all the paperwork to you in the next few days. It has been a pleasure, James." David extended his hand.

As he walked to his car, David's phone rang. He waved at James and answered the call.

"Hello, Beth. Okay, I'll be leaving now, before she arrives. I don't want to spoil the surprise. You have spent long enough planning it. See you later, darling."

After David had left, James retraced his steps. He was heading for the kitchen when he noticed that the sign was being painted on the wool shop.

He made his way across and noticed that the logo was the same as the one that he had seen earlier in the bar.

The sign maker was standing at the foot of the ladder. So this was the place that caused all the fuss. He decided to have a closer look.

"Nice work. Definitely worth looking at!"

"Thanks. I only hope the client will be happy with it. She was very specific about the exact shades of red and purple that were to be used. I've tried to mix the colours as close as possible but I'm not sure I've nailed it. She is due here any minute and I really need to get this right. This unit will receive lots of publicity and that could mean more work for me." Gary wiped his paintbrush on a piece of cloth.

"Well, it looks perfect to me. I'm sure she will be thrilled. I'd definitely hire you based on this," James reassured him.

"Thanks for the vote of confidence. I saw you earlier with Mr McGovern. You are in charge of the security. Eamonn mentioned that you would be coming today. My name is Gary Maguire."

"James Murray. I've been looking around. This is a great set-up and we will have all aspects of security in place in no time. I saw the other signs and I wouldn't worry about disappointing anyone. You are very talented. I once knew someone who was very fussy when it came to shades and tones. She was into knitting as well. I'll leave you to it. We will freeze if we hang around any longer and I would murder a coffee," James shivered.

"Well, you are in luck. Ann is still here. You won't drink better coffee anywhere else. I could do with one myself."

Ann looked up as the men entered the room.

"James, meet Ann. She runs the Cottage Tearoom and has been cooking up some great recipes here for the past few weeks," Gary smiled.

"Hello Ann, I have heard great things about you already. I spotted some apple tart earlier. Hope there is a slice with my name on it," James smiled hopefully.

"Indeed there is. Sit yourself down anywhere and I won't be a minute."

"This is lovely. It is like stepping back in time. My grandmother used to have tablecloths on the table all the time and tea was always served from a teapot – no teabags for her." James rubbed his hand along the green and white gingham tablecloth.

"Ann wants this place to be a blast from the past. She is recreating recipes from bygone times. Her soda bread is second to none and she bakes it in the fireplace over there." Gary told James.

"You sound like a fan of hers," James laughed.

Gary was saved from answering by the arrival of the coffee and tart.

"I hope you like custard, James." She placed the generous portion of apple tart on the table. It was accompanied by two little jugs, one with custard and the other with cream.

"This looks great. Thank you." James couldn't wait to get stuck in.

"The usual for you, Gary," she said putting the steaming bread and butter pudding down on the table.

"Thanks, Ann. If you continue to feed me like this, I will be as big as a house!" he smiled.

"Sure you're as thin as a reed." She placed the large teapot on the table.

"Enjoy. I will be out back tidying up. The evenings are getting a bit longer. It is only starting to get dark now. When the clocks go forward next week, the evenings will be bright for longer." She left the two to enjoy their food.

For a while they enjoyed their desserts in silence.

"That was perfect. I will be back again." James drained his cup and put the fork down on the empty plate.

"So, will I," Gary concurred.

"Yes, I think you probably will." James noted how the other man's eyes followed Ann wherever she went.

"Well, I must be off." James stood up, shook hands with Gary and made his way over to the counter.

"Thanks, Ann. That was beautiful. What is the damage?" He took out his wallet.

"On the house this time. That was a taster of what is to come," she assured him.

"You won't make much money if you keep giving food away." He placed a ten euro note on the counter.

"No, that's fine. There is method in my madness. You can tell all your friends about my Tearoom," she said as she picked up the money and handed it back to him.

"I will indeed. I wish you all the best with your venture. See you soon."

"Thank you, James. You are welcome here anytime." She extended her hand.

When he arrived back to where he had parked the jeep, the hotel itself was shadowed against the mottled grey and black sky. He sat behind the wheel and looked up at the imposing building. He recalled the numerous times that he and Clodagh had walked up those steps to the main entrance. They had come here at least once a week for over two years. He could almost hear the music. What he wouldn't give to see her, just for a minute. Still, no point dwelling on the past. He wasn't going to meet her and there was no point in dreaming that he would. It was time to get out of here.

He started the engine and drove slowly down the driveway. As he indicated to turn right, he was almost sideswiped by a car which pulled into Brandon Lodge without indicating. He jammed on the brakes and the engine cut out.

"Stupid fool! I should get out and give them a piece of my mind. Bloody dangerous driving!" He sat for a minute, restarted the engine and drove carefully out onto the main road.

Chapter Three

Clodagh
"Oh, Jesus wept!" Clodagh threw her mobile on the passenger seat. She was almost in the ditch. She could just about make out the outline of the hedges which were a purple blue colour in the darkening evening. The other vehicle had not moved. She wouldn't blame the driver if he had gotten out and approached her. She hadn't even indicated. She shouldn't have answered the phone but she had seen Beth's name and had almost caused an accident. What if he was some sort of psycho? She breathed a sigh of relief when the jeep drove off. Her mobile rang again.

"Mom? Are you alright? Did something happen?" Beth sounded scared.

"I'm fine. I almost missed my turn. I have just arrived at the shop so I will ring you when I get home. Bye Beth." Clodagh took deep breaths and dropped the phone into her bag. After parking beside the hotel, she locked her car and walked across the courtyard. Gary was putting the finishing touches to the sign on her unit. As she got closer she realised that the colour scheme was not quite as she had imagined it.

Gary watched her approach and pre-empted her reaction.

"I'm sorry, Miss Kenny. I'll redo the red tomorrow. I changed suppliers and am not sure that it's the correct shade. I really tried to get it right. I'll..."

Clodagh stopped him. "It's lovely, don't worry. I like it. Actually, it's perfect. Thank you, Gary. You did a great job."

"Thank you, Miss Kenny. I appreciate that. I've painted the other signs here as well."

"The other signs look perfect as well. As soon as people see these signs you will be inundated with offers. You can count on me for a reference. Right now I'd love a large pot of tea. Ann is expecting me, so I'll see you later. Thanks again, Gary." Clodagh turned towards the Tearoom.

Ann was filling the old-fashioned dresser with china ware when the door opened.

"Hello Ann, I love what you have done with this place. The table settings are wonderful. A touch of luxury is always welcome." Clodagh sat down at the table by the window.

"Tea or coffee, Miss Kenny?" Ann asked.

"I'd love a cup of tea. Please call me Clodagh." She sat by the big window which looked out onto the courtyard. On the opposite wall, she noticed the line of bells over the door. Under each bell was the name of a room.

Ann poured the tea into the china cup that was already on the table and noticed what Clodagh was looking at.

"I love those. They tell a real story."

"Sit down, Ann. Tell me what inspired you to take this place on." Clodagh indicated to the chair beside her.

"As you know I have a son, Leo. He is my number one priority. I wanted to set up a viable business. I guess it helps when your Dad is an accountant!" Ann added. "I did a bit of research and I spoke to the local people. They said that they would love a café in the area. And as there was nowhere to meet, they would love a focal point. I put two and two together and decided on the Tearoom. I have great ideas for menus to suit different tastes. My aim is that it would be a bit of a haven where friends can meet. It will definitely be an added bonus that it is so close to a place where people can enjoy their hobbies as well." Ann topped up Clodagh's tea.

"Well, I am delighted as well. Providing refreshments in craft shops has proved a big hit in England. The fact that people can relax as they choose materials for their next project is always good. Having a wonderful place like this so close to my shop is the next best thing. Tell me more about your menus," Clodagh said.

"The Tearoom will be open from eight thirty in the morning to seven, six days a week. As well as the usual tea, coffee, scones and pastries I want to focus on low calorie options and a gluten free menu. All my soups will be gluten free, I will have gluten free options of bread and cakes. A simple tasty menu is what I intend to aim for. I will visit the local markets to meet producers and buy from them. I will make my own scones and brown bread every day," Ann finished.

"Where do you think most of your customer base will come from?" Clodagh asked.

"Well, there are a number of factories and office blocks in the immediate area. I visited them and discovered that a lot of people would love more than a tired sandwich at lunchtime. Some of them go to work without a breakfast, so I said that I would provide a delicious breakfast menu until noon. This would include the full Irish or a 'healthy breakfast' with free range poached eggs, grilled tomato, mushrooms, spinach and homemade brown toast. I will also provide a breakfast bagel as well as a ciabatta stuffed bacon, sausage, fried egg and relish. That should bring the crowds in." Ann twisted her ponytail.

Clodagh was impressed.

"Wow, you are quite the business woman. If you are to carry all that off, you will need to employ more staff. How do you feel about that?"

Ann shifted in her chair.

"I'm hoping to employ someone part-time for a start. Gary's sister is in college and she has experience as a waitress. I intend to do all the cooking myself. My mother is a chef so she is willing to help me out as much as she can. The lunchtime menu will be fairly simple. I was thinking of warm salads and omelettes. Soups, wraps and sandwiches could be prepared in advance." The twirling became more frantic.

"You have it all worked out. I know your business will thrive. Indeed, I intend to be your best customer. I seriously need to lose a few pounds so I will rely on you to make me delicious healthy dishes, in fact I will insist on it!" Clodagh patted her stomach.

"Thank you so much for this opportunity. Let me get you fresh tea. Would you like something to eat with that? I could make you a lovely salad?" Ann rose and went behind the counter.

"That would be lovely. I haven't eaten much today. I have been trying to hire a manager to help me in the shop. I interviewed four candidates this afternoon but I don't think I have found the right person yet. I have three more lined up here tomorrow afternoon. Maybe my luck will change then. I have also spoken to Beth and she thinks that she has found the perfect candidate…someone she met today, a Gillian Roche," Clodagh said.

"I hope she proves to be the one you are looking for." Ann walked over with a plate. "I hope you enjoy this. I have been trying different combinations of herbs and spices to give the flavour. You can tell me what you think of it." She placed it on the table in front of Clodagh.

"It looks delicious." She poked among the colourful salad leaves.

After she had demolished the food and coaxed the list of ingredients from Ann, Clodagh looked out the window at the darkening sky.

"It's getting really dark here. We need to sort out the lighting and get the security sorted. I must get on to David. Strictly speaking, that's his department."

Ann stood up and gathered up the plates. "The security guy just left. He was looking around. You must have just missed him."

"I almost collided with a jeep on my way in. It was my fault, I was distracted when my phone rang." Clodagh shivered at the thought of her near miss.

Gary's entrance to the Tearoom interrupted their conversation. He smiled at Ann and placed his hand gently on her shoulder. Ann twirled her plait and blushed.

"I will be ready to drop you home whenever you are ready. Just give me a ring. Nice to see you again, Ms Kenny." He left them to their conversation.

"I won't keep you any longer. If you don't mind me asking, what is the story with Gary? I gather that you went to school together."

"We were in the same class. He was going out with another girl for years. Amy was her name. They went off to Australia together a few years ago. I didn't know that he was back home until the night of the meeting in January. I haven't asked him about Amy and he hasn't mentioned her. Maybe they are still together."

Chips in a Bag, Classy Mr Murray

Clodagh was intrigued.

"You like him?" she asked.

"I always did, but he only had eyes for her. She was beautiful and popular, and really nice as well. The whole package. They seemed so suited, the couple most likely to stay together," Ann said.

"You're getting on a bit. Your last year as a teenager began yesterday!" Claire dumped her weekend case on her bed and hugged her sister.

"Happy birthday Sis!"

"Thanks Claire. I can always rely on you for a reality check. You are not far behind me. Two years will fly by," Clodagh retorted.

"Ah yes, but by then you will be positively ancient. Anyway, enough about me, what did James get for you?" Claire asked.

"I don't know yet. He didn't turn up last night. He promised that he would. I suppose I should be used to his timekeeping by now. I know he's busy. Everyone wants alarms fitted these days, and they have just landed a big job in Killarney. Some new factory. All good news as far as I am concerned. Engagement here we come. That is if he ever turns up." Clodagh enfolded herself in the net curtain and hummed, 'Here comes the bride.'

"You really think that he will propose? You're still at college. Don't you think you are a bit young to be thinking about marriage?" Claire said.

"I might be, but he's not. Anyway we wouldn't get married for years, but it would be nice to be engaged."

"Well that's a nice thought. I have more pressing things to worry about. The dreaded Leaving Cert is just a few months away and I have lots of studying left to do. I really don't know why I bother. I'm going to become a hairdresser and own my own business. If you just want to marry James, then why are you doing the Art and Design course in Limerick?" Claire said.

"Well, little Sis, I guess I want to have it all. I'm going to be a famous designer and so I'll make lots of money. I'll be Mrs James Murray and live in Brandon Lodge. That's why I'm going to college. That place will cost a packet. You should study for your exams. You will have a better chance of making your dreams come true. Anyway, back to my present. James has mentioned

that he might be able to get me a little car for my birthday. I'd love a Mini. They are so cool." Clodagh answered.

"A car would be lovely though I think that is expecting a lot from him. He works very hard. Aren't you being a bit selfish?"

"Ah Sis, don't spoil my dreams. You know that I will be happy as long as James turns up. Anything else will be a bonus. God I'm still so full after the lovely birthday dinner Mam made yesterday! She made my favourite apple sponge as dessert." She rubbed her stomach.

"So why don't both of us get a bit of work done. I've a project due next week." Clodagh continued and handed Claire a maths book.

Claire sighed as she took the book. They worked quietly for over two hours. Claire closed the book with a flourish.

"I'm only doing the exam because Maura said that she would take me on as an apprentice when I finished the exams. I think Dad had something to do with that. He has an obsession with education."

"The exams will be over in a few months and I'm sure that you will make a brilliant hairdresser. After all you made a fabulous job of my unruly mop for the wedding last week. Maybe you could do something with it before James turns up tonight." She looked hopefully at Claire. "My 'old' man had better get here soon!" Clodagh checked her watch.

"Ah Clodagh, he's only twenty-six…and speak of the devil, here he comes now. Your hair is lovely the way it is. Mam will be putting on the kettle and slicing the apple tart as soon as she hears the car pull into the driveway. You've a bit of competition there!" Claire looked out the window at the approaching headlights.

"That's because he's a typical Kerryman and knows how to charm her. She is putty in his hands when he starts going on about what great apple tarts she bakes and how lovely her hair is. We will give them a few minutes to bond. I just need to rewrite this piece of the pattern. This is an important assignment. I can't seem to get the numbers to add up in the side panel," Clodagh sighed.

"I'm sure you will work it out. Please stop running your hand through your hair, you are destroying it." Claire rushed over to fix Clodagh's hair.

"What do you call that type of cardigan anyway?" Claire asked as she worked on her sister's hair.

Chips in a Bag, Classy Mr Murray

"That's called a batwing and this mohair wool is so luxurious. I'm going to make one for Mam. Pretty appropriate, don't you think?" Clodagh smiled wickedly.

"Ah, leave her alone, she means well. Speaking of which, I think I hear the kitchen door opening. Wait for it…one, two and…we have lift off."

Their mother's voice drifted up the stairs.

"Clodagh! James is here. Are you going to get off that bed and come down here? I've boiled the kettle twice and the apple tart is getting cold. He is sitting in the car waiting for you to go out and bring him in. Are you coming?"

"No, Mam. I'm not. He was supposed to be here twenty-four hours ago. Another few minutes won't make much difference," Clodagh continued to work on her calculations.

"So, he is a bit late…"

"Jesus wept! Mam that must be the quote of the year. You go out with him. I'm doing college work. I'm knitting."

"Less of your lip now, missy. Get down here this minute and don't be letting me down. What will the neighbours think of us? I did not raise you to be rude." Her mother lowered her voice.

"Ah… The ace card." Claire burst out laughing. "Come on now, Mam's going to have a kitten. You know how she loves your James. What colour are you planning on using for that?" Claire looked over Clodagh's shoulder at her sketches.

"Purple, I think."

Their mother called again.

"Well. I can imagine Mam's shade of purple face. I've seen it often enough. Please go down there before she has a fit." Claire took the sketch book from her sister and closed it.

"Okay, I'm going. He doesn't deserve me. My birthday was yesterday. He could have made more of an effort. He can sit out there until he is thirty for all I care. Which won't be that long in coming in his case. I needed to finish that sketch. I love the pattern. I designed it myself."

"CLODAGH. Get down here…n…o…w." The sisters froze.

"Coming, Mam."

A car door banged and footsteps approached the front door. Their mother's voice was now at a level that only an owl could hear.

"James is here. You have thirty seconds to negotiate those stairs. Stop acting like a spoiled brat." Her tone did not imply choice.

"She does have a point. You are acting the diva a bit. He is gorgeous. If you don't get a move on, I'll knock Mam out and go and seduce him myself." Claire pushed Clodagh out the bedroom door.

When Clodagh opened the kitchen door, James was sitting at the table. A cup of tea and a slice of tart were on the table in front of him. He stood up.

"Happy birthday. I'm really sorry about last night. I had to meet a client. Dad got tied up with another job and Conor is back in London."

"Really. Don't you have a lumpy black thing on your hall table? I'm sure I saw it there last weekend. It goes ring. We have an identical one here but not a squeak out of it all night. Get the picture James? Nothing matters more than Dan Murray and Sons!"

"That's enough, Clodagh." Her mother interrupted her tirade. "Stop acting like a spoiled child. More tea, James?" Mary Kenny continued.

Clodagh sighed. Deep down she knew that her behaviour was unacceptable but she didn't care. Turning nineteen was a milestone and her boyfriend wasn't there to share in it.

"Come on, James. Let's continue this discussion in the car. It's two against one here, and she's supposed to be my mother."

Sitting in the car listening to Jim Reeves, she let rip again.

"Calm down, please. I'm really sorry that I couldn't make it last night. I tried, I really did. You know that we have been awarded a big contract. I was the only one available. Did you want me to tell the client that I couldn't meet him because my girlfriend was celebrating her nineteenth birthday? I'm doing this for us. Conor is chasing up work in London. Lots of opportunities are there among all the Irish contractors running construction sites. I was working to secure our future. I did get you a present." He reached into the glove compartment and produced a carefully wrapped box. Clodagh's heart soared.

She undid the purple ribbon and peeled open the sticky tape to reveal a jewellers box inside. This was what she had been waiting for! Inside the box was a sapphire bracelet.

James watched her face.

Chips in a Bag, Classy Mr Murray

"I know it's not what you were expecting. I know you wanted that engagement ring that you have pointed out to me a hundred times," he tried to lighten the moment. "That ring is very expensive. I'll need to secure a few more contracts before I'll be able to afford that," he continued.

"It's lovely. Thanks."

James turned her towards him and gently kissed her.

"I love you, Clodagh Kenny. I have since I first set eyes on you in Brandon Lodge. I was gutted when I realised that you were going out with Richard. You know how we planned a weekend together? Well, I have booked a room in a really posh hotel. We can be properly together. No more half promises. I want to spend a full night with you. You promised." He kissed her again.

She shifted uncomfortably. "Ah James. That's really nice. When is it? Not next weekend or the weekend after? I have loads to do for college. Why don't we spend one night in Mary's again? I will be finished for Easter in a few weeks. We can go somewhere then." She twirled her bracelet so that it shone under the street lights.

"Ok, Clodagh. Whatever you want. You need to keep up with your work. We are pretty busy at the moment as well. Maybe it would be better for both of us if we didn't see each other until Easter. Then, when the exams are over and my work load lightens again we will go away for the weekend. Deal?" James hugged her.

"You're the best boyfriend ever. College is really busy at the moment. You need to relax too. Go out with your friends." Clodagh kissed him gently. He pulled her close and kissed her deeply. She wrapped her arms around his neck.

"Come on" he whispered. "Let's go somewhere more private and you can show me how much you love me." He caressed her breast through her thin sweater.

She pulled away. "Better not. Let's go for a drink instead. There is a good band playing in The Bridge Bar tonight." She straightened her clothes.

"Actually, I think I'll head home. It's a long drive to Killarney. You go to the pub with your friends. I'll ring you in the next few days." James sounded tired. "I'll drop you off if you like."

"No, that's ok. I've a few things to do first. I do love you, James. You know that. Okay?" She kissed him on the cheek.

James pulled into a gateway just outside the town. He sat in his car and banged the steering wheel. He was very annoyed and frustrated. She kept promising him and then changing her mind. There was always some excuse... Next week James, the week after James, on my birthday James. This had been going on for months, ever since she thought she was pregnant. That had been a scary time for both of them. He loved her and knew that they would marry some time yet he was glad when her period arrived. She had avoided sex since then. Yet sometimes she gave out signals and then changed her mind. She was pushing him to the limit and she knew it. She could be a real teasing bitch sometimes. He had booked a romantic weekend for her birthday but tonight she had made it clear that that would have to be cancelled. He had even planned to officially ask her to marry him.

He knew the ring that she had her heart set on. It was a sapphire surrounded by diamonds...at least that was how the shop assistant described it when he had pointed it out in the window. He had put a deposit on it. He was due to pick it up the following week. Tonight he was seriously pissed off with her...yet he loved her very much, but a man has needs. Unfortunately, Clodagh chose to ignore that fact. When he had told her about the hotel, she was not that impressed.

"How would we explain that to my parents? Dad would kill me if he knew," she had said.

"We can tell them that we are helping Mary out in the guesthouse. We have done it before. They know that she insists on us sleeping in different corridors! I'm beginning to think that you don't want to sleep with me," he added.

Clodagh had looked shocked. "You know that's not true. We are going to be together forever, so what is the hurry?"

"I love you, Clodagh. I just want to show you how much," James had put his arms around her and drew her close.

"If you don't want to go away for the weekend, then I will cancel it. I'll lose my deposit but if that is what you want..."

"Ok James, you win. We will go away at Easter. I will tell Mam and Dad that we are going to help Mary out during a busy weekend. They will be fine with that, though I hate lying to them," she finished.

That had made him feel worse than ever. He knew exactly how much she hated lying to them. She had told him often enough.

Chips in a Bag, Classy Mr Murray

He needed time to think, time alone. When he had suggested that they not see each other for a few weeks, he had hoped that it would have scared her enough to give in. He was such a bastard but he needed her. It didn't work and now they were on a break. She had told him to go out with his friends and maybe he should.

He started up the car.

As he drove towards home he didn't know who he hated more... Himself for almost begging or her for her constant teasing. He needed to put a bit of distance between them. Surely, she didn't expect him to live like a monk.

When he reached home, he parked the car in the driveway and locked it. The lights were on in the sitting room so he knew that if he went in now he would be given the third degree.

He decided that a walk would do him good so he headed towards the village. There was always a good session in O'Brien's bar every week. A few of the local lads got together and played a few tunes. At least it would be a distraction, take his mind off his troubles for a while. He wouldn't contact Clodagh for at least a week. That would give her a little time to appreciate him!

The cigarette smoke almost blinded him when he opened the door. The place was packed and the heat was tangible.

"Evening, James. The usual?" The barman held up the Guinness glass. James nodded.

As he cradled the pint in his hand the man beside him turned to him.

"Busy here tonight. Poor Jack the Mountain was buried today and young Kate Cashman is celebrating a birthday. The girls at the factory organised it for her. She's a lovely lass and deserves more than she has. Her father is a nasty piece of work who drove his poor wife into an early grave and will do the same with her if she doesn't get away from him soon. He makes her work on the farm and do all the housework after she finishes her shifts at the factory. Do you know her?"

"Yes, actually I do. She is a friend of my sister. She used to hang around with Conor as well. My Dad always said they her old man was a waste of space and he's supposed to be worse since his wife died."

"Your father is right about that. He has her on a short leash but some plan was hatched tonight so that she could stay in town after work. Her aunt went to the house and cooked his dinner and managed to persuade him that Kate needed a night off for her birthday," the man continued.

Paddy, the barman, was filling pints and making sure that everyone had their drinks while keeping an ear cocked to every conversation.

He watched the pints settle. He joined in the conversation.

"I cannot abide meanness or laziness and that man has more than enough of both. He has the best land in the country and it's all going to rack and ruin. There is only so much that poor young one can do on her own. That man has a lot to answer for, he's an evil cur, but I'm not one to gossip so I'll say no more on the subject. Anyway here she comes."

Kate staggered up and draped herself on the counter next to James.

"Hi, handsome. You are a more handsome, sexy version of Conor. I used to fancy the pants off of you in secondary school, and taking the pants off you, James, would be so much fun. How are you fixed for a shift? I don't get out much so time is of the essence. Miss Brandon Lodge is absent so you look young, free and single to me tonight!" she purred.

James smiled at her while gently removing her hand from his crotch.

"Hi Kate. I believe it's your birthday so allow me to buy you a drink. What's your pleasure?"

"Well now, sexy, my pleasure has more to do with you than with a drink! Since you asked I'll have a double vodka and coke. Will you join us?" She indicated to the table of giggling people behind her.

James nodded for another round.

"Guinness, double vodka and coke."

A few minutes later James was sitting beside Kate and getting reintroduced to her friends. Since he had started going out with Clodagh, he had lost contact with the crowd that he and Conor used to hang around with.

They were a fun crowd and he needed some fun. Kate was still touching his leg under the table. He wouldn't be human if he didn't like it. He knew that she used to fancy him, but he didn't think it was serious. After all she was the same age as Mary.

Closing time came and went and still the party continued. Eventually they staggered out on to the street and meandered to a friend's house. Kate was *still glued to James and kept touching his face and body as if he were very precious. It was nice to be desired.*

"James," she whispered. "You didn't give me a birthday kiss."

Before he could react she had him clamped to her as she kissed the face off him.

Paddy wandered into the room with a tray of drinks.

"None of that caper here, girlie. He's practically married to that young one from Cork. The Kerry girls are not up to his standard at all."

"Well, she's not here tonight but I am." Kate wound her arms around his neck.

James smiled at her. The combination of too many pints and her increasingly obvious attraction for him was pushing any thoughts of Clodagh out of his head. Anyway they were on a break until Easter. She had said that he should enjoy himself so what harm could a few kisses do? He was merely following orders.

Next morning James woke up and looked around him. He did not recognise the room but he certainly knew the naked girl that he was curled around.

His head was pounding.

Jesus. What had he done?

Clodagh sat on her bed, her needles clicking furiously.

Claire stirred in her own bed and turned over.

"Jesus, what the hell are you doing? It's bloody well only half six in the morning. Are you knitting a fecking sunrise or what?"

"Sorry Sis, I didn't mean to wake you. I'm very angry so I must knit. It helps to calm me."

Claire sat up and turned on her bedside lamp.

"Not sure that's working out for you, not with the racket those needles are making. They are practically crying out for mercy! Want to talk about it? Another Chapter in the James saga, I presume. You came in almost as soon as you went out and James stormed off into the night. We decided it was safer to leave you alone. It's no wonder you're awake; you were in bed by ten!" Claire pulled on her dressing gown and sat on the edge of the bed.

Clodagh put down the purple sweater she was working on and went to sit on her sister's bed.

"I'm such a spoiled bitch. First of all, I gave out to him for being late. They are very busy and I should be supporting him. Then, when he gave me a beautiful bracelet, I couldn't hide my disappointment that it wasn't an engagement ring! I can't imagine life without him, but he keeps going on about sleeping together. You remember how scared I was when I thought I was pregnant last year. I will never forget that. Can you imagine how the parents would react to that? I don't care how much Mam loves James. He would have been dead meat. If we were to sleep together again I would feel that Mam, Dad and the three in the frame in the kitchen…you know The Pope, John F Kennedy and what's his name would be looking at us!" Clodagh shivered.

Claire burst out laughing.

"You two are made for each other. The fact that he is older than you means that he expects more from the relationship than you do. Men always want more sex than we do. Why don't you just pretend that you are married! Book a nice hotel room and add a few candles and a nice bottle of wine. Ring him later and suggest it. I'm really good as an agony aunt, even if I say so myself!"

Clodagh picked up her knitting again. She considered Claire's suggestions.

"You are perfectly right, but I can't ring him tomorrow. We agreed not to meet until Easter…but that's only two weeks away. I will write him a really romantic letter. Then he will know exactly how much he means to me. Hopefully he will be able to change the dates on that weekend he had booked. I can't wait to show him how much I love him! How did you learn to be so smart, Sis?"

Claire yawned.

"I guess it's my role in life. You're the creative one and I'm the sensible, intelligent one." She ducked as Clodagh threw a pillow at her.

"Now that we have sorted out all your problems, do you think that we could go back to sleep for a while? Why don't you give those needles a rest and dream about the happy life ahead for you and James?" Claire climbed back into bed.

"Thanks, Claire. I feel so much better. I was getting really worried. James couldn't wait to get away last night. I'm going to make sure that it will never happen again. I'm going to…"

"GO TO SLEEP CLODAGH."

Chips in a Bag, Classy Mr Murray

Clodagh settled down to think about how much James would want her at Easter. After all he would miss her so much.

"Happy Easter, Clodagh. I missed you so much. I have a surprise for you. Mary has finally changed her car. The Mini is now yours. We will sort the insurance out and hopefully you will pass your test soon!" James paused for breath.

She threw her arms around him. "I love you so much, James Murray. I will love you for ever. We will grow old together. Well, you'll get there faster than me! I'm so looking forward to this weekend. I can't wait to show you just how much I love you." Her hand travelled up and down his leg as she kissed him deeply.

James held her close.

"I'm so glad everything is back to normal," he whispered in her ear as her caresses became more urgent.

"Nothing will ever come between us again."

2 months later

"Please, Clodagh. Just listen."

His tone silenced her. She looked at his profile and he looked haunted. She felt uneasy. Maybe the weekend away wasn't as good as she thought. She didn't have much experience with sex so he was tired of her inexperience. She hadn't heard from him in over a week.

"Okay. I'm sorry. I am going on a bit. What is wrong? Was it the weekend away? It was okay – us sleeping together? You said that it was great. I love you, James. I'm sorry if I kept you waiting too long. It won't happen again. I just love you." She was pleading.

He turned and looked at her. He grabbed both of her hands and kissed them. "Please, Clodagh. Stop talking. I need you to listen to me. I have to explain."

Cold terror gripped her heart. To her horror, his body began to shake and she realised that he was crying.

"I'm so sorry, Clodagh. I wish I could turn the clock back."

"Jesus wept! James. Will you please tell me what is going on? Whatever it is, I'm sure we can fix it. You haven't killed anyone, have you?"

"It might be easier if I had. I don't know how to explain, where to start. I want you to know that I will never love anyone like I love you. Never"

"For feck sake, James. WILL YOU PLEASE TELL ME WHAT IS GOING ON?"

"I'm so sorry, Clodagh. I swear to you that it only happened once. I know it is no excuse but I was drunk and she was too…"

"What are you talking about, James?" Clodagh whispered.

"Kate is pregnant," James spoke quietly.

"Who the hell is Kate?"

The previous day

Kate had asked him to meet her in the pub at eight. He hadn't seen her since the morning after the night of her birthday. They had both agreed that the whole thing had been a reaction to too much drink. It had haunted him for a while afterwards but he had managed to put it out of his head. Clodagh had been like a different person after their self-imposed break. The weekend away had been a revelation. She had been like a tiger between the sheets!

They were back on track and Mary had told him that Kate was seeing someone – Pat. He worked the farm with her father. James was delighted. She was a lovely girl and he wished her the best. He had no idea why she wanted to see him.

She had sounded upset on the phone.

Kate was sitting alone at a table in the darkest corner of the pub. He sat down opposite her. "I wanted to get you a vodka but Paddy insisted that you were on orange juice so I got you one of those." He placed the drink on the table. "Will I get you something stronger?"

Kate fiddled with the table mat.

"No thanks. I'm fine with this. Look, James. There is no easy way to say this. I'm pregnant and you're the father."

"Oh shit. Are you sure?"

She nodded and burst into tears.

Chapter Four

Gill
Gillian Roche wrapped her new scarf around her neck and fastened it with her favourite brooch.

"Not too bad for an unemployed, overweight menopausal woman!" she told her reflection.

Tucking her blonde hair into a scarlet, felted cloche hat, she grabbed her coat and banged the door behind her. The cold air froze her breath so she hurried to the bus stop.

"God, but its bloody cold today. I wish this month was over. I hate March." Gill handed the fare to the regular driver on the city bound bus.

While waiting for her ticket, she stumbled as the bus took off suddenly.

"Falling for me?" Tom smiled.

"I did that years ago but you never noticed," she quipped.

"You sure about that? What if the feeling was mutual?" He negotiated through the estate and onto the main road.

Gill looked around her. "I know that it's almost April first, but I'm certain that we shouldn't continue with this conversation. Maybe I should sit down. Like, it's a bit early to be playing April fool jokes." She turned to walk down the bus.

"Ah, come on, keep me company for a while longer. This job is boring enough as it is. We are only talking. What's the harm in that?"

She turned back. "I guess there isn't any as long as we chat about general stuff. I was only joking before. I'm sorry if you, like, got the wrong impression." Gill flashed her wedding ring.

"I love the way you put the word 'like' in your sentences. You can never hide the fact that you are a pure Cork city woman! Did you know that each person falls in love five times during their lives? But only once very deeply. Then they go and marry one of the other four," he said, finally handing her the ticket.

"I don't know about you, but my Joe is my number one, two, three, four and five all rolled into the love of my life."

"Jesus, that's a scary thought. Maybe I'm still in with a fighting chance so." He winked at her as he pulled in at the end of the hill to pick up more passengers.

The regulars saluted Tom as they flashed their passes which he acknowledged with a nod. He checked his mirrors before indicating and pulling out into the busy early morning traffic. This gave Gill a chance to gather her thoughts as she wondered why she was still standing. She realised just how ridiculous and inappropriate the conversation was. She had known Tom for years. When she used to commute to work, she was a regular on this bus. The longer she was unemployed, the more her self-confidence was ebbing away. Joe was probably fed up of listening to her moaning. She was definitely to blame for the fact that their love life had become almost non-existent. She had turned into a fat moaner and she felt like an unattractive whale. Maybe that was why she was still standing. In some remote corner of her brain, she needed to hear that someone still fancied her. Her life had slipped from her control. It had all spiralled after that bloody holiday last year. She should have trusted her instincts and refused to go with her cousin Caroline. They were chalk and cheese. Caroline was game for anything.

Having negotiated his way back into the flow of traffic, Tom turned his attention back to Gill.

"I'm glad to see that you haven't deserted me yet. That's a good sign, at least."

Gill was saved from answering as the bus shuddered to a halt on a steep hill. Tom swore.

"Bloody road works, been going on for weeks. They know by now the number of buses that pass through here every day. Look at the little space they have left. You couldn't drive a nail through there, let alone a bus. Look at that eejit!"

A workman in a high visibility jacket was signalling to Tom to reverse as he attempted to direct an articulated truck driver out of the building site.

"I'm not reversing this. The traffic is backed up behind me. If he locked hard all the way, he will make it." Tom sat and waited.

"I hate reversing too. I'm no good at it, like," Gill said.

"I'm sure that's not true. You can reverse into me any time, and I don't mean while I'm driving the bus," he looked at her meaningfully.

"For feck sake, like. You on Horny Goat Weed or something, Tom? It's just as well that most of the passengers are wearing hearing aids because they do not need to hear this. Get a grip, like. We're not teenagers."

"I don't smoke any type of weed. Though you are right. Wrong place, wrong time. I'm taking advantage of the fact that we are neighbours, well almost. There are only about eighty houses separating us after all. A better place to discuss this would be in that new hotel near the Museum. Say around three o'clock?"

She gaped at him. Surely, he was joking. She would never cheat on Joe. So why were her feet glued to the floor? Was there something seriously wrong with her? Her head began to spin and the sweat began to pour out of her. Brilliant...a bloody hot flush! Perfect timing! Just because Joe no longer found her attractive didn't mean that she should entertain any random offers of afternoon sex.... especially from randy bus drivers.

The longer she remained standing on the same spot listening to this drivel, the more it seemed that she was buying into the possibility of actually agreeing to something that she would definitely regret later. She didn't even fancy him. He was far too skinny. She loved a cuddly bear of a man. Just because it had been a few months since she and Joe had even slept in the same room didn't mean she was desperate. Not yet anyway.

"Look Tom, I appreciate the offer but no thanks."

"Nothing ventured and all that," he shrugged.

As she started to walk down the bus aisle, she turned back.

"Horny Goat Weed is a health supplement which he definitely does not need," she murmured to herself.

Gill sat. What was happening to her? She was twice the woman Joe married, and cranky as hell most of the time. He had moved into the spare bedroom months ago, so that must mean that he didn't fancy her anymore. The last time that they had attempted to have a romantic encounter in the bedroom, he hadn't risen to the occasion. So, he must be really repulsed by her. I suppose that was the reason that, in the remotest corner of her brain, she had considered this ridiculous liaison, just for a second. She was still attractive to someone! A little harmless flirting was okay. What Tom had suggested – that would never happen.

Her mind was in turmoil. The recession had taken her job, and with it a lot of her self-esteem and confidence. She had a few close friends but she felt guilty going on too many outings as Joe was the only breadwinner. Her life was a mess but sleeping with a total stranger would not solve anything. She would look on it as the last weird moment in her present life. She would turn things around.

The bus pulled in the stop by the shopping centre and all the passengers got off. As she passed Tom, he pressed a paper into her hand.

"Think about it. Who would know?"

"I would." She handed the paper back to him

"I'm sorry if I offended you. I'm being moved to another route at the beginning of the week and I may not see you again. I took a chance. You are a very attractive woman and you look so sad lately."

"Good luck with the new route. I'm going to take a new route myself."

Walking through the shopping centre and out into the main street Gill suddenly felt attractive and light-hearted. Considering that she was usually a quiet person, she would have to think seriously about giving up the Horny Goat Weed as it seemed to be attracting the wrong sort of attention.

She would be fifty in a few months' time and by then she intended to be in a more positive place. She would lure her husband back into her bed and show him how much she loved him.

"Excuse me, madam, would you mind returning to the store with me, please?" Gill looked down at the hand clamped onto her arm. "What?"

"Please madam, let's not make a scene. We will go back inside and sort this out in the privacy of the office."

Gill looked at the man beside her. Who the hell was he and where had he come from?

Surely he was mistaken. He definitely had to have the wrong person. She would put him right in no uncertain terms! The bloody cheek of him. She pulled herself up to her full five foot two and eyeballed his chest.

Looking up, she noted that he was at least seventy.

"I don't know what you think you're playing at, but you have made a serious mistake. Please remove your hand and I will forget all about this incident." She tried to shake off his vice like grip on her arm.

He wasn't having any of it and they were beginning to attract curious looks from the people passing by on the street.

"Please return to the store with me. I have reason to believe that you have a number of unpaid for items on your person," he said calmly.

"The bloody cheek of you! Who do you think you are? I realise that you think that you are doing your job, but I can assure you that everything I have in my bag has been paid for. I have receipts to prove it." She was fuming.

"If that's the case, madam, then you will have no objection to accompanying me back in and producing said receipts. You might also be able to explain why the security barriers bleeped while you were exiting." He pushed her towards the door.

Gill decided that the best option was to go back inside and vent her anger on the manager. A shoplifter indeed! The very thought was hilarious. The most she had ever stolen was a lipstick in a pound shop when she was twelve and that had been for a dare.

"Madam?"

"Will you please stop calling me 'madam' in that tone of voice? You make me sound like a brothel owner. You have the wrong person." She finally managed to shake off his hand.

"Please, madam. We really should go back inside."

Gill sighed and allowed herself to be led back into the shop, confident that a mistake had been made.

She was not a thief. The bleeping was probably caused by that bloody magnet that she wore in her knickers. It was supposed to help ease the hot flushes. She had noticed that she had often 'gone off' as she went in and out of shops. This was the first time that she had been apprehended by security. The only consolation was that she had made her criminal debut in Smithfield's, one of the most exclusive stores in the city!

At least if she was going to end up in court, her crime would be upmarket.

Joe would love this story. It was just the type of practical joke that he would pull…at least he would have done back in the time when he had still loved her. These days his sense of humour seemed to have evaporated, along with his desire for her.

As she was being frogmarched to the rear of the store, Gill actually felt like laughing out loud. What a very strange day this was turning out to be. What else could go wrong? If this fell into the dream category, then it was definitely a nightmare.

As she waited in the office, she suddenly realised that things were not going well for her, and that they hadn't been going well for a very long time, ever since the Celtic Tiger had reared its ugly head, bared its teeth and bitten everyone in the arse. She had lost the job she loved in The Wool Shop and Joe had suffered as well. Taxi drivers had multiplied like baby mice and their only remaining income had taken a nosedive.

She caught her cabled scarf and twisted it between her fingers. She looked up as a very young woman entered the office. She prepared herself to have to protest her innocence. She knew that she had not stolen anything from the shop. All she had bought was a Molten Brown body lotion for a friend's birthday. She was clutching the receipt in her hand.

The girl was young, pretty and dressed in a smart black trouser suit. Her black hair with the red streaks made her look like a character from a fairy story. She also looked very young.

'Great!' thought Gill, 'I'm dealing with Snow White!'

"My name is Beth Kenny. I'm a buyer and the trainee manager. Mr Mulroney usually deals with customer relation issues but he is in the Tralee branch today. I'm really sorry about this. I'm sure we can resolve this matter as quickly as possible." Her English accent did nothing to ease Gill's anxiety.

She sat opposite Gill. "I'm very embarrassed about this and I apologise for keeping you waiting. I know that you haven't stolen anything. Jack used to work here. He retired some years back. Problems with his memory. Sometimes he manages to make his way back to the store. He has never gotten as far as arresting anyone until now. We have called his daughter and she is on her way in to collect him. We have been very lucky so far in that nobody has sued us. I hope our luck holds out today and that you will forget about this incident."

"My name is Gillian Roche. Gill, to my friends and I swear I was beginning to doubt myself. I've been so preoccupied lately that I thought it was possible that I had forgotten to pay for something. Of course I won't be taking this any further. The poor daughter has enough to worry about." Gill twisted her scarf again.

"I appreciate that. Thank you on behalf of the management. Of course we will be providing you with gift vouchers as a token of our gratitude. In the meantime, I hope you will allow me to buy you a coffee. I was about to get one just before this incident." Beth stood up and indicated towards the coffee shop visible through the glass partition that divided it from the retail section of the huge store.

Beth

Gill stood up and twisted her scarf again. Beth noticed both the scarf and the action.

"That's a beautiful scarf you're wearing. It's not one of ours. It looks fabulous but then winter white is one of my favourite colours. Do you mind me asking which label it is?" They walked towards the coffee emporium.

"I suppose it's the Roche label! I made it myself. I prefer to create my own patterns," Gill answered.

"It's beautiful. The pattern is very classy. If I am not mistaken you have used a mixture of cables and double seed stitch."

"Wow. You know your patterns." Gill looked impressed.

"I studied Art and Design in London. I was brought up by a yarn addict. Clodagh Kenny. She's a well-known knitwear designer in London."

"Wow! I know her. I've seen her stuff and I always follow her articles in the Knit and Natter magazine. I was thrilled when I heard that she was opening in Brandon Lodge. I intend to go there as soon as I can. I used to manage a wool shop but it closed a few years ago. The owner retired and at the time I couldn't afford the lease. It was always my dream to take it over. But that's life…" Gill looked sad.

Beth looked at the other woman and made a decision.

"Would you mind walking through the store with me? I would like to show you our scarves. They are not a patch on yours. We are always looking for new talent. I might have a proposition for you." Beth stood up.

Walking through the different aisles, Beth pointed out the different ranges of designer goods on display. The price tags on the scarves made Gill gasp.

"I could buy groceries for a month for the cost of one of those!" Gill gasped.

"Your one is so much nicer and it has the added advantage of being a one-off." Beth stopped to fix one of the displays.

"You remind me of Clodagh. She loves creating one-off pieces. I think that you two would get on well together. The shop in Brandon Lodge should be up and running in the next few weeks. She has been trying to hire a manager with both management and design skills. She has interviewed quite a few candidates, but has had no luck so far. Some can design and some can manage. I think that you would be perfect. Might you be interested?"

"Are you serious? I'd love to meet the famous Clodagh Kenny. That would be a dream come true. To work in her shop would be amazing. Until a few minutes ago, I was having the strangest day of my life. This would change that life. Thank you so much." Gill gushed.

Joe

Joe could not believe his eyes. His suspicions were proving to be correct. His wife was having an affair. It certainly explained why she kept her mobile phone glued to her body and jumped every time it beeped.

Sitting in the taxi rank across the street from Smithfield's, he had a bird's eye view of the comings and goings in the shop. Lately he was spending a lot of his working day parked here. He had become a people watcher by necessity. It passed the time between fares. That and fast food. The street had lots of fast food outlets dotted around and he was known in all of them. What he did not expect to see was his wife arm and arm with another man. A much older man at that! He was well dressed so he must have a couple of bob. Shopping in Smithfield's no less. Joe had spotted her earlier coming out of the shop and had been about to call her when this older gentleman had come out of the shop and persuaded her to go back in again. He must have decided that he needed to buy her some more stuff! They had been in there over an hour. He would have to sit and wait until they came back out even though he wanted to rush in and demand an explanation. Ask her why she was cheating on him with a man who was clearly old enough to be her father. She had never struck him as the sugar daddy type, but then her husband had turned into a fat impotent slob.

The rear passenger door opened.

"Blackstone Castle, please. The coffee shop."

Torn between earning a living and finding out what his wife was up to, Joe pulled away from the kerb. He wondered when the affair had started. He really couldn't blame her. He was twice the man she married and earning half the money. The last time they had attempted to make love had been a total disaster. He couldn't rise to the occasion... He moved into the spare room shortly afterwards, using his unsocial hours as an excuse. He said that he didn't want to disturb her. She was upset at this; he could see it in her eyes. He loved her more than life itself but he couldn't risk a repeat non-performance. He missed her in bed. It looked like she had sought solace elsewhere. He loved her enough to let her go, but it would break his heart.

He was jerked back to reality when a woman, partly hidden by an umbrella, dashed across the street in front of the car. He had to slam on the brakes.

"Sorry about that. I don't know what some people think pedestrian lights are for!" He looked in the rear-view mirror. His passenger shrugged.

Joe tried not to let his mind wander back to the events of the past hour. Life could not get any worse. The recession had really fucked up their lives. He used to earn decent money and Gill had loved her well-paid job in the wool shop. All that had changed. Their world was falling apart and he could not see any way of fixing it. Blackstone Castle wasn't the only thing on the rocks.

Gill

Five minutes after Joe had driven off, a much happier Gill danced onto Thomas Street. At last something good had happened to her. She had the opportunity of getting a new job, doing something she loved, and all thanks to a confused old man and her new cabled scarf. The Law of Attraction was beginning to make sense to her at last. Her vibrations must finally be aligned! She couldn't wait to tell Joe all about it. She could have sworn that she had seen his car in the taxi rank earlier. Hopefully, he had gotten a fare.

In the store earlier, Gill had to resist the urge to grab Beth and hug her. Once was enough to be arrested. God bless Jack. She would pray for him every day.

She hummed to herself as she waited for the pedestrian lights to turn to green. A quick coffee, a look at the knitting magazines and then home to plan her new future. Though if she had any more caffeine this morning she would be able to fly home. At least she wouldn't be getting anymore offers of afternoon quickies.

Joe

Joe sipped his coffee and watched a group of school children enjoying their packed lunches on the benches in the castle courtyard. If life had been kinder to them, their child would have been old enough to be here today. He often wondered, as he ate his lunch, how their son would have looked now. Would he have had Gill's beautiful green eyes and her sallow skin or would he have looked like his father. God help him! Whoever he would have favoured, he would have been loved.

They had waited a long time for him. It was a dream come true when Gill had finally become pregnant. Hugh was a beautiful baby, very quiet.

Today Joe decided to go for a very long walk by the water's edge before entering the Castle Café for a black coffee. Seeing Gill with that man had shaken him up, and made him realise that, if she left him, life wouldn't be worth living. He would have to win her back. The first step would involve a lifestyle change. He would stop eating rubbish, get more exercise and win back the love of his life.

Everything would be on the up. Hopefully.

The problem was, how could he best go about it? Should he confront her with what he had seen or wait and see if she would tell him about it. Maybe his over active-imagination was to blame. There could be a perfectly innocent explanation. What about the way she continually clutched her mobile – was that innocent as well? He needed to sort things out in his head before he could decide how he would progress.

"Can I get you anything else, Joe?"

"No thanks, Laura. This coffee is plenty. I'm thinking of trying to lose a few pounds and maybe try to get fitter. Any suggestions?"

"Sure, you're lovely the way you are. A cuddly teddy bear," Laura said as she refilled his cup.

"Maybe that's where the problem lies! I'd like to be fitter and healthier. It's easier for women, there are plenty of classes to suit. Could you see me in a leotard prancing around to loud music? Now that would be something that would attract a crowd!"

"Look Joe, if you are really serious about this, then I can help you. My Mam attends a guy who has really helped her to lose a lot of weight. I will ask her for the details. I'll ring you later when I get more information. She also goes walking with a group a few times a week. I think that they are called 'Like Minded People.' Interested?" she enquired.

"I most certainly am. Thanks Laura. You have just improved a very bad day for your old taxi driver." He drained his cup.

"You're welcome. You have never let me down for a lift home. I think I have a magazine here that has an article on that weight loss fellow. I'll find it for you before you leave."

Beth

Beth was thrilled with herself. She had just solved a huge problem for Clodagh, who had been really stressed for the past few weeks. She had interviewed ten people already. She needed someone that she could trust to run the shop single-handed. She decided to phone her with the good news.

"Hi Mom, you'll never guess what happened today! I've found a manager for your new place in Brandon Lodge. Her name is Gillian Roche and she seems perfect for the position. I gave her your number and told her to ring you this afternoon. I'll give her number to you, in case you want to contact her straight away. She actually didn't mind that the place was in the middle of nowhere! That has to be a plus." Beth laughed at her own joke.

"It is not in the middle of nowhere, missy. I will have you know that I grew up near here and look how I turned out! If this Gillian is half as good as you seem to think, then I will be delighted to talk to her. It's all beginning to come together. Ann is thrilled to have the extra business so if I had a manager, then that would be great. Thanks Beth. Oh, Jesus wept!" She muttered as she ended the call.

Beth checked the window display as she left the shop. She had worked up the extra hours so that she was able to finish work earlier than usual and had booked a hair appointment. One of the girls had recommended the salon and this would be her second visit. She was meeting David later for dinner so that they could finalise the plans for Clodagh's birthday surprise. She loved spending time with her 'Mom.' She had called Clodagh by that name since she was three years old. She barely remembered her own mother. Clodagh and Aunt Lizzie had raised her between them. A very old woman and a very young girl had done a marvellous job. David and his family had taken all three of them under their wing. All things considered, Beth had been very lucky.

She was looking forward to the surprise. Clodagh thought that it would be a dinner for just the two of them. They hadn't had a proper chat for over a week. They had a lot of catching up to do.

She had felt a little out of her depth earlier when she had been sent to sort out the issue that arose with Jack and his supposed shoplifter. That had turned out to be a blessing in disguise. She had trusted her gut instincts on that one. She had been worried that Mom had taken on too much with this new venture, but Gill Roche was heaven sent. She would be perfect for the job.

As she set off towards the quays, she marvelled at how well she had settled in Ireland. She could have stayed in London but she wanted to sample the country that Clodagh had raved about for as long as Beth could remember. The house in London was still there. She could return any time she wished. Clodagh was on cloud nine. This Brandon Lodge was where she always wanted to be. Now her dream was coming true. The new shop was already on the radar, orders were flying in.

As she turned onto the square towards 'Hair by Colin,' her mobile rang.

"Hi, David. How are things with you? Did you manage to get away before Mom arrived? It would have been terrible if the surprise was ruined at this late stage. She thinks it's only the two of us! I can't wait to see her reaction. I'm on my way to the hairdresser. I'll see you tonight."

Dropping her mobile into her bag, Beth smiled to herself. Mom would kill her when she discovered that the cosy meal for two would actually be a dinner party for twenty-two! Clodagh's sister Claire, her family and friends from London would be waiting in the restaurant when Beth and Clodagh arrived. Clodagh never celebrated her birthday. She was vague about the reasons, she just preferred to ignore them. This one was a milestone and she wasn't getting away without celebrating it. Fifty was the new forty and Mom could certainly pull that one off.

She was still smiling when she entered the salon.

"Hi girl! Welcome back. What can we do for you today?"

"I'm not sure. It definitely needs a deep conditioning treatment. It feels dry." She draped her handbag across the back of her chair as Colin hung up her jacket.

"My Mom was fifty this week and I have a surprise dinner planned for tomorrow night." She settled into the chair.

"That's great. Have you any ideas for how you would like to wear your hair?"

"I have been thinking about cutting it shorter, but maybe I will just try an up style. What do you think?" she looked at him in the mirror.

"Well I agree with you about the condition. We need to refresh the red streaks and give it a trim. It will keep the ends strong. I'll get you a coffee and send Alan over to you." He pointed to the man who was busy applying colour to the girl in the chair next to Beth.

"Coffee would be great thanks. I take it that Alan is the King of Colour here then?" she joked.

"Yup, he is the best. Though I think he would prefer Queen of Colour. See you later!" he laughed.

Beth flicked through the pile of magazines in front of her as she waited for Alan to finish with the client he was working on. The salon door opened just as her coffee was placed in front of her.

"Hi all, I'm here to brighten up your day. Come here Colin and give me a hug. What's new?"

The blonde arrival grabbed Colin and air hugged him.

Turning to sit in the only available chair, she spotted Beth's handbag.

"LOVE your bag!" Blood red nails picked up the diamante studded bag. "This is a beautiful bag. It would make a perfect present for my favourite cousin. It's even in her very favourite colour. She adores purple. Who is it by?" She addressed Beth as she replaced the bag.

"It's by Clodagh Kenny. She just moved back to Ireland from London. She has a shop in Killarney and a new one about to open in Brandon Lodge near Mallow. The collection is also available online." Beth couldn't keep the pride out of her voice.

"I must get one. I don't care how much it costs. It's felted and I know someone who would simply adore it. She is into knitted stuff, so this will be right up her street. I will get on it as soon as I leave here. Thank you. I'm Caroline O'Connor and you are?"

"Beth Kenny. Pleased to meet you, Caroline."

"Beth, Clodagh and Kenny! Would I be correct in assuming there is a connection between you and this designer?" Caroline asked.

"You would indeed. I will give you a card that will entitle you to a twenty-five percent discount. It will make the bag a little less expensive. The crystals are Swarovski so that adds a lot to the price." Beth rummaged in the bag and pulled out a card.

"Thank you. I appreciate that. I'm more of a shoes person myself. I don't suppose there is a shoe shop opening up as well?

I'm not that into bags but I will definitely check it out. Thanks again." Caroline smiled.

Robert

Robert was delighted with his bookshop. It was not connected to the converted stables but was a little stone cottage that had once been a gate lodge. It faced directly onto the courtyard and so he had a view of the Cottage Tearoom. It was nice to know someone else in the courtyard. Ann was a nice young girl who had been very kind to him anytime he had gone into the bakery where she had worked before embarking on this venture. In the past few weeks, even though she had been busy setting up her own business, she often popped over with a coffee and sandwich.

He could see her and Clodagh Kenny chatting inside the window. This was the second day that Ms Kenny had been in Brandon Lodge. He had seen a few people coming and going so he assumed that she was holding interviews. Greta had told him that Brandon Lodge was not the only shop that she had in Ireland. There was already one open in Killarney. He was so deep in thought that he didn't notice Ann approach.

"Hi Robert, are you busy? Come on over and have a coffee. I don't think you have been formally introduced to Clodagh. I have told her all about you," Ann said cheerily.

"I'm sure Mrs Kenny has more important things to occupy her rather than meet me," he answered.

"Would a blueberry muffin help persuade you?" She knew they were his favourite.

"You said the magic words. Lead the way," he laughed.

"Clodagh, this is our neighbour Robert Munroe. He is a self-confessed bookaholic. Robert, meet Clodagh Kenny, a self-confessed knit-aholic. You should get on famously, what with you both being aholics." She laughed at her little joke and ran off to put the kettle on.

"Pleased to meet you Robert. I'm sure we aholics will get on famously."

"The pleasure is all mine. Every time I mention Brandon Lodge, I get asked if I have met the famous Clodagh Kenny. At last I will be able to answer in the affirmative. My daughter Greta will be thrilled. She is a big fan. I'm afraid I know very little about what's what in the world of wools." He smiled and her heart gave a little flutter.

"That's ok. From that beautiful sweater you're wearing, I take it that your wife takes care of your knitwear requirements."

Ann bustled over and placed two steaming cups of coffee in front of her guests. She had heard Clodagh's comment.

"I'm a widower," he answered quietly.

"Oops," Ann said quietly.

"I'm sorry to hear that." Clodagh could have kicked herself. "Are you from around here?"

Robert stirred his coffee and took a muffin from the plate that Ann had placed on the table. "Yes, about ten miles away. I used to dance here years ago, when dancing was an art form and not just a series of gyrating moves on the dance floor."

"I couldn't agree more," Clodagh nodded.

"I like to dance regularly. Thank God for ballroom dancing sessions. There are quite a few of them around here. Do you dance?" he asked.

"I used to, in London when I first moved over there. It was great fun. I haven't danced in years. I'd like to get back into it sometime."

"Maybe you could join one of the local groups. It is usually a good laugh. We could go together sometime." Robert surprised himself by saying.

"Thank you, Robert. I would like that," she smiled.

"That's great. I will let you know when the next few sessions are on and you can see when you are free. I had better get back to the shop. Still lots to do. See you later. Bye, Ann." Robert waved.

"See you, Robert."

"What have I just agreed to do?" Clodagh asked.

"Joining a class with a fellow tenant? Sounds harmless enough," Ann reassured her.

Chapter Five

Joe
Joe had become addicted to reading his horoscope. It had all started months before when Laura had given him a magazine on one of his frequent visits to the coffee shop. He knew that she went to college as well as working in the Castle Coffee shop. She was a lovely girl and always very efficient and friendly. She used to sit with him on her break. She loved to read her horoscope.

"I just love reading these. There is always something interesting. What's your star sign, Joe?"

"I don't believe in that rubbish. It's just made up claptrap."

"Then it won't make any difference to you if I read it anyway. Come on Joe, when is your birthday?"

"It's on November third. Whatever sign that is." He gave in gracefully.

"You're a Scorpio. Let's see what it says."

He had barely listened while she had been reading.

One or two small things had proved accurate so he had gotten into the habit of reading it on a regular basis. Of course he would never admit it to Laura!

He was still shaken by what he had witnessed in town that morning. He wondered what the stars would have to say about that!

It's a good time to finally get to grips with an issue that is affecting your wellbeing. You give the impression of being on top of the world most of the time, however there are certain times when your energy levels drop and you feel like you are unable to lift a newspaper. Don't ignore what your body is trying to tell you. Your lifestyle needs to undergo a gradual transformation. Start now.

He had to admit that it was on the ball once again. He could barely fit in behind the steering wheel.

"Did you find the article you wanted, Joe?" He was so engrossed in his own thoughts that he hadn't heard Laura approach his table.

"I did indeed. I'll definitely go and see him. He was overweight himself, so he will know where I am coming from. It will be easier facing another man. Most of the weight loss places are usually full of women. That's a bit too daunting for me."

"I'm sure Gill will be delighted to help you with the food plans," Laura added.

"Actually, I might keep it to myself for a while. Just in case it doesn't work out. I'll have to change my eating habits completely. I can't wait to get started. I can't even sleep properly because my weight. I wake myself up with my snoring! I really need to be alert in my job so I'll have to find a solution sooner rather than later. Thanks for listening to a grumpy old man. I'm really looking forward to joining the walking group. I hope your mother and her friends won't mind." He folded the newspaper and placed it on the table.

"Not at all. New people join every week. I'll text you later this evening with the details. Usual number okay?"

"No, that is the work phone. Here is my own mobile number."

Laura put it in her phone.

"I'd better get going now. I must collect Matt from the airport. I'll talk to you later. Thanks again, Laura." He stood up.

"No problem, Joe. Bye."

Laura began to clear the table. Joe was at the door when she called him.

"I remember Mam not being able to sleep after Dad died. She found something in the health shop that worked. It didn't make her drowsy during the day. I think it was a girl's name. I will ask her about it. She might remember the name."

As Joe drove away from the castle, he was amazed at how accurate the horoscope had been and what good advice it had held for him.

Sometimes he was so exhausted that he could barely keep his eyes open. In order to keep his energy levels up he would eat chocolate and guzzle fizzy drinks. The quick sugar fix only lasted for a short time so he had to keep topping it up. It was a vicious circle and here he was – fat and guilty. Sleeping in the spare room was not where he wanted to be. He had told Gill that he didn't want to disturb her on the nights when he worked late. The truth was that he was ashamed of his weight and the fact that his belly always got in the way of any uplifting ideas that he might have had. The last time they had tried to make love had been a complete disaster. He was afraid that he would never be able to perform again. He loved Gill more than life itself but he was not a real man anymore. Maybe she would be better off with the sugar daddy. As soon as he had dropped Matt off in town, he would make an appointment with his doctor and with the weight loss guru. He would do anything to win Gill back even if it involved running naked up the marina. He hoped that Laura would text him about the walking group.

He was in much better form as he headed to the airport. While he waited for the plane to land, he searched for his mobile. He suddenly realised that he must have left it on the kitchen table. He had intended to make that appointment with his doctor. He would have to wait until he got home.

Gill

Gill arrived home around three o'clock. She had treated herself to a knitting magazine. She loved looking up the wool sites and seeing what was new. She put the kettle on and rummaged around in her bag for her phone. God knows how people managed before mobile phones. She checked her messages. There was one from Beth Kenny telling her that Clodagh would be in contact later. She was delighted with that but a little disappointed that there was no message from Joe. He usually texted her around lunchtime. Things were not the same between them for a while. She had been upset when he had moved into the spare bedroom a few months back. He tried to tell her that it was for her benefit, but she knew the real reason. He didn't fancy her any more. Maybe he had found someone else and was trying to pull away gradually. If he ever knew what she had almost done on that bloody holiday.

God how she wished that Caroline had never mentioned it in the first place.

She should really try to get fitter and lose a few pounds. The treadmill which was rusting away in the spare room would be a good place to start. No time like the present!

She heard Joe's phone beep. Looking around the kitchen she located it under the newspaper on the table. One new message.

Hi Joe, she would be delighted to meet you. Her name is Maria and she is certain that you will be delighted with everything. She said that you should also try Melissa Dream…should work a treat for your problem. Should perk you up no end. Laura x.

The mobile number was included.

"Damn you, Joe." He couldn't make love to her lately because he was getting plenty elsewhere. He had mentioned a few months back that some of his regular customers were a group of women who worked in a city centre brothel. She had joked that she hoped he was not being paid in kind. Damn. This Laura must be running the place. Melissa dream, bloody stupid name for a prostitute!

What was she going to do about it? Would she confront him with the evidence and face the consequences? Did she want to lose him after all this time? She had to think. She needed time to sort it all out in her head. Did she want to save her marriage or was it way too late for that? She knew that it was partly her fault. Since she had returned from Turkey, she had been restless and had taken his presence for granted. She couldn't remember the last time that they had enjoyed a romantic night in or out together. Joe loved to cook and was much better at it than she was. Lately it had seemed that he just got takeaway or grabbed a quick sandwich. Cooking for one wasn't much fun, so she was almost as bad. She seemed to be existing on white bread and cheese. No wonder he needed Melissa Dream to perk him up.

After another two cups of coffee and the last sandwich she was going to eat, she had come to a few decisions. She deleted the message. She needed help and she knew just the woman to call. She found Caroline's name and pressed the call button.

Caroline

"I think your phone is ringing," Colin said as he placed a fresh towel around Caroline's shoulders and passed her the bag.

"Hi Gill, how are you?" Caroline smiled down the phone.

"Hi Caroline… I know I haven't been in touch. I need to talk to you about something important. Can you call today?"

"Breathe woman. Of course I can. I will be there as soon as I can. I am at the hairdressers but am almost finished. Everything okay? Do you want me to come now?" She held up her hand to Colin who was approaching her with scissors at the ready.

"Everything, okay?" asked Colin.

"See you later then, bye Gill." She nodded and Colin set to work.

Gill

Gill pounded the treadmill. She had been on a high after her morning in town. It had been the best day in years. Then she had arrived home and her world had fallen apart. She had been looking forward to telling Joe all about it. He would have gotten a great laugh over the shoplifting story. She was still trying to take in the events of the past few hours. Was this how it was going to end for them? They had survived so much together. They had known one another in school, had grown up together and had married when they were only twenty. The waited for their fairy-tale to continue but she didn't get pregnant. Each month brought disappointment.

She and Joe had tried everything. Eventually they had succeeded. Happiness for a while and then despair. They had lost their beloved Hugh. He had simply been too weak to survive.

She had wallowed for long enough. It was time to get her life back on track. Hence the treadmill! She had to remove piles of winter clothes before she could step onto it. She was going to get a fabulous new job, lose weight and reinvent the sexy woman that she once was. She hadn't heard from Joe all day which was unusual. He still had his work phone.

The iPod had been nearly as redundant as the treadmill. She had forgotten how much she enjoyed Martina McBride.

Gill jumped as she felt a tap on her shoulder. Pulling the earplugs out of her ears, she slowed down to a walk and then stopped.

"Hi Joe, I didn't hear you come in," she grabbed a towel and dried her face.

"I'm not surprised. You were working hard there. I haven't seen you in this room for a long time. Maybe it's time I revisited it myself," Joe patted his expanding stomach. "Did you do anything interesting today?" he enquired innocently.

"Yes, I went to town to pick up a few things. I picked up a new knitting book and was dying to start a vintage inspired dress I saw in it. I've some beautiful yarn that will be perfect for it. I also had a pretty interesting experience in Smithfield's. I will tell you all about it over coffee. You look tired. I thought you would lie in this morning since you worked last night. Was it busy?"

"Busy enough. The conference ended early but there were a lot of students around. Some cheap drink promotion. The aftermath is not so pretty. I got a few messers. One guy didn't want to pay the fare and a young one nearly puked all over the back seat. I collected two mobile phones, a ring, one glove and a pair of black knickers, though to be fair, that was in a Penney's bag. What's the story with the treadmill?" he yawned.

"I've just decided to get fit. I'm going to ditch the chocolate and crisps and eat more healthily. I'm not getting any younger and I read that a healthy diet cuts down on the number of bloody hot flushes a woman can get. You are lucky that you have your own bed or you would be sleeping in a swimming pool. I've had to strip the bed again. I'll be washed away from showers. Pity water doesn't dissolve fat particles – I'd be stick thin in no time. You men have it easy. No tropical moments for you lot."

"You look perfect to me, even with sweat dripping off you," he reassured her.

"Thanks, Joe. You should rest for a few hours." Gill could see how tired he looked.

"I had a few regular customers. Anyway Matt needed to be collected from the airport. I couldn't let him down. Anything exciting happen to you? No sugar daddy tried to steal you away from me then?" he joked.

"You'd be surprised. Listen, I'll have a shower and then we'll have something to eat. You sit down and relax. I'll only be a few minutes. Caroline is calling later. She is in town for the day." She grabbed the towel and headed for the bathroom.

When Gill entered the kitchen Joe was putting the plates on the table. The coffee was already made. She looked out at the driving rain.

"God, I hate this weather. Oh for some sun." She walked to the table and sat down. Joe poured milk into his coffee. She passed him the sugar bowl.

"No sugar for me. I'm going to try to do without it. You enjoyed your holiday last year, didn't you? Caroline would go again in a second. At least that was the impression I got the last time she was here. I'm glad she is dropping in. I haven't seen her in months." Joe grimaced as he tried to drink the coffee.

Gill looked at her husband. How she wished she could ask him about Maria and Melissa, but she needed to get her head around it first. Hopefully Caroline would be able to advise her. Since the holiday in Turkey, Gill had avoided her friend. The truth was that Gill was so guilty about what she had done that she couldn't face talking to Caroline. She just wanted to forget all about that damn holiday.

Joe worked hard. He was a big gentle giant who deserved to be loved. She did love him very much but since that holiday and the onset of the bloody menopause, not to mention the weight that crept into the house every night and attached itself to her hips, she had lost interest in sex. She had read somewhere that Horny Goat Weed was a good supplement. She had started taking it months before. So far all it had done was to make her seem fair game to the bus driver.

"Sorry Joe. What did you say? I was miles away. I guess the treadmill was tougher than I thought."

"Food is ready. Poached eggs on wholemeal toast. You can tell me all about your interesting morning. Matt was asking for you. He was at some exhibition for the past week. I meant to text you earlier but I left my phone here. Have you come across it?" Joe poured the coffee.

"Yeah. It was on the table. The battery was dead so I plugged it in. It's over there by the dresser. I couldn't check it." She was amazed at how easily she could lie.

Joe checked his messages.

Gill recounted the events of the morning.

"You mean, he actually thought that you were a shoplifter. You, of all people. At least some good came out of it. When are you expecting to hear from this Clodagh Kenny?" Joe asked.

"She left a message. I hope to meet her sometime in the next few days. I'd love to work again. This job would be a dream come true. The shop is in a place called Brandon Lodge. I'd be there in less than thirty minutes," she added.

After they had eaten, they watched television in the sitting room. Gill picked up her knitting and Joe snored softly.

At half six Gill's phone rang.

"Hi Gillian, this is Clodagh Kenny. According to Beth, you are the answer to all my prayers. I usually trust her judgement, so when can we meet?" Gill couldn't believe that she was actually talking to the famous Clodagh Kenny!

"Hi Clodagh, I'm delighted to hear from you. I can meet you anytime. Tomorrow too soon for you?" Gill enquired.

"How about Friday? I'll be staying in the city on Thursday night. I am having dinner with Beth. I can meet you in the afternoon if that suits you?" Clodagh sounded apologetic.

"Friday will be great. I can meet you whenever it suits you. I live just outside the city centre so any place you choose will be fine with me." Gill said.

After the arrangements had been finalised Gill went back to the collar she was working on. She was almost finished when Joe woke up.

He looked at the clock.

"Jesus, my neck hurts. I would love to chat with Caroline but I need some exercise. I will go for a quick walk before she arrives. Did you hear any more about the job?"

"Yes, Clodagh Kenny rang me. I am meeting her on Friday at four in the Metropole. Beth should be with her so at least she will know me. I can't make up my mind whether I will drive or take the bus." She tidied up her knitting.

"I'll drop you in. It will save you the hassle of trying to find parking." He stretched and stood up.

"Thanks Joe. That would be lovely. Caroline should be here by seven. Do you think this collar would be too much to wear at the interview?" She held up the delicate, beaded lace collar that she had just finished.

"Perfect as usual, pet. I will see you soon." He bent and kissed her cheek. "You'll knock them dead. You're clearly a very talented lady. When you get the job, you might be able to sell some of the beautiful stuff that you keep making...before the two of us will have to be rescued from under a mountain of designer hand knits," he joked.

"Very funny. I'll have you know that all the blankets are being given to the girl's club. There was a stand in the shopping centre last week. They were looking for blankets to give as a gift to people diagnosed with cancer. I'll tell you what, if the interview goes well, we will go out to dinner. That new place in Washington Street is supposed to be excellent. Do you think we could get a reservation?" she added.

"I'll book it in the morning. See you later, love." Joe kissed her cheek and grabbed his jacket.

When Caroline had first suggested going on holidays, Gill had declined. A week on the west coast was usually as far as she and Joe got. It suited them. They didn't have much spare money but Caroline was very persuasive, even offering to pay for the whole thing. Money was no object to her and she didn't mind sharing it. Joe sided with Caroline. Gill eventually agreed but only because

Caroline insisted that she needed a break from her long-term partner Dylan. He had suddenly decided that he wanted to get married after years of being 'perfectly happy' together.

Caroline had been excited as she showed Gill the hotel complex online.

"It's lovely, right on the beach. You could do with a break and a good laugh. You'll get both in Turkey. Sun, sea and sand or any other s you fancy."

"Slow down on the s-words. Technically you might be considered to be single, but I most certainly am not. Sun is the only s that interests me," Gill giggled.

"Don't worry, I'm only joking. We will lie in the sun all day and hit the town at night. Turkey, here we come." She hit the button and confirmed the booking.

Standing at the reception desk, she waited for her key card. The handsome guy behind the desk looked at her passport and then at her. He shook his head and spoke.

"Sorry Madam but there appears to be a problem!"

"What do you mean, a problem?"

He smiled at her. "You cannot possibly be the age that it says here."

Beside her Caroline started to giggle. "Welcome to Turkey." she whispered.

"Let's look around before we unpack," Gill dumped her suitcase onto the single bed.

"Just give me a minute to freshen up." Caroline grabbed her make up bag.

As they walked the short distance from their room to the beach, they stopped to pick up a drink from the cocktail bar.

Dropping their towels onto the sunbeds, they went for a quick dip in the crystal clear water.

Making their way back, they noticed that two umbrellas had been hoisted over the sunbeds.

"That's service for you. I could get used to this!" Gill laughed.

"The restaurant is so close to the beach that we can order our food and wait to be called when it is ready. That's the Turkish way. After my last holiday I was back home three days before I realised that I had to pour my own tea!"

Passing through reception later, he had winked at her. She was definitely flattered. It wasn't every day that a younger man showed interest in you, even if it was all part of the service!

The evening was warm and as they walked along, they noticed that restaurants and shops were evident all along the street. Waiters in crisp white shirts tried to lure the passing tourists into their establishment with promises of great food and even greater entertainment.

Offers of Turkish baths were shouted out from all the hotel foyers along the way.

"How do we decide where to go?" Gill whispered.

"We will go up to the top of the street and have a drink at the bar. It is really well recommended. We can decide then. That alright with you?" Caroline winked at one of the waiters who was trying to get their attention.

It was after three am when they staggered to the hotel pool bar. It was still packed.

"I need a drink of ..." slurred Gill.

"Good on you girlie, getting into the spirit of things!" Caroline burst out laughing.

"I meant water. You know I can't hold my drink and I've already had more than enough for one night."

Caroline caught Gill by the arm and swung her around to the beat of the music.

"I'm so funny. Two very large Sex on the Beach cocktails, please, handsome, sexy man... Look Gill, it's the hunk from reception."

"Shhh! He will hear you!"

"Na, I'm being really quiet. His name is TJ. You fancy him too?"

As they waited for the drinks, Caroline started dancing with a group of young holidaymakers by the bar. Gill felt dizzy so she sat on a stool. She rarely drank more than two drinks but they had been in every pub on the street. God only knew what was in some of the drinks they had bought.

TJ put the drinks on the counter.

"I would like to kiss you, pretty lady. You like me too. Your friend she say that. I hear her say it. You come for walk with me? I have apartment uphill. I find friend for your friend."

Caroline wandered back.

"Jesus, I'm knackered. Let's take this drink back to the room. It's been a very long day."

Gill paid for the drinks.

"Good idea. Goodnight TJ."

"Night beautiful Gillian...We meet soon, no?"

Back in the room, Caroline put her drink on the table beside the bed, laid down on the bed and promptly fell asleep.

Gill suddenly felt old. She knew that it was all part of the Turkish way, but for a split second she had been sorely tempted. She threw back her drink in one go and followed it with Caroline's one.

She decided that she needed to get more water from the bar and left the room quietly.

When she awoke the following morning, she had no recollection of how she had gotten back to bed or of what had happened after she had left the room. Surely to God she hadn't slept with that waiter.

Gill dragged her thoughts back to the present. She shaped her collar and rolled it in a damp cloth. Walking to the kitchen, she hit the switch in the kettle

Caroline walked up the beach and flopped down onto the sunbed.

"God, the sand is so hot but the water is lovely. You should try it at least."

Gill looked up from her book.

"Where did you get to? I was beginning to worry. You've been gone over an hour and I'm starving."

While they waited for their food to arrive, Caroline giggled as she told Gill about her swim.

"I was minding my own business, enjoying my swim when the hairiest man I've ever seen swam up to me. He began to chat so I thought he was someone we had met here. He told me that he worked in one of the small hotels further up the beach. He wanted me to be his friend. He said that he would meet me out in the sea again tomorrow. He will bring a friend. That

must be the strangest offer I've ever had. You ok Gill? You are very quiet," Caroline said.

"I'm fine, just not used to late nights and so much alcohol."

"I know the feeling." Caroline stretched out on her towel.

After lunch they went back to getting a tan and stayed glued to the sun loungers until almost seven o'clock. A quick shower, into the glad rags and off they went to explore the resort. They had already made a reservation for dinner, so they had to avoid being talked into every bar and restaurant that they passed.

"Did your father steal the stars from the sky and put them in your eyes?" one guy called out as they made their way up the street.

When they reached the top of the hill, they decided to stop for a cocktail.

"What will it be, my angels?"

"We will have whatever cocktail you recommend?" Caroline smiled.

"I give you Sex on the Beach. Later I give you triple orgasm."

"You can give me a triple orgasm any time. It would be three more than I've ever had!" A woman at the next table slurred.

Her husband glared at her.

Caroline and Gill burst out laughing.

"Christ, I've jeans that are older than him," Gill giggled. As their drinks were placed on the table, the woman started up again.

"You have some sex for me, lovey? This fellow here is only beans on toast. Tonight I fancy steak."

The waiter smiled at her. "I serve these ladies, then I come back to you. You wait?"

"Ooh, can I come too?"

Her husband stood and left the bar.

"Good riddance," she slurred. "Now I'm all yours."

"Is she for real?" Gill whispered.

"Probably. That fellow is about thirty, which is old enough for a waiter here. It could be worse. Some of them are very young. Hopefully she will sober up and go back to her husband." Caroline sipped her drink.

Gill thought about TJ and the look that he had given her as they had passed by the reception desk on their way out. If only she could clear her head and remember.

She thought about Joe working all the hours he could get and felt deeply ashamed of herself. She didn't deserve such a good man. She would make it up to him when she arrived home.

The ringing of her phone disrupted her thoughts.

"Hi Caroline. You on the way?" Gill took a bottle of wine from the fridge.

"Open the door. I'm laden down," Caroline laughed.

Caroline was barely visible behind the huge bouquet of lilies. Carrier bags dripped from her arms.

"Help me here." She pushed the flowers towards Gill and dropped the bags in the hall.

"These are my favourites." Gill led the way into the kitchen and placed the blooms carefully in a cut glass vase.

"Wine?" She waved the bottle in the air.

"Of course. I will get a taxi later. Dad is in town as well, so I promised that I would call to the hotel." Caroline took the glass that Gill held out. Put these in the fridge." She handed Gill the cheesecake and bottle of Moet.

"Wow. What are we celebrating?" Gill asked.

"Friendship. We haven't had much of that lately," Caroline looked at Gill.

"I know and I'm sorry. I have been feeling so… displaced. It is as if I am not me anymore. My life seems to be falling apart and I think that Joe has found someone else." Gill tried to explain.

"I doubt that. He adores you." Caroline hugged Gill.

"I think we had better open that bottle now. Glasses in the usual spot?" Caroline reached above the sink and opened the press.

"This tastes great. I love a good champagne. Do you want to talk about why you think Joe is…?"

"What am I doing that needs talking about?" Joe entered the kitchen.

"Hi Joe! Long time, no see. It seems you are working too hard!" Caroline hugged him.

"How are you doing, Caroline?" He took the glass that Gill held out.

"I am great. You?" she answered.

"Not too bad," he told her.

"Anyone for cheesecake?" Gill asked.

"Why not!" Caroline and Joe answered together.

"You seeing her again soon?" Joe asked as he and Gill waved Caroline off in a taxi.

"Yeah, I will ring her tomorrow." Gill locked the door and switched off the outside light.

"I will go up so. That champagne went straight to my head. See you tomorrow. Night Gill." He hugged his wife and made his way upstairs.

"Night Joe." She was gutted.

Gill patted the empty space in the king size bed and was just about to turn out the light when her phone beeped.

Sorry we didn't get to talk about what is bothering you. I will ring you tomorrow xx

Gill lay in bed and listened to the cars pass by on the road outside. If her life was about to improve, then why did she feel so empty.

Joe

Joe tossed and turned. He knew that when he had walked into the kitchen earlier that he had interrupted a conversation between Gill and Caroline.

He wished he knew what was going on with his wife. She had explained about the incident at Smithfield's so he knew that there was no sugar daddy. He loved her more than life itself and yet they lay in different bedrooms divided by a wall that may as well have been a continent.

Margaret Kelleher

Chapter Six

Beth
Beth gave a final check in the full-length mirror, flicked back her hair, grabbed her bag and left the apartment.

Thirty minutes later she was sitting opposite David in the plush surroundings of the hotel that would host Clodagh's birthday party.

"I hope that this goes according to plan, David. She has always refused to celebrate her birthday. She thinks that it is only the two of us having dinner in Green's next door!" Beth sipped the champagne that David had poured for her. "Mmm…this is really nice."

"Dom Perignon never fails to please. This is what I have ordered for the toast tomorrow night. Clodagh likes a good champers now and again," David remarked.

"Well I hopes she appreciates it so much that she will overlook the fact that we have done exactly what she asked us not to do." Beth giggled as the bubbles hit her nose.

"Well it has made you quite happy already, so I must be on to a winner!" David quipped.

"I am tiddly because I haven't eaten much all day. You promised me a taster of what is on the menu tomorrow night and I wanted to do it justice. If I inhale any more bubbles then I won't be able to remember what the food tasted like." Beth drained her glass.

"Excuse me, Mr McGovern. Your table is ready."

"Thank you. We will be right there."

"Come along, you lightweight." He held his hand out to Beth.

Clodagh
Clodagh looked around the cottage that had become her latest shop. She still could not believe that she had ended up back in Brandon Lodge. She thought of all the times that she had danced

the night away with James and of the dreams they shared of being able to live happily ever after as the owners of the hotel. Now she was here…but without James Murray. She was delighted to be here and James was firmly in the past.

"Morning Ms Kenny. My name is Megan Kelly." Clodagh's trip down memory lane was interrupted by the arrival of the first of her Thursday morning interview candidates.

"Good morning, Megan. Please come in."

Ann

The Tearoom was busy and Ann was glad that Gary had stepped in to help. While he and his sister took the orders, Ann and her mother filled them. If business continued at this rate, then she would have to consider taking on someone on a full-time basis. Gary was still painting signs on the units and her mother could only help out on her days off. Still this was what she had hoped for when she took on the lease.

"You okay, Ann? It is a bit quieter now so why don't you grab something to eat. The table in the alcove is free and I see Clodagh heading this way," Gary told her.

"Thanks, Gary. You have played a blinder. I will take ten minutes, if you don't mind. Clodagh had a few interviews for the manager's position this morning so I would like to know how she got on." Ann took off her apron and hat and placed them behind the counter.

"You and Clodagh have become good friends in a short space of time." Gary observed.

"Actually we have been in contact since the first meeting about Brandon Lodge. She has been really helpful with business tips and we have become good friends," she answered.

"That's great. I am glad that things are working out here. You sit down and I will show Clodagh to your table."

"I seem to spend all my time in here with you. I'm hoping that I will get immune to the smell of fresh scones and cakes," Clodagh sat down opposite Ann.

"Don't worry. We serve much more than that. How did the interviews go?" Ann asked.

"The first girl, Megan, was quite impressive but has little experience. I am waiting until I meet the woman that Beth recommended." Clodagh bit into the toasted sandwich that Gary had placed in front of her.

"It must be a huge change for your daughter. Does she like it here?" Ann sipped her tea.

"Beth works in the city, but she likes it here. She is a city girl at heart. What makes you think that she is my daughter?"

"Oh, I just assumed that she was. She was with you at the meeting. Your shop is called after her. God this is awful. Please forget that I said anything." Ann was mortified.

"Relax Ann. It's fine. A lot of people assume that for the reasons you have mentioned. In a way she is a daughter to me. The fact that she has a habit of calling me Mom is also a bit confusing. If you are still here later then you can meet her."

"That would be lovely. Would you like a refill?" Ann held up the pot.

"No, thanks. I am fine. I will chill out here for a while. I have another interview in twenty minutes."

Beth

"Wow, this place is unreal." Beth stood in the doorway of Beth's Knits and admired the view across the courtyard.

"Yes, I must agree." Clodagh stood behind her.

"I used to think that you exaggerated the beauty of this place but it is truly fabulous. Is that place still open? I would love a cup of tea." Beth looked across the yard at the Cottage Tearoom.

"Yes. Ann stays open until everyone else leaves. Actually I would like you to meet her. She has a great business head on her shoulders," Clodagh answered.

"Sounds like someone I know." Beth deadpanned.

"Ha ha. You are just like me too. Ann actually thought that you were my daughter. We must be more alike than either of us thought," Clodagh said.

"Really? Do you fancy a coffee?" Beth asked.

"Why not! I am all finished here. Let me lock up and we will get going. What time is dinner booked for?" Clodagh answered.

"Eight o'clock. We have plenty of time." Beth looked away.

While she waited for Clodagh to close up the shop, Beth hoped that she and David had not made a serious mistake by organising the birthday party. She would not hurt Clodagh for the world but she felt that turning fifty and returning to her roots needed to be celebrated.

"Ready, Beth?" Clodagh turned from the door and dropped the keys into her grey felted bag.

"Yes, indeed. Let's grab that coffee and then we can set off. We can't spend more than an hour in your place so I hope you have your clothes laid out on the bed!"

"Indeed I have. It won't take me too long to get ready. Anyway, since it is only the two of us…" Clodagh started to walk across to the Tearoom.

"Just because it is not a big event does not mean that you should drop your standards!" Beth joked.

"I wouldn't dream of it," Clodagh answered.

Ann was dashing around filling orders when the two women entered the Tearoom.

She pointed at a free table, Clodagh and Beth sat down.

A few minutes later Ann came over to take their order.

"Hi Ann, you are very busy. This is Beth." Clodagh looked at the menu that Ann had handed her.

Both women shook hands.

"Delighted to meet you at last," Beth said.

"Likewise. Clodagh keeps singing your praises. What can I get you both?" Ann's pen was poised.

"Just a decaffeinated tea for me, thanks." Beth answered.

"I'll have an Americano, please." Clodagh put down the menu.

"No problem. I know that you have a fabulous meal waiting for you in Cork." Ann went to get their drinks.

Beth looked across the yard at the view of the darkening hills.

"The view is lovely from here. I can see everything that is going on in the courtyard. It is very impressive. I must visit that bookshop opposite. I haven't read a good book in ages," Beth added.

"I'm not sure that Robert stocks the type of book that appeals to you. He is into some serious stuff… first editions and suchlike." Clodagh told her.

"Maybe I will have a look anyway. You never know what catches your eye until you have a look." Beth answered.

"He is a lovely man, a widower. I hope he will be successful." Clodagh swallowed the last of her coffee.

"You seem to like him. Any ulterior motives?" Beth inquired.

"Of course not. I have agreed to go dancing with him, but only as a friend." Clodagh busied herself tidying up the table.

"I see," Beth answered.

Ann was moving around the room, removing empty ware and refilling cups. She approached the table where Clodagh and Beth sat.

"Do you need anything else?" she asked.

"I'm okay. Clodagh?"

"I am happy as long as I have caffeine," Clodagh laughed.

"Thanks Ann. We are fine." Beth smiled at the other woman. You have a lovely set-up here. It is so Downton Abbey."

"I know. I love it too. I hope to get a chance to explore it properly some time." Ann wiped down the table.

"Maybe we can explore this place together. I haven't had a chance to have a proper look around. Did you know that this fine lady here was a teenage delinquent! She and her friends used to climb through a window into the basement. She wouldn't get away with it now, especially with the top notch security firm that David hired." Beth checked her watch.

"Actually I've met the boss of the security firm. A person could do worse than to get caught by him. He is quite handsome. Too old for me though!" Ann smiled.

"You never give up. You're as bad as Beth. She is always trying to set me up. I've already agreed to go dancing with Robert.

security. Been there, done that. What's the name of this security firm anyway?"

"There's the sign over there. CJ Securities."

"Never heard of them, thank God." Clodagh sighed with relief.

Beth and Ann looked at her.

"It's okay girls, don't mind me. Come on, Beth. Drink up your tea. I'm sure Ann wants to close up."

"It is time I left. Gary is going to give me a lift." Ann began to collect the cups.

"You will love her, Mom. She wore a beautiful scarf that she had designed herself. It was made up of seed stitch and cables. Your favourite combinations. She used to work in a yarn shop but it closed down a few years ago. She would love to get back to work. She would be perfect for your shop. She has the experience, the interest and the talent. You were worried about getting the right person – I think she is it. I felt the shiver. Aunt Lizzie still makes her presence felt. I hope you will follow it up." she glanced at Clodagh.

"I rang her already. I have learned to trust your instincts. We are meeting tomorrow at two. Anyway to more important issues, Claire told me that she gave you my present. I know that she was a bit put out when I told her that I didn't want a big party. I'm just not the party type."

"You will have to wait until tomorrow for your presents. We are lucky the traffic is light. I'm glad that you have decided to stay with me tonight. We can share a bottle of wine."

"Me too. Things have been hectic for the past few weeks."

"We don't see as much of each other since we came over from London. I'm glad you persuaded me to come over with you. I wasn't sure about it when you first mentioned it." Beth slowed down as she reached the first set of traffic lights.

"I know you had doubts, but it wouldn't have been the same without you. Aunt Lizzie's house is still there so you can go back any time you like. I know that this is my dream, so thanks for trusting me."

"I'm happy for the moment. I like my job and I have made some good friends. Shirley is really lovely and she has a handsome brother! I am going back to London in December for the annual reunion. It's always great fun. No matter where we are, the six of us promised that we would meet every year on December the sixth. This year Amy is travelling from Australia, so I can surely make it over from Ireland." Beth waited for the lights to turn green.

"How long are you planning on staying over there? I could go over for Christmas if you were still there?" said Clodagh.

"It depends. My work contract ends at the beginning of December. I don't know if I will stay any longer than that. Mike is opening a new boutique in January and he said that I can manage it if I want. It's going to be the largest one in the chain so far and would be a great challenge. Still that's all months away. Who knows what life-changing events will come along before then?"

"You are right, of course. It is way too early to be discussing Christmas. You could wake up one morning and discover that your whole future has changed," Clodagh sighed.

"You okay? I know that you went to London when you were very young. Is that what happened to you?" asked Beth.

"Something like that. Still my life turned out pretty good. I don't regret any of it. I met lots of people that helped to shape my path Aunt Lizzie was a huge influence. Then there was David and his family, not to mention your mother who entrusted her precious daughter to both Lizzie and me. I wouldn't change any of that for the world."

Clodagh

"*Clodagh, you don't have to go all the way to London.*"

"*It's not what I want. It's what I have to do.*" *She folded the sweaters ready for packing.*

Chips in a Bag, Classy Mr Murray

"Well maybe if you stay around you can get back together again. I wish you would tell me what happened. Maybe I could help. He is a nice lad and being a few years older than you, well I thought he would take care of you."

"Mam, if you like him that much then you can sit and listen to his explanations over tea and tart. Let him explain to you that, while we were on a short break, he went off and got another girl pregnant. Not just any girl, mind you, but the one who has tried to break us up since the night we met! She made snide remarks every time she saw us together. It wouldn't surprise me if she planned the whole thing just to get him for herself. Well now she has him and I am not staying around here to be laughed at. I never want to see that conniving bitch or that bastard again." She sat on the bed.

"Language, Clodagh. Though to be honest I feel like calling him something awful myself!"

"Go for it Mam, you won't melt." Claire entered the bedroom.

"I'm sorry pet, I didn't know any of this. Your father will kill him for treating you like that. He had better not darken my door again or I will take the poker to his bits!" she muttered.

Clodagh and her sister giggled.

"Sure if she goes to London, she will have great fun. Aunt Lizzie is the black sheep of the family so who knows what adventures await. I'll have a whole bedroom to myself and she will have a new life!" said Claire.

"This is about more than a room. This is about your only sister leaving home, over that scoundrel. She is changing the course of her future. She can go to college here. She shouldn't have to cross the water just because of this."

Clodagh walked over and put her arms around her mother.

"Look Mam, Aunt Lizzie had already offered me the chance to go to college in London. I only said no because I didn't want to leave James. I will be perfectly safe. It is the eighties, and not as if I am going to Australia on a coffin ship! Aunt Lizzie and I will visit at Christmas. I can stay then if I don't like London. I need to get away for a while. I know that you were delighted when I met James. He reminded you of Dad with him being older than me. We both thought he was a lovely person. I wanted to spend the rest of my life with him. We had even put a deposit on our engagement ring. It was a really beautiful ring... a sapphire in the middle surrounded by little diamonds. So now I hate him. It was his idea to have a break while I was doing my exams. I thought he was just giving me space to study. I didn't know *that he had another girlfriend lined up to keep him company. The heartless bastard. I never want to feel like this again." Clodagh burst into tears.*

Her mother and sister hugged her.

"James Murray can go to hell. I'm going to London," Clodagh sobbed.

"Where are we going? Isn't the restaurant this way?" Clodagh asked as Beth started up the alleyway towards the hotel.

"It is but I want you to try a cocktail that this place is famous for. We still have twenty minutes so you might as well try it. After all you are only fifty once!" Beth kept going.

"I suppose so. What is this drink called? I hope there aren't too many spirits in it!" Clodagh struggled to keep up on her heels.

"Middle-aged woman!" Beth joked.

"Very funny. What is it really called?" Clodagh persisted.

"Actually I have narrowed their selection down to two and since it is your birthday we are going to try both." Beth pushed opened the door.

A few minutes later the barman placed the drinks on the counter in front of the two women.

"There you go ladies, Aqua Marina… Enjoy."

"What is in it?" Clodagh sipped it cautiously.

"Champagne, vodka, green crème de menthe and lemon juice."

"Okay. It has all my favourites in one glass. Cheers!"

"Cheers, Mom. Happy birthday!" Beth raised her glass.

"This is lovely. I will definitely have it again." Clodagh placed the empty glass on the counter.

"Not tonight you won't! I want you to try their Pisco Sour… It is made with grape brandy, lime juice, syrup and an egg white. Sounds disgusting but tastes unreal." Beth assured her.

"You sure about that?" Clodagh wasn't convinced.

"Try it." Beth picked up the white foamy drinks and handed one to Clodagh who took a sip.

"Wow, this is lovely but I will be too tipsy to enjoy my dinner if I drink anymore," she laughed.

"Don't worry… This is the last one. We will be leaving as soon as we have finished these. I am just nipping to the bathroom," Beth said.

Outside the door, Beth texted David and told him that they were ready.

"We are good to go. Claire, you're on." David told Clodagh's sister.

"On my way." She made her way down the winding staircase to where Beth was waiting by the entrance to the bar.

"Hope this works."

"Me too," Claire agreed.

Clodagh was wondering what was taking Beth so long and was just about to go and find her when the door opened and Beth, followed by Claire came into the room.

"Claire… what are you doing here?"

"I came to help my favourite and only sister to celebrate her birthday!"

"That's great. Let me get you a cocktail," Clodagh beckoned to the barman.

"We had better get going, Mom," Beth interrupted.

"You are right… I hope the restaurant won't mind an extra guest!"

"Don't worry Mom…" Beth picked up their jackets.

"I am staying here tonight. Tim had some meeting in town and won't be back until later. Come on and let me show you our room. It is really luxurious." Claire took her sister's arm.

"Do we have time?" Clodagh looked at Beth.

"I will give them a ring and let them know that we will be a few minutes late. You go on up. I will meet you both in the restaurant in ten minutes. I also want to say goodbye to the handsome barman over there," she smiled mischievously.

"He is very good looking. If I was only twenty years younger!" Clodagh giggled.

"Come along, Sis. We will leave the young people alone." Claire led Clodagh towards the lift which would take them to the Yeats Suite where all the other guests waited.

"Which floor are you on?" Clodagh asked.

"Third. Here we are."

The lift opened directly opposite the function room.

"The room is down here," Claire pointed to the left. "But let's be nosey and see what the function room looks like. If Beth and the barman hit it off, you might be looking for a wedding venue," Claire headed across to the door.

"Surprise!"

The lights came on and Clodagh was momentarily blinded.

"Jesus wept!" Realisation dawned on Clodagh.

"Happy birthday, Clodagh!" David hugged the startled woman.

"Thanks, David. I will murder you later," she whispered as all her friends gathered around her.

Gill

Gill fiddled with her scarf as she entered the hotel. She turned and waved at Joe who gave her the thumbs up before pulling away from the kerb.

Once inside she looked around her. It was busy as people queued to be checked in. In the comfortable armchairs scattered around the lobby, people were relaxing with coffee and newspapers. Some worked on their laptops or chatted in groups. She hoped that she would recognise Clodagh Kenny in the flesh. She was glad that Beth said that she would be here as well. Somehow, she knew that the beautiful girl with the red streaks in her waist-length jet black hair would help her to feel more comfortable about meeting the famous Clodagh Kenny.

"Gill, I hope!"

She hadn't noticed the alcove behind her, from where the woman had come.

"Yes. Was it the shaking hands that gave me away?" she smiled nervously.

"No, indeed. Beth gave me a pretty good description of that scarf and she didn't exaggerate at all. It's absolutely beautiful. She will join us later. We can sit over here and talk. I've ordered coffee but you might prefer tea. I'm afraid I need the caffeine hit today. A quiet dinner for two didn't go as planned, but that's another story. Shall we?"

Clodagh

Two hours later the women were still deep in conversation. They made an odd pair. Clodagh, extremely tall with vibrant auburn hair, and Gill over a foot shorter. Her hair was short and blonde.

"Oh look, they are over there. Come on, David. Let me introduce you to Gill." Beth's soft English accent interrupted their interview.

Clodagh stood up and hugged the newcomers.

"This is Gill and I hope that she is going to be my right-hand woman in Brandon Lodge. Beth, you already know Gill and this is David McGovern, who is someone that I should not be talking to since he is partly responsible for my hangover! The rest lies with the lovely Beth."

David shook her hand. "Delighted to meet you and so glad that Clodagh will have someone that she can rely on. She's getting on in years now, you know!" he quipped.

"That's why she is grumpy today. She had a big birthday yesterday," he continued.

He ducked as Clodagh went to hit him with her bag.

"Okay kids, that's enough. How about a drink to celebrate? I'm buying since I found Gill for you. What will it be?" Beth took out her wallet.

David signalled to a passing waiter.

"Champagne please and put it on my tab."

"Right away, sir."

Hours later, after a more than slightly drunk Gill had been collected by Joe. Clodagh, Beth and David decided to order dinner in an attempt to sober up. As they waited for the food to arrive,

Beth asked Clodagh when she had first decided that Gill was right for the shop.

"As she walked in to the hotel I felt a shiver run down my spine. After that the scarf sealed the deal. It must have been the most unorthodox interview that she's ever had. I hope she doesn't change her mind. After you two came along the whole thing just degenerated into a drinking session." Clodagh sipped her water.

"It will work out. Aunt Lizzie's shiver should never be ignored! We only had a few glasses of bubbly. That stuff just goes straight to my head," said Beth.

"What's a bloody shiver? Is it another Irish thing?" David looked perplexed.

Beth leaned forward. "You mean you've never experienced the 'shiver'? You know how Aunt Lizzie was always making decisions based on her gut instinct. She said that it never let her down. Since she is no longer here to help us, she sometimes makes her presence felt, especially if important decisions need to be made. We christened it the 'shiver.'"

"You two are quite mad. We need a little more wine," he signalled to the waiter.

Joe & Gill

Back in the house, Joe helped Gill onto the couch. He knew that she hadn't eaten much before the interview and champagne never agreed with her. He would have put her to bed but he wanted to keep an eye on her. Indeed, she rarely drank at all and could get drunk on the smell of alcohol.

Right now she was giggling to herself as she rummaged around in the couch.

"Where is my knitting bag?" she slurred as she tossed the knitted cushions onto the floor.

Joe handed her a glass of water before putting the kettle on.

"Here, drink this. You will have a stinker of a headache in the morning. I'll make some coffee and a slice of toast to settle your stomach. I presume you had your fair share of the contents of the two champagne bottles that were on the table! Maybe you should leave the knitting alone until tomorrow."

She peered at him through half closed eyes.

"Joe and Joe. Why are there two of you, Joe? Will one of you please stop the ceiling from spinning around? It's making me feel really sick. Anyway Joe, I got a job in... in... somewhere Lodge. Did I tell you that?"

She flopped back into the couch, then pulled herself up again and looked around.

"Where is my knitting bag?" She fell back again and started to giggle.

Joe walked over to the couch and lifted her legs onto it. He covered her with a multi-coloured throw and went back to the kitchen to make the coffee and toast. It was only eight o'clock.

When he went into the front room to give her the coffee and toast, he found her snoring loudly. (For a split second he felt like recording it and playing it back to her in the morning).

He tiptoed out of the room and returned to the kitchen to make himself a sandwich.

After he ate his food, he settled down to read the newspaper. A few minutes later he heard a bang and a curse. Rushing to the door of the room he found Gill on the floor trying unsuccessfully to get back up. She started to cry in frustration.

Joe picked her up and she promptly threw up all over his shirt. This made her cry even more and she started to babble.

"Oh Joe, I'm so sorry. Please don't leave me. I don't blame you, like, for the whore and Maria. It's a stupid name for one, isn't it? I mean Melissa Dream. Is she a dream to be with? Is Maria good too? Did she perk up your pecker? I can't perk it up because, like, I'm a fat bitch. Bet she has lovely hair, not like this yellow nest on my head. I want to be a thin bitch not a fat bitch. If only Caroline hadn't given him the number. It will take the twins to get rid of him and his bloody 'labtobs'. I don't think but I don't know for sure like. Then the horny goat turned out to be the bus driver instead of you. It's a mess. Please don't have any more affairs. I rang Caroline. It's her fault too. Jesus, Joe, you smell. Are you sick? I make you sick, don't I?" She started to cry again.

He gently removed her soiled cardigan and put her back on the couch.

Joe was shocked. What in God's name was she talking about? Who is Melissa or Maria? What twins? Being turned on by a horny farm animal was not high in his bucket list. He was not having an affair, she was.

Now he wasn't so sure. There was something going on and he would have to get to the bottom of it. He considered ringing Caroline and demanding to know what had happened during that holiday. Instead he decided to leave it for a few days. Maybe Gill would remember the conversation and they could clear the air. Whatever was bothering her needed to be addressed. Their marriage could depend on it.

She slept soundly after that. Joe watched television for a while. At about eleven o'clock he got a pillow and some blankets and settled down on the other couch. Before he drifted off to sleep, he remembered the dinner reservation that he should have cancelled.

"I guess they have figured out by now that we are not coming."

When she awoke the next morning, her head was pounding. It took a minute to realise why she was not in her own bed. She dragged herself over to the mirror and was shocked at her appearance. She had dark circles under her eyes and her skin had a grey pallor to it. Boy, did she smell!

Joe came into the room with tea, toast, water and paracetamol. He placed the tray on the coffee table.

"Morning, madam. Have you seen my wife?"

She glared at him. "Please don't shout. My head is splitting and I look awful."

"Well, that's what you get for drinking a barrel of champagne. Sit down and have some of this. Your stomach is empty as my shirt will attest to!"

"I'm so sorry. I took two strong painkillers yesterday before I left. I should have eaten something but I was too nervous. I didn't know that I would be having a drink. It was supposed to be just the one to celebrate my job. Like, only one. It just went on. I didn't have that much but I think I'm allergic to champagne! I missed our dinner as well. Was I really bad?" said Gill.

"Well now, where do I begin? Firstly, you can snore for Ireland, secondly should get an Oscar for projectile vomiting. You melted onto the floor on numerous occasions and attempted to knit. Other than that, you were the perfect drunk," he laughed.

"Ugh...I'm disgusting. What if Clodagh thinks that I'm unfit to do the job? What must they think of me at all?"

Joe crossed the floor and enveloped her in his arms. She leaned against him.

"I wouldn't be too worried about that if I were you. They seemed like very nice people, very down to earth. You would never think that she was a famous designer or that he owned half of north Cork. Anyway they were as tipsy as you were. When are you supposed to meet her again?"

Gill rubbed her head and tried to remember.

"She said that she would ring to arrange for me to see the shop early next week. I can't wait. What if I have really messed it up? I shouldn't drink at all. It always gets me into trouble. I must have a shower and then I'll wash your clothes. I'm so sorry."

"The laundry is done, but I just soaked the sweater and that lovely collar you made because I didn't know what else to do with them. Stop saying sorry. It could happen to a bishop. Now eat this before it goes completely cold and have your shower. I'm going to work for a few hours. We can celebrate your new job tomorrow night. I've rebooked the table."

Snippets of conversation shot through her mind. She couldn't piece it together but the parts that she could recall made her come out in a cold sweat. She shivered.

"You ok? Want me to put the heating on?" Joe asked.

She nibbled on the toast.

"Yes, please. Was I really that awful last night? What was I saying? Was I talking crap?" she looked at him anxiously.

"I can assure you that I have heard much worse. You should hear some of the rubbish that I've been exposed to at three on a Sunday morning. It would make your hair curl!" he laughed.

"I know all that, but like, what did I really say?"

Joe busied himself tidying the cushions. He didn't want to lie to her face but he needed time before he asked her what she had meant, and to whom she was referring.

"Mostly you went on about your new job, your new best friends and a shiver. Then you snored your head off. Of course you wanted to knit, but I still remember that episode with the waistcoat at Christmas and since this one is for me I didn't want to end up with two left fronts, so I hid the bag. It's in the wool press on the landing. Now go have your shower because, Mrs Roche, we may be together for better or worse, but right now you smell! You should go to bed for a few hours before the hangover sets in. I must drop Matt to the airport at three. He is off to New York this time. Who would have guessed that things would turn out this way between me and him? See you later, Gill." He dropped a kiss on her head before heading out the door.

As the hot water cascaded over her, Gill knew that she had said more than she should have. Fiddling with cushions was not Joe's style.

On his way to the suburbs to collect Matt, Joe was deeply disturbed. He couldn't figure out why Gill thought that he was having an affair. The idea was ludicrous. He was an overweight, almost bald middle-aged man. Unless she was blind, one legged and badly stuck, Maria or Melissa or any other woman would not give him a second glance. Indeed, he considered himself lucky to be married to such a beautiful talented woman. She didn't seem to notice how she attracted admiring looks when they were out together. She looked ten years younger than she was. Caroline with her Botox and fillers, looked like a dried-up prune next to his Gill.

He had a lot to think about but he would sort it all out. He would start with his own health.

After parking in front of the large Victorian house which Matt Vaughan called home, Joe checked his phone. He had hoped to have heard from Laura by now. He needed proper advice on how to lose weight and begin a suitable exercise regime. He would have to drop by the coffee shop on his way back from the airport. A walk around the pond would clear his head.

Inside the house, he could see Matt putting some papers into his briefcase. Since deciding to give up smoking, he had become cranky as hell. He was rummaging – probably for the last of the paperwork that he needed to close the deal. Joe chuckled, knowing how Matt hated running late.

Minutes later Matt threw open the rear passenger door, threw his briefcase on the seat and scrambled in after it.

"Jesus, Joe this non-smoking lark is hard. If I have to sit next to someone like the spanner I met last week, all bets are off! He kept going on about forecasts and spreadsheets and how he weatherproofed himself against the recession, or claptrap to that effect. He was lucky that I didn't wrap him in a spreadsheet and hang him out to dry, on the wing on the plane. His short term forecast was looking very dicey there for a while! Stupid prick."

"Hello to you too!" Joe handed Matt the nicotine gum that he kept especially for pre and post flight stress.

"Okay, point taken," Matt took the gum. "How are things with you?" he asked while frantically chewing.

"Oh you know, the same old crap, different day. Too many taxis, not enough customers. You keep the wolf from the door with the custom that you put my way. I really appreciate that. I'm really glad that your business is booming."

Matt began to relax. "Me too. Actually I might have a very lucrative contract for you. I'll know more in a week or two. I'm in the middle of negotiations. I'll let you know as soon as it is settled."

"Thanks a million, Matt. You're a lifesaver," said Joe.

"No worries," Matt answered.

Watching the ducks floating serenely across the pond, Joe pondered the advice Matt had given him. Matt was not only a well-known and respected business man, he was also Joe's best friend. He had noticed that Joe was distracted and managed to prise the story from him. He had gotten to know Gill at the same time as he and Joe had become friends and didn't believe that she would ever cheat on Joe. He had laughed out loud when Joe had told him about Melissa the whore.

"You need to take the bull by the horns and ask her straight out about what she had meant. It is probably just a case of crossed wires. Cook her one of your signature dishes with her favourite wine and have a heart to heart. Tell her exactly what she had said. You said that you think that she already suspects that she mentioned some of these names," Matt had told him.

After he had completed the circuit around the pond, he decided to get a coffee. He hoped that Laura would be working.

"Hi Joe. How are things with you? Did you get my message?" she asked with a smile.

"I'm doing, okay. How about you? My phone seems to be acting up in the past few days. When did you send it? I walked around the pond there and it was tough. I really need to get this wreck of a body sorted out before it gives up the ghost," he replied.

Laura placed the black coffee and a large glass of water on his favourite table by the bay window.

"I have a break due, so I'll sit with you for a few minutes if that's okay?"

"That would be lovely."

Laura fished her mobile out of her pocket and found the message. She showed it to Joe.

Hi Joe, she would be delighted to meet you. Her name is Marie and she is certain that you will be delighted with everything. She said that you should also try Melissa Dream...should work a treat for your problem. Should perk you up no end. Laura x.

Joe took a gulp of his drink and began to piece together and make sense of Gill's drunken ramblings. It was becoming clear that she had read and deleted this message. Why would she do something like that? It didn't make any sense.

"I'll take down the number and put it in to my work phone. This one needs replacing. Do you know what this Melissa Dream is?" he asked.

"I think it is a tablet made from Lemon Balm. It's natural so there are no side effects. After my Dad died, Mam couldn't sleep so she took sleeping tablets for a while. She was like the walking dead so she stopped taking them. Someone recommended these and they really helped. I take them around exam time so I can vouch for them. They keep me calm and give me a good night's sleep. You told me that you have a problem sleeping so they could be the answer that you are looking for. You have nothing to lose. Mam is due here any minute so you can meet her if you have time to hang on. I think there is a walk arranged for tomorrow morning," she said.

"That would be great. The sooner the better," he said and sipped his coffee.

Chapter Seven

Pamela

Pamela O Neill was obsessed with Danny Murray and was determined to make him hers at any cost. She had been waiting for the right opportunity for ages and her patience had been rewarded. Now she was thrilled with her good fortune. She had managed to persuade Danny to be her partner at a mutual friend's upcoming wedding. She knew that he only thought of her as just another member of the crowd that they both hung around with. She had been trying to catch him on his own for ages so when she had spotted him rushing past the chemist where she worked, she had unashamedly followed him into the local man's shop where he was searching for a shirt and tie for the wedding.

"Hi Danny, fancy meeting you here. I am looking for a jumper for my brother," she lied.

"Oh, hello Pamela, I need to get a shirt and tie for the wedding tomorrow. I am usually more organised but this time I am cutting it fine. What do you think?" He held up two striped shirts for her opinion.

"They are a bit on the dull side. What about that one?" She pointed to a vibrant purple shirt that was draped on a model nearby.

"Cripes…it's a bit…out there! I would outshine the bride in that one!"

"I don't agree. It would be lovely on you."

"I hate shopping for formal clothes. I'm more of a jeans and t-shirt guy. Thank God the whole gang were asked or I would have had to coordinate my clothes with my plus one!" he joked.

"I know what you mean. You do realise that all the others happen to be couples. It's just you and me that are spare wheels," she quipped.

"I didn't actually, but we have all known each other for years, and we are all at the same table so it will be fine. I thought you were dating some hot shot from Cork," he replied.

"Yeah, that's over. Since we are the only two singles at the table, maybe we could be one another's plus one for the day. I have the perfect outfit to match that shirt!" she joked.

"There's no need for that. I don't think I will buy that one anyway." He looked horrified.

"I didn't mean that we would pretend to be a couple, I was just joking," she murmured.

Danny felt horrible. Just because he didn't fancy Pamela was no excuse to be so rude.

"Don't mind me. Bad day. Look, I'll pick you up and we can travel together. Just remember that if you spot the love of your life across the floor, feel free to chase him. This is just a convenience travel thing. We are only friends." He tried to lighten the mood.

"The same applies to you, of course. I will leave you to your shopping. I must be getting back to work."

Danny looked at the purple shirt again. It was just a bit too vibrant for him and he didn't want Pamela to get any ideas about matching colour schemes. Rumour had it that she could be a bit intense in relationships and he didn't want to encourage her.

"You going for that one, then?" John the shop manager asked.

"It is lovely, but you know I'm not sure it's me. I think I will go with the cream one and maybe that tie over there. I would be able to get more wear out of it. I think showing people around prospective homes in the other one might dazzle them too much." He put back the purple one even though he actually liked it. He might get it anyway as soon as the coast was clear, though he wouldn't risk wearing it the following day at the wedding. In his group, it meant 'couple' if you shopped together.

"You not going to coordinate then?" John joked.

"No way, mate. I am not interested. A bit too clingy for my liking," Danny shuddered.

"I agree. She can be a bit bunny-boiler."

"What do you mean? I didn't know that you knew Pamela," he said.

"I don't really, but my cousin used to date her. Granted that was a long time ago. They broke up but she wanted to try again. Turned up wherever he went for a long time. Scary shit really. Still she has probably grown up by now. I shouldn't have said anything. I could be wronging her. We all did stupid things when we were younger. Anyway, back to business. You actually serious about that dull colour? Your old man wouldn't be seen dead in that. Let's find you something more fitting. It's your friend's wedding, not a meeting with the bank manager!" John picked out a few options.

After she left Danny, Pamela decided that she would try and buy an outfit that could do justice to the shirt that Danny had picked out. Dull cream was not in her usual colour palette but the tie did have a hint of gold so all might not be lost. Pity he didn't go with the purple one, it was so much more her and would have matched the designer dress that she had intended to wear. Still, if she ended up with Danny permanently, then the added expense would be worth it. She wanted him for herself and now she would stop at nothing to make him hers. What Pamela wanted, Pamela got! She would have to tread carefully as Danny was not into long-term relationships. God help anyone who got in her way!

Beth

Beth woke up to the sound of the rain on the window. For a second she couldn't figure out where she was. She turned over in the bed. Her head hurt. She hoped that she was not late for work but when she went to check the alarm clock, it wasn't there. This was not her bedroom. She shot up in bed. Where was she? What day was it?

Slowly the events of the previous night began to creep back into her brain. Champagne and wine, lots and lots of it. She stumbled out of bed and reached for the bottled water on the bedside locker.

Clodagh stirred in the other bed in the room that David had booked for them.

Beth looked at the time display on the television: 9.10. She tried to remember if she was due in work but her brain was wrapped in cotton wool. She couldn't figure out what day it was. The battery in her phone was dead so she couldn't check her messages. She found Clodagh's phone. It was Saturday. She collapsed back onto the pillow and promptly went back to sleep.

The knock on the door woke them both.

"Room service."

Clodagh answered the door.

A smiling waiter pushed a breakfast trolley into the room.

"We didn't order room service," Clodagh yawned.

"Mr McGovern ordered this, madam. May I set it up for you? He included a note." He handed the folded sheet to Clodagh.

Good morning to both of you. Hope you both had a good rest. I felt that you might need some sustenance so I ordered breakfast. I'm off for a look around the city. Will see you later. Enjoy xx

The smell of kippers was overpowering. David liked to make a statement.

Clodagh sat back down on the bed. She dragged her hand through her hair, and saw her reflection in the mirror.

"Jesus wept! I look awful. How much did I have to drink last night? My head feels like it has been invaded by a team of tap dancers. I'm a great role model for you! Aunt Lizzie would be horrified not to mind what your mother would have thought. Is there any orange juice on that trolley? My tongue is welded to the roof of my mouth."

Beth came and sat on Clodagh's bed. She handed her a large glass of freshly squeezed orange juice and a slice of buttered toast. She put her arm around the older woman.

"You are the best Mom in the world and don't you ever forget it. If it wasn't for you and Aunt Lizzie, David and his mother, God only knows where I would have ended up. I love you very much.

Now we will have some breakfast, though I think I will pass on the kippers. We can go for a swim later and use the sauna and steam room. It will help sweat out the alcohol," she added.

Clodagh drained her glass.

"God only knows what Gill thought of us. I hope she is not having second thoughts about working in the shop. At least she had left before the last bottle arrived. I must ring her later. She is perfect for the job. I just know it!" said Clodagh.

Beth poured coffee into two cups and added lots of sugar.

"I'm sure it will work out. Give her a ring and you will see. She was sent by Aunt Lizzie to help you out. The 'shiver' never lies. Anyway we have more pressing things to sort out. We must go back to my apartment and collect our luggage. The hotel is booked for two nights in Killarney. Aunt Claire found out that it was the same hotel where Aunt Lizzie worked before she moved to London. It was called Hammersham House back then. Now it's the Quayside Hotel. Queen Victoria had supposedly visited it once by boat. The ruins of the quay are still there. I hope I will be able to find them. Aunt Lizzie used to tell great stories about the place. We might find some photographs from that time. Apparently, it has a room with all the old stuff in it. It also has a spa and I'm looking forward to having a few treatments," she said.

"What time are we meeting Claire at?" enquired Clodagh.

"She is off today so she said to ring her when we get to the hotel. She is also booked in so that the two of you can really catch up. You must admit that it is a lovely birthday present to get!" added Beth.

"Yes, it is and so was the huge party that you and David organised. I'm not usually a party person but I really enjoyed myself. Thanks pet." Clodagh smiled.

"I'm glad. I wasn't too sure about it. You have never celebrated your birthday so I was a little scared that it would just make you angry," Beth said.

Pamela

Pamela was not a happy bunny. She had spent a small fortune on an outfit that she would probably never wear again. When Danny had turned up to collect her (after he had collected Mick and Sophie) he was wearing a multi-coloured shirt of different shades of purples and lilac matched to a deep purple tie. He looked fabulous. If he had arrived alone, then she could have made an excuse to change her outfit. Now it was obvious to all that they were not a couple. When she heard that he hadn't told her that the group had booked one of the holiday homes, she was furious. It would have given her an opportunity to move her plan on. After all, weddings were great places for drunken sex!

The hotel bathroom was crowded. The bride and groom had not yet arrived so the guests were freshening up.

"I love that bag, Pamela. Isn't it from the Beth's Knits collection? It matches your outfit perfectly. I love the gold glitter in it," Sophie smiled.

"Yes, it is, though I wouldn't have thought that you were a designer handbag type of girl," Pamela retorted.

Sophie blushed as Pamela brushed past her.

"You okay, Sophie? Take no notice of that bitch. It's beyond me why Danny would hang around with her. He's such a nice guy and she is a wagon!" Jane hugged the other girl.

"Anyway she looks like a cappuccino in that get up." They both burst out laughing.

Beth

Claire waved when she saw Clodagh and Beth. She was sitting in the alcove by the window. There was a wedding on in the hotel so the bar was crowded. As the two women fought their way through the crowd, Beth's bag strap caught on the back of a high-backed stool and she found herself being jerked backwards. An arm reached out to steady her.

"I know that my aftershave is irresistible but at least look me in the eye before you fall for me!" Danny joked.

Beth burst out laughing.

"You okay?" he added.

"Yes, I'm fine. No harm done," she answered.

"Ah. An English accent. My name is Danny and you are?"

"Beth. Nice to meet you." She held out her hand.

"Lovely to meet you too. I knew that coming to this wedding would bring me luck. Did you cross the sea just to meet me? It must be fate." He kissed her outstretched hand.

Clodagh came back through the crowd and beckoned to Beth.

"Sitting by the window when you are ready," she mouthed.

"Sorry, must go. Enjoy your day. It was nice to meet you." She turned to leave.

Danny took a card from his pocket.

"This is my number. You might decide to stay in Ireland. I could help you if you wanted to buy a house. I could arrange a private viewing, just you and me! You would be surprised at how helpful I could be. You could pick my brains or do other stuff. I'm versatile." Danny stroked his beard.

"I'll vouch for him. He is a very good auctioneer," interjected Mick, who had been watching the exchange with interest.

Red talons encircled Danny's arm.

"My boyfriend never misses an opportunity to expand his client list. That is what you were doing, isn't it? My name is Pamela and you are?" she extended her hand.

"I'm Beth. Your boyfriend was trying to interest me in buying a house. He thought he had the perfect proposition for me, property wise of course," she added mischievously. "If you will excuse me, I must go," Beth continued.

She turned to Danny. "I will be sure to let you know if I decide to take you up on that offer. See you."

She turned to Pamela and Mick.

"Nice to have met you both."

Clodagh waved at Beth and pointed to the place where she and Claire were sitting.

"Is that Clodagh Kenny the designer? I have one of her bags," she gasped.

"Yes, it is and so do I... she's my Mom. If you will excuse me. Nice to have met you all. I'll keep this safe." She put the card in her bag, winked at Danny, turned and walked away.

Danny was intrigued and Pamela was livid.

"Those red streaks are so last year and that hair is way too long for someone her age," she huffed.

Danny put his pint on the counter.

"There was no need to be nasty and what was all that crap about boyfriends? We are here as friends and I would appreciate it if you would remember that. If I want to talk to some other woman, then I will. She is very nice and I hope that she will ring me," he finished.

"I thought you looked like you needed to be rescued, that's all," she answered.

"From one of the most beautiful women in the room! I think not," he retorted.

Mick had never seen a woman go that shade of angry in all his life!

Beth 1 Pamela 0, he thought.

"Did you meet someone you know?" Claire asked.

"No. Just chatting to a few people at the bar. They are going to the wedding here. I still can't get used to how friendly everyone is in Ireland. What time did you book the treatments for?" Beth changed the subject.

"In about forty minutes. We just have time for a quick drink beforehand," Claire answered.

"I am going to wander around while you are getting the treatments. I will meet you both afterwards," Beth told them.

"That's okay. We should be finished in about two hours." Clodagh sipped her coffee and admired the outfits of the wedding guests. The bride and groom had just arrived and all the guests were heading out into the hallway.

"I haven't been to a wedding in ages. I love getting glammed up. I am just going out to see the bride. You two coming?" Clodagh stood up.

"You go ahead."

"She loves a good wedding!" Claire said.

"I know. She is always asking me about the possibility of me getting married," Beth laughed.

"Maybe you will meet a nice fellow and settle down," Claire answered.

"Hey. Give me a chance!" Beth thought of the card that Danny had given her.

"Just joking, pet. I was thinking of that nice barman that you met the other night," Claire laughed.

"He was very nice. I may even call him!" Beth told her.

"She is really lovely. Her dress is vintage." Clodagh sat back down.

"Vintage seems to be the trend at the moment. Did you see the hen party that arrived a few minutes ago… all flapper dresses and headbands?" Beth observed.

"This hotel is really busy. The function room where the wedding reception is being held is huge and I spotted two smaller function rooms as well," Clodagh answered.

"Are you casing the place, Sis?" Claire sipped her wine.

"Just looking around. I was looking for the treatment rooms. We must head over there shortly. We can spend some time in the relaxation suite afterwards. I am really looking forward to the massage. You sure that you don't want to join us, Beth?" Clodagh asked.

"No, thanks. I am going to wander around here. There is supposed to be a room which features old photos and the history of the hotel. I might find out something about Aunt Lizzie. You two can catch up or I will come and find you later." Beth stood up.

"See you later so."

Beth left the bar and headed for reception.

"May I help you?" The receptionist asked politely.

"Hi, I was wondering where I could find information on the history of this hotel," Beth smiled.

"There is an alcove beside the function room on the first floor. The lift is just down the hallway to your right or you can use the stairs. There is also an information booklet in each of the guest rooms or you can get one here," the receptionist said handing Beth the booklet.

"Thank you." Beth headed for the stairs.

Pamela

Pamela was not happy. She had overlooked the fact that name cards had been placed on the tables and she was not beside Danny. If she had realised it earlier she would have sneaked in and switched cards. Now she had to put up with the soppy conversation of the lovebirds beside her. Danny had been moved to another table to amuse two cousins of the bride! She watched him laugh and joke with the girls on either side of him. Pamela felt a red hot poker of pure rage engulf her. How dare they monopolise her man! She needed air before she attacked someone. Forcing a smile, she excused herself and left the room.

She stood outside the function room and tried to compose herself.

"Breathe… one, two, three in. Three, two, one out…" She repeated the mantra that she had been taught in the hospital.

Suddenly she spotted Beth going into the bathroom. She decided to follow her and make sure that she would never contact Danny.

Beth was washing her hands when Pamela entered the bathroom.

"Hello again, we met earlier at the bar." Pamela faked a smile.

"Oh yes. How is the wedding going?" Beth dried her hands and held them under the hand cream dispenser.

"Oh you know… same old thing. The meal is just being served but I felt a bit faint," Pamela sighed.

"You okay? Can I get you something?" Beth enquired.

"No, I am fine. It is just that ever since the miscarriage, I have been feeling a bit unwell." She leaned against the washbasin.

"Oh, I am sorry to hear that. Was it long ago?"

"A few weeks. Danny is very upset about it but he tries to hide it by pretending it never happened. We had been talking about getting married but then this happened..." She trailed off.

"That is terrible. Have you two been together long?" Beth asked.

"About seven years. Everything was great until this happened... I think that he is going off me..." Pamela started to cry.

"Please don't cry. I'm sure everything will work out between you two." Beth hugged Pamela and felt guilty about even considering contacting Danny.

"Thank you for your kindness. I had better get back now. I know that Danny liked you today but please don't tell him that we talked. I feel so silly now," Pamela dabbed her eyes with the tissue that Beth had handed her.

"No worries. Your secret is safe with me." Beth was going to tear up that card as soon as she was alone.

"Thank you so much. You are really kind. I had better go back." Pamela threw the tissue in the bin and left the bathroom.

"Good job Pamela!" she told herself as she re-plastered on her smile and went back to the reception. Nobody had noticed her absence and Danny was still deep in conversation with the two girls.

Clodagh

Claire and Clodagh relaxed side by side as their stresses were massaged away.

"This is sheer heaven! It is the best birthday present ever. I must have consumed more wine in the last three days than I did in the last three years. I just wanted to creep silently into the dreaded fifties but my family had other ideas," Clodagh smiled.

Claire smiled sleepily.

"We couldn't let that happen. It was a great night. The food was fabulous in that restaurant that Beth and David booked. David looks great. It was ages since I had a chance to have a proper chat with him. At least we will see a lot more of him once this joint venture takes off. I'm looking forward to seeing Brandon Lodge when it is up and running. Remember when we used to climb in through the basement window and play Upstairs Downstairs. You always wanted to be Lady of the Manor and now you will be. A dream come true."

"Yes, I suppose it is. I will finally end up where I always wanted to be. What about you Claire? Are you where you wanted to be? I'm only asking because you seem distracted. How are things since the new owner took over?" Clodagh asked.

"You know me. I hate change. The salon is full of young ones in skimpy black tops masquerading as hairdressers. Add multi-coloured hair and enough piercing to enable a jeweller to retire early and you can picture exactly where I work. I feel like a dinosaur next to them! Only for the fact that my customers have stuck by me throughout it all."

"They have stayed with you because you are very good at what you do. You are not just good at what you do; you have won awards almost every year since you finished your training. If you opened your own place in Mars, all your clients would still follow you. That should tell you something." Clodagh sat up suddenly and grabbed her sister by the hands.

"That is what you should do. It's brilliant. Why didn't we think of it before? Mars might be a bit of a stretch but I'm sure there is somewhere nearer."

"I've been thinking about it for a while but with the boys still in college, I'm not sure it's the right time to do it. I know that my clients are unhappy with the glass and chrome type salon. It is just so impersonal. They would prefer a cup of tea and a good old chinwag to lattes and copies of the latest celeb magazine. If I am seen to be too chatty, I get the evil eye from The Dragon otherwise known as Ms Doyle. She is very young and knows very little about people skills. Being the niece of the owner was all the experience she needed! As for the prices, they just keep going up and up. A lot of my clients are on a pension and have to budget to get their hair done. I've been going to some of their houses but it's not ideal," said Claire.

"Then you must open your own salon. We can use the money that Mam and Dad left us," Clodagh said.

"Half of that is yours and we decided to keep it for emergencies," Claire answered.

Clodagh got up to refill their glasses with water.

"I don't need it and this is as good a use for it as any. You are clearly unhappy, so go for it. You will make a lot of your older clients happy and I'll bet that a lot of the younger set will follow you as well. You have upskilled every year since you started so you are one of the best hairdressers in Killarney. That award you received for your wedding styling has meant that every bride in the county is coming to you. Take a few days to think about it. Here's Beth."

"Hi Beth, I was just telling Claire that I thought you might have deserted us for some attractive wedding guest."

"There was one possibility but he was spoken for. His girlfriend was clung to his arm like a limpet! I wouldn't fancy an up close and personal encounter with those nails!" Beth shuddered. "Anyway, I've ordered afternoon tea for us. You two look about ready for cucumber sandwiches and drizzle cake! Then we can go and explore the grounds. Maybe we will find the quay where Queen Victoria landed when she came to visit. Meet me in the bar in fifteen minutes." She turned and left the relaxation room.

"Bossy boots." They spoke to her retreating back.

After Beth had left, the sisters showered, dressed and walked towards the bar.

"I'm really glad that you seem happy, Clodagh. I was so pleased when you decided to come back home again. I've hated James Murray every day for over thirty years. We should have spent all those years together. If he walked in here now I wouldn't be responsible for my actions! What he did to you was unforgivable and yet you don't seem bitter about it. You have made a very good life for you and Beth. Aunt Lizzie was lucky to have you when Elizabeth died. That was so sad. Her poor mother was heartbroken, especially when she was not allowed to raise Beth herself. That bastard she was married to, had a lot to answer for," Claire said.

"It was all such a long time ago. I know that I said that I would never come back again, but never is a long time. I was very young and a different person. Going to London changed my life for the better. I wouldn't be here but for the people I met, and the choices I had to make. James Murray did me a favour. Aunt Lizzie was such an inspiration. She was brilliant to me, Elizabeth and Beth. We were quite the little family! I don't regret a single day of it, so don't be wasting any of your precious thoughts on Mr Murray. I like my life the way it is. I'm very happy. I would like for Beth to meet someone nice. Who knows maybe that nice barman from the night of my party might be the one!" she finished.

"Well then, why don't you take your own advice and find someone to share your life with?" Claire stopped at the entrance to the bar.

"Sister, I may already have someone in mind. It's early days yet but the shiver has been busy in my private life as well as in my business one. Watch this space."

"I'm intrigued now. There's Beth. At least most of the wedding guests have gone in for the meal."

At the table Beth was poking in her bag.

"Lose something?" enquired Clodagh.

"Just a card with a contact number. It's not that important. Look at all this food. We will have to walk for hours to justify this lot. Anyway I have a surprise for you both. I found a photograph of Aunt Lizzie upstairs!"

Pamela

The speeches finally ended and the guests began to mingle. Pamela moved her chair next to Danny but he barely acknowledged her presence. He was very popular because of his easy-going and kind manner. People gravitated towards him and he liked to have a large circle of friends. Eventually, he turned to her.

"You alright, Pamela? Can I get you a drink?" He stood up.

"Thanks Danny. A gin and tonic, please. Do you need a hand?" she smiled at him.

"No, I am fine. We will have a dance later. Do you see anyone here that you fancy?" he asked.

"One or two maybe. You?" She attempted to sound calm.

"Not here but I hope to see Beth from the bar again. I have a good feeling about her," he said.

"Well I wish you the best of luck with that," she lied.

Danny took ages to return with the drinks. He had met a group of people at the bar and had spent ages chatting with them. When he had finally returned, he had a girl with him.

"Remember, Sophie?" He had his arm around the other girl.

"Yeah sure, hi Sophie."

"Hi Pamela, can I sit here?" She indicated to Danny's chair.

"Sure."

Danny placed the drinks on the table.

"Excuse me ladies, but I need to make a few calls. I will be back in a few minutes." He picked up his pint and headed towards the door.

"How long have you and Danny been together?" Sophie sipped her drink and noted that Pamela swallowed most of hers in the one gulp.

"Ages. We have been getting to know one another. It is quite serious now." She drained her glass.

"I wish you both the best. Danny is one of the good ones. I have known him since we started primary school together."

"You fancy him! Well, don't get any ideas about taking him off me," Pamela threatened.

"I am engaged. My fiancée Gary is on a training course in Dublin." Sophie flashed her ring.

"That's lovely… mine will be much bigger, of course." Pamela barely glanced at Sophie's hand.

They both looked up as Danny approached the table.

"All well here? Managed without me?" he joked.

"Of course, I will leave you two love birds together." Sophie stood up.

"See you later, Sophie." Danny watched her walk away.

"What did she mean by that?" Danny asked.

"I have no idea. I suppose she presumed that since we came together that we were a couple," Pamela slurred.

"Sophie knows me very well. I would have told her if I was dating. I have promised a few of the ladies here that I would dance with them. I will see you later," Danny walked across to another table and was soon laughing and joking.

Over the next few hours, things got steadily worse. Danny danced with every girl in the room. The angrier Pamela became, the more she drank.

She was practically falling asleep on the table when she saw someone approach her.

"You okay, Pamela?" Sophie's voice came from a distance.

"Get lost, you loser. Just because you have a boyfriend and a miniscule diamond."

"What's going on here?" Danny appeared beside her.

"I was only trying to help. She has been drinking rather a lot and since you are supposed to be with her… you have behaved badly, Danny and that is not like you. You have spent the evening talking about some girl that you met for a few minutes. Cop on, Danny." Sophie stormed off.

"Good riddance to Miss Goody Two Shoes." Pamela stood up, stumbled into the table. Glasses shattered.

"What is wrong with you?" Danny took Pamela's arm and practically carried her out of the function room.

Pamela's head was pounding. She had woken up fully dressed and lying on a couch she didn't recognise. She vaguely remembered the night before. Once Danny had met that woman, he had spent all evening talking about her. He had even gone looking for her in the bar. If Pamela hadn't told him that the groom was looking for him, he would have found her.

She couldn't even object because Danny had made it perfectly clear that they were not an item and she had agreed. All her plans to try to make him notice her as more than a friend had come to nothing. Clodagh Kenny's daughter had ruined her evening. The more Danny went on about 'the love of his life' the more Pamela drank. Gin became her friend. When Sophie had tried to get her to slow down, she had turned on her.

"Get lost, you loser," she had shouted.

Danny had practically carried her out of the function room.

As she tried to focus on her surroundings Danny came into view. He was sitting opposite her and he was not happy.

"How are you this morning?" He handed her a glass of water.

"My head is splitting. I'm sorry about last night, Danny. I made a right fool of myself. Everyone must be talking about me," she murmured.

"It's not that bad. It was very late so lots of people had a little too much to drink. Don't worry about it. I was a bit of a prick myself. We went to the wedding as friends and I shouldn't have kept going on about Beth. Sophie gave me an earful. She was worried about you," he added.

"Oh God, I was horrible to her all day. I am such a bitch. I will have to tell her how sorry I am when I see her." She gulped the water.

"You're okay. A group of the lads had booked this house so we brought you here. Sophie and Alice came with me to protect your reputation. They will be back in a minute with juice and the makings of a good fry up. That will sort you out. I will drop you home then."

"Thanks Danny. I don't deserve a friend like you. No one would have blamed you if you had just left me there. Maybe you will let me buy you dinner sometime as a thank you, just as friends of course," she added.

"Sure we will see. Here come the others now." He got up to get the frying pan ready.

Chapter Eight

Kate
"Too bloody right I'm tired. I'm bloody knackered. This place is dragging me down." Kate Cashman threw the magazine across the kitchen just missing her son who had chosen that minute to come through the door.

"Jesus Mam. You nearly took my eye out. You okay? That sister of mine been giving you grief again?" Danny picked up the magazine and placed it on the table.

She couldn't help but smile. He always had the knack of cheering her up.

"No, it's not Kathryn. She is very happy at the moment. She likes her job and her romance is going from strength to strength. Speaking of which. How did the wedding go? Did you have a good time? Who did you say you went with again?" She got another cup and poured out the tea.

"Yes I did. I went with Pamela who is only a friend. No romance there, just a scary moment."

"What do you mean by that?" his mother asked.

"I was in the hotel bar before dinner having a pint with a few of the gang when a girl, a beautiful girl with long black hair with the most beautiful red streaks, walked in. She was just passing by when her bag caught in the back of my chair. When she spoke, she had the most amazing English accent. We were still chatting when Pamela came back and nearly speared me with her nails. She was acting like a very jealous girlfriend. She even told Beth, that was her name, that I was her boyfriend. I was not too impressed at all. I managed to give Beth my card so I hope that she will ring me. I really liked her Mam. It was like a shiver went down my spine when I saw her. That has never happened to me before. It was weird," he said.

"I hope it works out for you. She has your number, so it is up to her to call. Do you know anything else about her? If she was just over for the weekend, then you may not hear from her again," she answered.

"Pamela said something about her mother being a well-known designer in London. I think Sophie knew something about it as well." He finished his tea.

A knock on the kitchen door was followed by the entrance of Pat, who managed the large farm with Kate.

"Hello Pat, come on in. There is tea in the pot. Help yourself."

"Sorry to intrude, Kate. I was just checking on the animals. I need you to sign some cheques. Hi Danny, how is life treating you?" he poured himself a cup of tea.

"He is having a bit of a love life crisis at the moment. Your advice usually goes down well. Give me those cheques and then I am going to leave you two to sort out the world. You can give him the benefit of your experience!" She scribbled her name on the cheque book.

"That will be a short speech. What this bachelor knows about affairs of the heart could be written on a postage stamp. Still I'm prepared to listen to the favourite son that I never had!" Pat smiled at Kate.

"I'm off to the Outlet Centre. The usual Sunday Craft Fair is on. I need to pick up a few new ideas for my crochet project. I might also go for a walk through the park so you two enjoy your chat. There's the making of a salad in the fridge if the love summit drags on," she joked.

"Right son, talk. I'm a good listener."

When Kate arrived home a few hours later, her head was spinning. Thankfully the place was in darkness. Danny's jacket was slung across the back of a chair and his shoes were under the table. She could hear the soft snoring coming from across the hall. His phone rang in the jacket pocket. While she waited for the kettle to boil, she made herself a sandwich with the remains of the salad. She had some decisions to make and was not looking forward to it.

It had turned out to be an interesting afternoon. After leaving the Outlet Centre she had parked in the grounds of the Quayside Hotel and gone for a walk. She was familiar with the area so she had chosen a path that would be off limits to hotel guests as it was overgrown and extremely muddy at the best of times. It led down to the ruins of the quay so it was pretty wet. Kate knew it well and was well prepared. There was a large out crop of rock where she liked to sit and think. She had been feeling very restless lately so she really needed to sort herself out.

Surrounded by the beauty of the mountains, she tried to make sense of her life. It had not turned out as she had planned. She had effectively been on her own for over thirty years. Her sex life had consisted of a torrid few weeks with James. The rest was a sham. Even the children didn't know the whole truth. They thought that she had decided to keep her maiden name when she had married. The truth was that she was still a single woman, with grown up twins. James had refused to be forced into marriage. Even the image of her father shouting at him from behind a loaded shotgun hadn't changed his mind. He still had hoped to somehow fix things with Clodagh.

They were already back together again and Kate had started to date Pat when she found out that she was pregnant. It was a terrible shock and it changed all their lives forever. She hadn't actually set out to trap James but she had been delighted when he and Clodagh had taken a break. In a drunken moment he had confided in her that their problems were due to the fact that Clodagh wasn't too keen on sleeping with him. Kate was unhappy at home so the thought of finding someone and moving out of that loveless house was so appealing that she was only too happy to provide James with all the sex that he wanted. So maybe she had trapped him after all. She had always fancied him so the rest was easy.

Her father had used every opportunity to belittle her. He used to tell her that she was fat, stupid and ugly and that she would end up alone. He had that one right! She was almost sixty and she was alone. Danny and Kathryn were leading their own lives and she wanted something more than this. James was a great father and to be fair to him, he was a good friend. He didn't love her and he never would.

He used to come to the house every day to help her with the children. It was years before anyone realised that they were not living together, except their closest neighbour, Gertie. She spotted James leave late at night and arrive in the morning before work. She had taken an instant dislike to him and blamed him for everything. Kate had never put her right. It was nice to have an ally.

There was no need for him to visit now that the twins had left home but he still dropped in once or twice a week. She enjoyed those visits. She still loved him but now only as a dear friend. She knew that he had not gotten over Clodagh Kenny and she wished that she could do something to help him. He still kept the knitted scarf in the drawer in his office. Then there was the letter. Kate had come across it and in a fit of rage, she had copied it. She had regretted it almost immediately.

Reading that letter, she had known that he had wanted to go to London and leave his unborn child behind. She knew now that it was the hopes and dreams of a young man who had found himself facing fatherhood and the possibility of never seeing the woman he loved again.

She never knew whether Clodagh answered the letter or even if she had actually received it. James had moved into the farm for a while. They had taken a short holiday to Rome and when they returned they had told everyone that they had married. People had thought that it was so romantic.

Over the past few months her feelings for Pat had resurfaced, but as far as he was concerned she was a married woman. Telling him the truth now would mean telling Kathryn and Danny that their whole life had been a sham. She suddenly shivered and realised that she had been sitting on the rock for over an hour.

Straightening up she gathered her things and started back along the path, picking her steps to carefully avoid the water filled potholes.

"Oh, thank God! Can you help me please? I'm lost."

Kate nearly jumped out of her skin.

The young girl looked frightened and cold. She was sitting on the remains of a low stone wall surrounded by bushes and muddy puddles. Kate could imagine how she would feel if Kathryn or Danny had gotten lost and she felt a rush of maternal concern.

"Hi, I'm Kate. You are?" she smiled at the girl.

"Beth. I'm staying at the hotel over there. I can see it but I can't find my way back there. My mobile died. Can you show me the way out, please?" she spoke in a soft English accent.

"Yes, of course. You are not too far away but the path is messy. I'll walk you back. What made you come this way? The tourist trails are well signposted."

Beth held out the history book that she had bought at the hotel.

"I was looking for the ruins of the quay. There is a map at the back of it and I was trying to follow it. Boats used to come up here in the past. This is my Mom's Aunt Lizzie. I was trying to find the place where this was taken," she showed Kate a black and white photograph of pretty young girl standing by the water.

"That's at the other side of the wall. It's about a mile away but the path is completely overgrown. It's getting late so we had better head towards the hotel. Your friends will be getting worried about you. What part of England do you come from?" Kate asked.

"I'm from London. We moved back to Ireland a few months ago." Beth accepted the chocolate that Kate handed her. "Thank you. I was beginning to get really scared. You would think that I was ten instead of thirty! I'm more used to city streets than country lanes but I really wanted to discover Aunt Lizzie's roots." She finished the chocolate.

"It's nice to be able to find out where your relations came from. It's also alright to be frightened. Getting lost can be scary at any age, though to be fair, you don't look thirty. What is your birth sign?" Kate asked.

"It's Capricorn, born in January." She smiled at her rescuer.

"Same as my twins. They were born in January as well. They are thirty same as you," Kate added.

Kate guided Beth through the almost hidden opening in the ditch and across the field towards the hotel.

As they neared the entrance, they could see two women frantically waving at them.

"There she is. Oh Beth! We were just about to send out a search party. It's nearly dark!" Clodagh was almost hysterical.

Kate froze. Clodagh Kenny was running towards her.

After Clodagh had enveloped Beth in her arms and hugged her, she had turned to Kate and hugged her as well.

"Thank you so much for bringing her back. I was so scared that she had fallen somewhere. She has been gone for hours. Can I buy you a coffee, or a drink to thank you? You must be frozen as well," she asked.

Kate gently dislodged herself.

"No, thank you. That won't be necessary. I had better be getting home myself or my son will be sending out a search party for me." She couldn't wait to leave so that she could process all that happened.

Beth threw her arms around Kate and hugged her again. They were one touchy feely pair.

"Please have lunch with us tomorrow before we leave," Beth begged.

"Yes, please do. Here is my number. We would love to thank you properly. I'll just put Beth's number on here as well. Please try and make it." Clodagh handed Kate the card.

"Thanks again, Kate. Hope to see you tomorrow," Beth said.

After Kate had driven out of the car park, Clodagh turned to Beth.

"You know I actually forgot to introduce myself properly. Did you say her name was Kate? Reminds me of someone that I used to know a long time ago. Her name was Kate as well," Clodagh added.

Back in her own kitchen, she couldn't believe what had just happened. What were the chances? There was no way in hell that she would have lunch with Clodagh Kenny! She couldn't risk the other woman realising who she was. Then there was Beth. Long black hair with red streaks and 'an amazing English accent.' The one person Danny chose to get interested in would have to be the daughter of the only woman in the world that his father ever loved. A horrible thought suddenly struck her. Before Kate discovered her pregnancy, both she and James had moved on with their lives. He was back dating Clodagh and she had found Pat. Beth was born around the same time as Danny and Kathryn. If James and Clodagh had been sleeping together, then Beth could be his daughter! Clodagh had moved to England and never had any contact with James so he would not have known that she was pregnant.

Jesus Christ, her beloved son might had fallen for his half-sister!

What in God's name was she going to do with this information! The future happiness of James and Danny could rest in her hands! The past was coming back to haunt her in the most horrible way of all.

Danny looked sleepy as he ambled into the kitchen. He found his phone and checked it. Three missed calls and several texts from Pamela.

Kate poured him a cup of tea and passed him a piece of her sandwich.

"Why don't you stay here tonight?" she told him.

"Maybe I will. I didn't get much sleep last night and that bed is so comfortable. How was your afternoon? Anything exciting happen?"

She stood up to make another sandwich and put a few slices of cake on a plate.

"No, nothing strange. Bought a few bits of wool for Gertie in the Outlet Centre and went for a walk in the park. Usual stuff, nothing new," she lied to her son. It really was for the best.

"I might drop in on Gertie for a few minutes later, Mam. I haven't seen her for ages. Do you want to come with me? You could give her that wool you bought." He hoovered the cake crumbs off the plate. "Nice cake. Well done, Mam."

"No son, I'm very tired. You can take the wool over for me. Tell her I will call tomorrow. I'm going to have a bath and start that thriller you got for me." Kate picked up the book.

"I won't be too long. Enjoy your book. Love you."

"You're a good lad. Gertie will be delighted to see you. I'll see you later, love."

After Danny had left, Kate went to her bedroom and took down a handbag from the top of the wardrobe. Underneath some scarves and costume jewellery she found what she was looking for. Sitting on her bed, she read the copy of the letter that James had written to Clodagh all those years ago.

Kate had tried so hard to push the guilt away. She had almost succeeded. Her children were the most important people in her life and she would die for them. James loved them and they adored him. If James had loved her, then life would have been perfect. She had gotten away with it for over thirty years. Her guilt in trapping James had been offset by the fact that he had two wonderful children. That had been enough. Now Clodagh Kenny was back in town, with her daughter. Putting the letter back into the box, her eye caught the title of the book that Danny had given her.

"The Game Changer... How apt..." she sighed.

David

Brandon Court was a hive of activity. The place was already proving to be a wise decision for the developers. James had spoken

Chips in a Bag, Classy Mr Murray

to David on Saturday. They had agreed to meet again before the Englishman flew back to London.

David had found out everything he could about CJ Securities. The two brothers had a reputation for honesty and hard work. They delivered what they promised. The meeting should not take long. They were all pleased with the progress being made. Looking across at the building that Clodagh had chosen for her shop, two of the girls from the Killarney outlet were stocking the shelves in Beth's Knits. The new manager, Gill, would be coming to look over the place and it would be up and running in a few days. That had been some evening. Thankfully the afternoon in the Metropole hadn't scared the poor woman off. Clodagh had been part of the McGovern family ever since the day when she had literally bumped into David and his mother on a freezing December. David loved both her and Beth and would go to the ends of the earth to ensure their happiness.

The Tearoom was full. Two people were kept going serving teas and delicious cakes, salads and soups to the customers. David waved at Ann who pointed to a table that had just been vacated.

"It is nice to see you again, Mr McGovern. There is a table free here. We are quite busy here today. The local community have organised a Farmer's Market to promote this place. Sit here and I will be with you in a minute." She went to get a menu.

James saw David as soon as he entered the room.

"Hello again, Mr Murray. I'll see if I can find you a seat," Ann greeted him.

"Hello Ann, actually I can see David over there."

David stood up as James approached. "You found me. Have you ever had an authentic afternoon tea? They do some great ones in London but I have never had the pleasure here," he indicated for James to sit down.

"You can count me in as long as it includes apple tart!" he answered.

Ann appeared beside them.

"What can I get for you, gentlemen?"

A while later the two men tucked into the tiers of sandwiches, pastries – including apple tart, scones with cream and jam all washed down with tea from a huge china pot.

After they had concluded their meeting, James turned to David.

"Would you like to join me in a walk around the market? I have heard that it is one of the best in Cork."

"I should but I am going to take a rain check. I must get back to the city and deal with a few things before I leave. I may not be back in Ireland for a while. You have my number and email. Eamonn should be able to answer any queries that you may have." He stood up.

"No problem. I hope that you will have a safe flight home." They shook hands.

James

James walked David to his car and then began his tour of the stalls.

"Excuse me. Are you okay? I am so sorry. Did I hurt you?"

He looked at the woman who had backed into him and embedded her heel in his ankle. His first instinct was to reach down to check for damage but the woman had a captivating smile and so he sucked up the pain and smiled back at her.

"I'll live, though I will probably have a limp," he joked.

"I really am sorry. I don't usually walk backwards but I was trying to get a better view of this painting. What do you think of it? By the way, I am Caroline O'Connor."

"James Murray. I am not really the right person to ask about art. To be honest it looks like a lot of squiggles to me. It's very large so you must have some size of a room that you intend to put it in," he told her.

"It's not for my house. It is intended for the lobby of a hotel. Bobby Mulcahy is a new talent so I came here to buy some of his pieces before he becomes too well-known. What's your excuse for being here?" she flirted.

"Work. I'm involved in security here." He reached down to rub his ankle.

"I really am so sorry about your leg. Can I buy you a coffee to make up for stabbing you with my shoe? I hope it is not too sore. I'm afraid that Christian L does not take prisoners."

"Sorry?" James looked confused.

"I'll explain over drinks."

Caroline

Caroline woke early the following morning and thought about James Murray. He was a very attractive man and she was definitely interested. It had been a while since she was in a relationship and to be honest she missed the feeling of being the most important person in someone's life. She also missed the sex. If she was brutally honest with herself then she would have to admit that she really missed Dylan. Eight years together and it had been a great relationship. She missed him so much... but marriage? She had never wanted that. It wasn't as if she had a ticking biological clock. They were way past that. He had been married before and had children. If his ex-wife had not remarried, then life would have gone on as usual. His marriage proposal had put the cat among the pigeons.

Today was the first day that she had felt like a woman in a while and it was thanks to James. An intelligent conversation was always important to her and he certainly ticked that box. He wasn't married, though he did have grown up children so she presumed that he was divorced. She would never date a married man. She recalled the night that they had spent together. It had been fantastic. Early that morning she had sneaked out of bed to have a shower. He had followed her. Wow.

So today was a very good day. She had found a man that she really liked. Who knows? James Murray might be the one to stop Dylan from creeping into her mind at every opportunity. When she had gone to Brandon Lodge to get a preview of the new shop she had expected to find a nice handbag for Gill, a new painting for the hotel and perhaps a few organic suppliers, but a man. That had been a bonus.

She smiled at how devious she had been. She had been in the Tearoom when she had seen him come in. For a split second she had thought that he was Dylan and her heart had skipped a beat. She had ordered extra coffee from the very pretty Goth girl who was dashing around keeping everyone happy and fed. She had watched him go and sit with the gay fellow. And thought how that would have been a waste…

When Tall, Dark and Handsome had left, she had followed him. He went walkabout for a while and eventually came back to browse around the Farmer's Market. She waited for her opportunity to accidentally bump into him.

After they had chatted for a while over tea, she had offered to show him the hotel that had been recently bought by her father. It was on the road to Killarney so it would be on his way home. It was empty at the moment as the renovations had not been started. Some of the fully furnished bedrooms were quite quaint. James didn't seem too put out by the speed with which they proceeded to the bedroom.

They had arranged to meet again at the weekend and she was really looking forward to that. She would dress up and flirt, eat fabulous food, drink expensive wine and hopefully spend a very satisfying night with a very handsome, successful and sexy man… her idea of a perfect date.

The second reason that she felt so good was because Gill wanted to meet her. Ever since the holiday in Turkey, Gill had been very cool towards Caroline. This worried her. They had been best friends forever and Caroline spent most of her childhood in Gill's house. It was more of a home than the fancy hotels that she was forced to call home. When her parents had divorced, she had been devastated. Gill and her family had been amazing. Caroline's mother had eventually remarried and moved to the States leaving her only child to be raised by her over-indulgent father. Apparently, her new stepfather Gus didn't 'do' children.

She had missed her chats with Gill. They used to be able to talk about anything. When Gill had not returned with the bottled water on the first night of their holiday, Caroline had gone looking for her. Thankfully Gill had fallen asleep on one of the loungers and had not gone off with that waiter. Caroline would never have forgiven herself if she had ruined Gill and Joe's marriage. Gill woke up the next morning with a massive hangover and hadn't mentioned the previous night at all. It was as if she had no memory of it. She had been quiet for the remainder of the holiday and they had only met a few times since.

Their friendship had been damaged by that holiday and she could not figure out exactly how that had happened. Now she was going to try and repair the damage and would never put their friendship at risk again. She was thrilled with the beautiful black and purple felted handbag that she had bought in Brandon Lodge. She would give it to Gill as an early birthday present. She might tell her about James, though she knew that Gill loved Dylan and always thought that they were perfect for each other. She might not approve of Caroline's new man.

Hi Gill. Can I call later? She pressed send.

James

James was shell-shocked. He had never behaved in that way before. He had slept with a woman within hours of meeting her and it had been great. He was meeting her again at the weekend. Maybe this might be the start of something wonderful.

Gill

Caroline had arrived bearing gifts – an expensive Merlot and the felted handbag.

"I know that you will be working with the designer of this bag but I just couldn't resist!" Caroline handed over the bag bearing the Beth's Knits logo.

"This bag is absolutely beautiful and way too expensive. I can't take this!" Gill protested.

"Of course, you can. It is to wish you luck with your new career. Crack open the wine and I will tell you all about Brandon Lodge." Caroline opened the cupboard and took out two wine glasses.

Gill poured the wine and went to the fridge for the salads that she had prepared for them.

"Must have soakage since I cannot drink more than an eggcup full without getting tipsy!" She laughed.

"Good plan. Sit down and I will tell you about the shop. It is in a really cute little cottage. Clodagh wasn't there herself but there was a really nice young girl serving. I think her name was Megan. She was really helpful. The shop is lovely and even though I know absolutely nothing about wool and stuff, it was a nice place to be. There is going to be a millinery and vintage shop next to the wine emporium. When that happens, I will be a very regular customer! I am so pleased that you are going to be working there. Managing that wool shop is the perfect job for you. It had lots of knitting stuff on one side and some great accessories like bags, scarves, and hats. It is a dream come true for you. You can't leave town without going into all the wool shops. Now you will get paid for doing what you love best." Caroline buttered a bread roll and started to eat.

"I can't wait to see the place for myself. I have arranged to meet Clodagh there tomorrow. She is going to show me around and let me get a feel for the place. I am so excited," Gill said.

"Have you seen Dylan lately?" Gill continued.

Caroline shook her head.

"I avoid the places that he is likely to be. I send someone else to some of the meetings and Dad has been very good. He attends some of the conferences in my place. He thinks I am totally wrong but he supports my decision."

"You and Dylan are good together. I agree with your father. Why are you so against marriage?" Gill asked.

"Marriage is not all that it is cracked up to be. Then there was his daughter to consider. Do you actually see me as mother material? I can just about mind myself," she laughed.

"You did love him though. You were in a relationship for years, at least your version of a relationship. His daughter is hardly looking for a mother. She had one already and she is an adult. That is not the reason, so what really changed for you?" Gill looked closely for the other woman's reaction.

Caroline hesitated before answering.

"He was quite happy with how things were until his ex-wife remarried. I was shocked when he produced that ring! I thought that we were doing great. We spent about half the week together and it was the best of both worlds. Marriage is so committed! Surely you don't need to be married to prove that you love someone? Look at my parents... I rest my case," she shrugged.

"Your parents are perfectly happy. They both have partners that they love. Your childhood may not have followed the norm but your parents did their best. Maybe it is time that you got over yourself? Let go of that old chestnut and marry the man. I'll even wear a pink meringue dress!" Gill laughed.

Caroline also burst out laughing.

"Well, well. At least you haven't changed. Now that you have laid your cards on the table, let's talk about the elephant in the room. Ever since the holiday you have basically ignored me. What did I do?"

Gill paced the room and hesitated before answering.

"The truth is that you didn't do anything. It was all my own doing. Meeting with you meant that I couldn't wipe that holiday from my mind. I'm sorry, Caroline. I slept with that waiter on the first night after you went to bed and I've felt so guilty, and now I think Joe is having an affair..." she murmured.

"Hold on there, girl. What do you mean? If you slept with that waiter, then it must have been the fastest sex in history! I came looking for you about five minutes after you left the apartment to get the water and you were fast asleep on one of the sunbeds. Your man was still serving drinks behind the bar, so I don't know where the notion that you slept with him came from. You remember the group of girls from Limerick? One of them said that you just wandered out, sat down and fell asleep. They were going to keep an eye on you for a while and wake you up before they went to bed. I arrived and led you back to bed. I was feeling guilty because you are not a drinker and I practically do it for a living! So set your mind to rest on that one. That waiter has no part in your memories." Caroline smiled.

Gill flopped down on the nearest chair.

"I felt so awful. I couldn't remember a thing but somehow or other it was stuck in my head that I could have slept with him. I thought that you knew it and so I thought it would be easier if I avoided you. I'm so sorry, Caroline. I wish that were true. Somehow or other he got hold of my mobile number and he sends text messages. I'm so afraid that Joe will see one of them so I keep my phone practically glued to my body. It's creating a terrible strain between us. He moved out of our bedroom a few months ago on the pretence of not disturbing me at night. I know it's because he has found someone else to have sex with. I should change my number but I like the one I have and I don't see why I should have to." Tears filled her eyes.

Caroline stood up and put her arms around Gill.

"I don't believe it, not for a minute. Joe adores you. He would never cheat on you. Please tell me why you think that he is having an affair."

"He is changing. He has started watching what he is eating and has been staying out when I know that he is not working. He left his phone charging here one-day last week and when I found it, I checked the messages. We always looked at one another's messages. Anyway there was one from a Laura telling him about a Maria and a Melissa Dream. Said that they would solve his problems and perk him up! I can hardly blame him. Look at me. I'm fat and menopausal and to be honest I'd rather knit than have sex! I tried Horny Goat Weed, but all I got for my trouble was an invitation for a quick afternoon shag in a city hotel. I was hoping to attract Joe back into my bed but instead I got a horny bus driver and messages from a Turkish waiter who would sleep with the entire population of a retirement village for a mobile phone!"

"Jesus girl, your life is much more exciting than mine. I've heard about that Goat Weed. It is supposed to be good. It comes in a blue box for men as well as the pink one for women so maybe you and Joe could take them together! Before long you would both be at it like rabbits!" she joked.

"Oh my God, I've been taking the ones in the blue box! No wonder they haven't worked." Gill pulled the box out of her bag.

"What did you say the name of that dream person was? Something sticks in my mind about that," Caroline took out her phone.

"Melissa," Gill answered.

"You are not going to believe this. Melissa Dream is not a woman. Look." Gill took the phone and laughed out loud.

"Look Gill, you need to talk to Joe. Tell him everything. He will understand about the messages. I've no idea how that waiter got your number but he will get tired and move on to someone else. I don't know who Maria is but there could be a simple explanation. If you two ever broke up, then my theory about marriage would be proven beyond doubt. Promise me that you will talk to him."

"Ok Caroline, I will. You must also promise me that you will meet with Dylan. You need him as much as he needs you. You do not function well on your own."

"What makes you think that I am on my own?" Caroline enquired.

"Do go on."

"Well actually, that bag was not the only thing that I picked up in Brandon Lodge. I also found a very attractive man. His name is James and I'm meeting him again at the weekend. We will have to wait and see how it goes."

Gill drove into Brandon Lodge and parked in front of the hotel.

"Wow. What a fabulous building!" she said to herself.

Getting out of her car, she walked around the huge house for a closer look. Scaffolding covered one side and as she walked all the way around, she came to the courtyard that housed all the units. Her phone beeped with a message from Caroline.

New month. New beginning. Hope April brings you all you wish for. Best of luck. Knock them dead. Ring me when you can x.

Gill was so nervous. So this was Brandon Lodge. She stood by the side wall and watched people coming and going. Some of the units were still in the process of being set up so there were quite a few delivery trucks around. She recognised the Cottage Tearoom as Caroline had described it so well. The sign for Beth's Knits was clearly visible across the courtyard.

She texted Joe to tell him that she had arrived safely. She was about half an hour early for her appointment with Clodagh Kenny. The smell of fresh baking drew her into the Tearoom.

"Hi, please take a seat. I will be with you in a moment." Ann smiled at her.

Gill sat in a little table beside the huge window which overlooked the entrance to the courtyard.

"That's a beautiful scarf you are wearing. I hope all that twisting won't harm it," Ann smiled as she handed over a menu.

"Oops. It's a habit I have developed when I'm nervous. I'm waiting for Ms Kenny. I will be working with her in Beth's Knits. My name is Gill."

"My name is Ann. Welcome to Brandon Lodge. Clodagh parks beside her shop and usually comes in for a coffee so you will be able to see her as soon as she arrives. Can I get you something while you are waiting?"

"Just a green tea please. The smell of baking is very inviting but I am too nervous to eat anything," she admitted.

"No problem. I will drop it right over," Ann answered.

Ann had just placed the tea on the table when Clodagh arrived.

"Glad you are here, Gill. Have you had time to look around? I will grab a coffee and maybe a scone and I will give you the grand tour!" Clodagh waved at Ann.

"I just walked around the hotel itself. It must have been pretty impressive when it was open!"

"Yes, it was… a real Downton Abbey. The dances were a huge attraction. Lots of love stories began there," Clodagh told her.

"You must be looking forward to seeing it restored to its former glory?" Gill said.

"Yes, I am. It will not be ready for a few months so the official opening will be held over until then. Most of the units are up and running already so the reopening of the hotel will be the icing on the cake." Clodagh swallowed the last bite of her scone.

"I am so looking forward to being a part of all of this. Thank you again for giving me this opportunity." Gill twisted her scarf.

"I am the one that is lucky to have found someone who is creative, experienced in management and loves yarn as much as I do. We will have a look at the shop as soon as we are finished here. The shelves should be stocked by now but I have left the window display for you. When I spoke to your last employer, she told me that your displays were exceptional," Clodagh said.

"Thank you. I hope I can live up to Maggie's standards." Gill blushed.

"I'm sure that it will be brilliant. Would you like some more tea before we go?"

"No, I would love to get started." Gill stood up.

"Oh my God! This is so, like, fabulous!" Gill gasped as they stepped onto the stone floor of Beth's Knits.

"It is, isn't it?" Clodagh agreed.

The room was a kaleidoscope of colour. Colourfully stocked shelves lined opposite sides of the large rectangular shaped room which opened onto another room also lined with shelves. Glass cabinets filled with Clodagh's signature felted handbags, delicate lace gloves and intricate neckpieces filled the back wall. A large wooden table surrounded by chairs sat in the centre of the room. Wicker baskets filled with silks, baby alpaca, mercerised cottons and silk lace sat on the table beside pattern books and knitting accessories.

"We hope to have regular workshops here. How do you feel about sharing your skills?" Clodagh asked.

"I have done it before so that would not be a problem. I have never seen such a variety of yarns. Do you source them all yourself?" Gill walked over to one of the shelves, picked up a hank of sari silk and held it to her face.

"A habit of a true yarn lover!" Clodagh laughed.

"I know that it probably looks strange to anyone else but I love the feel, smell and touch of yarn." Gill put the hank back on the shelf.

"To answer your earlier question, I have a number of suppliers worldwide. I travel to Europe on a regular basis and less often to the States. I especially love Prague. Have you ever been there?"

"No, but I have heard a lot about the Christmas markets there. I would love to go sometime," Gill answered.

"Well, we will have to change that. You will have to visit the Filium store which is inside the Palladium shopping centre. Then there is The Braken which is across the street. They both stock a lot of German wool but they also have a fabulous selection of buttons, ribbons and sashes. There is also my own favourite shop. It is owned by a young Czech woman who sells fabulous fabrics as well as yarns. I could stay there forever," Clodagh said.

"Sounds like my idea of heaven," Gill agreed.

"See! We really are kindred spirits! I spend a few days a month in London and I try to spend as much time as I can in the Killarney shop, so it is nice to know that I will be leaving the place in the capable hands of someone who loves yarn as much as I do. I think this deserves a little celebration." Clodagh took a bottle of champagne and two flutes from under the counter.

"Welcome to Brandon Lodge and to Beth's Knits. Here's to the future!" They clicked their glasses.

Chapter Nine

Joe
Joe was proud of his achievements. He was now able to run all the way around the pond without a problem. Three months ago he could barely walk around it. God bless Maria, Melissa and Gill. So much had changed since March, and it was all good. He had lost over twenty pounds in weight and was feeling on top of the world. His doctor had insisted on conducting a number of tests in order to rule out any major health issues. The bottom line was that he had a very unhealthy lifestyle, too much fast food and too little exercise. He had tackled the problem head on and felt so much better. All he needed at this moment was a coffee and a wrap. He had earned it.

"Hi Joe, looking good. What will it be today?" Laura placed a pint of iced water in front of him.

"A very large coffee and a chicken salad wrap, please. Hold the dressing. Any exam results yet?" he enquired.

"No, not yet. Anytime from July fifth onwards. The waiting is the worst part. Mam says that you are getting on really well with the diet and the walking group. She thinks a lot of you, talks about you all the time. You have become a really good friend to her. Thanks Joe. I really appreciate it. After Dad died, she stayed in all the time and just turned to food as a crutch. I'm so glad that she got her life back," Laura added.

"Sure, I owe her. If she hadn't taken me to the weight loss class and introduced me to the walking group, then I would be still struggling with my health problems!" he said.

"Here you go Joe. Enjoy." Laura placed his food on the table.

"How is the taxi business going?" she enquired.

"Not too bad now. I have a few regular contracts so they keep me going," he answered.

"I'm glad. You deserve it. See you later."

"See you Laura," Joe waved.

Parked in front of Arrivals, Joe had time to study his surroundings. Lots of people returning from holidays were surprised to find that the weather here was as good as it was in the continent. At least when they walked off the plane, their flip flops didn't freeze to the soles of their feet! He had seen some blue feet in his time.

Matt kept him in business. Joe had at least twenty regular runs to the airport each week, either to drop or collect Matt himself or for some of his clients. Matt preferred not to bother with the hassle of parking charges and he could also work on his laptop so he paid Joe to do the driving. At times Joe even donned a chauffeur's hat and drove one of Matt's fleet of top of the range cars. He loved those occasions. He had one coming up in a few weeks' time. An overnighter in Galway to value the contents of some ancestral pile after the owners had become victims of the recession. Matt had a well-earned reputation for fairness so he would do the best he could for his clients.

"I thought you had ditched smoking! You would think that the stint in hospital would have put paid to that habit," Joe chided as Matt sat into the back seat.

"I'm doing okay. That is the first and last one today. I only smoked half of it before I put it out. Anyway, how are you, skinny? You are fading away before my eyes. How does Gill feel about her shrinking man?" Matt countered.

"She is happy enough about it. We are both embracing a new lifestyle. She is really happy since she started working in Brandon Lodge. We have dinner together most evenings and she fills me in on the daily happenings. She isn't edgy anymore. She had built the phone thing up into something huge. I know my wife and I know that she would never cheat on me. Caroline is back on the scene again, so that is good. All said and done, life is good. I might even have a business proposition for you that could make it even better," he finished.

"I'm all ears. Give me the bones now and we can discuss it properly later. Any gum?"

Joe passed back some nicotine gum.

After he dropped Matt off, Joe headed home. He felt that it was now time to get back into the bedroom with Gill. She had been very understanding when he had explained about his fears. He prepared her favourite fish pie and made a fruit salad. He was going to seduce his wife. It was time!

Gill had just finished serving the last customer from the tour bus. Since the Farmer's Market had become a regular weekly occurrence, buses on the way to Killarney from Cork usually stopped for food and a bit of shopping. Convincing the yanks that they could make their own Aran jumper had proved to be a double edged sword! Tutorials involving cables, diamonds and moss stitch had become part of Gill's job description. She loved it all! The last three months had flown by.

She heard her phone beep a message.

Going for a run at seven. Will be home by eight thirty. Fish pie ready for oven. Wine chilling. See you soon xxxxxxxxx

The message surprised her a little. Joe hadn't added so many kisses to his messages in a very long time. Maybe he was ready to have sex again. She hoped so. Since she had discovered that Melissa Dream was a health supplement that helped you sleep and that Maria was just a friend, things had been improving daily. After she had discovered that she had not slept with that waiter and had spoken to Joe, life was on the up and up. The proper Horny Goat Weed was also doing its job!

"Well done Joe. You hardly broke a sweat," Maria drained her water bottle. They were back in the car park and all the others had left.

"Thanks. It's a good feeling. I've lost the equivalent of a set of obese twins and I can really feel the difference. I'm back cooking again instead of picking up fast food all the time. I just eat more regularly now and snack on fruit or a handful of nuts. It's all working and it's all thanks to you. My wife is delighted with the new model," he added.

"That's great news, Joe. I am really pleased for you," Maria smiled.

"You have a great daughter in Laura. I hope the exam results go her way," Joe said.

"Yes, I have. She is great with the boys. They can be a handful at times. Being at home all day can be trying. I used to love my job. When Dan got sick, I had to give it up in order to care for him."

"Gill used to feel like that until she got that new job. Have you ever considered going back to work?" he said.

"I would love to do something part-time but my thing was restoring old and rare books. There are very few people doing that anymore. If you happen to know of anyone in that line of business then please let me know," she laughed.

"Will do. I'll ask Matt. He is in antiques and if anyone knows, then he will. Must get off. Cooking dinner for Gill. Same time next week. Bye Maria."

"See you, Joe. Enjoy your night," she watched as he sat into his taxi and drove off.

Gill

Gill reached home just after seven. Plenty of time to put her plan into action. She dropped her bag in the kitchen.

Opening the fridge to get a bottle of water, she noticed the fish pie and fruit salad. Joe had also prepared some asparagus and broccoli. She spotted a couple of bottles of her favourite Sauvignon Blanc. She knew that if she looked in the freezer she would find Bailey's ice cream. This was great. Since Joe had started cooking again in March, their diet had become much healthier. A blow-out like this was not usual. She would have to make sure that they worked it off together! She rummaged under the cushions in the front room where she had hidden the book on seduction that Caroline had given her.

Joe

Joe was delighted to see Gill's car in the driveway. He had picked up some red roses on his way. He put the flowers in water before checking the oven. The washing machine was on. The contents swirling around looked like the sheets from his bed in the spare room. What was going on?

"Gill? Where are you?" he called out.

Gill

Gill parked her car and hurried to the shop. She hoped that the huge smile on her face would not be noticed. Though it was a very hot day in July, they were expecting a shipment of yarns suitable for autumn/winter.

Brandon Lodge was busy. The opening of the crèche and Montessori playschool had brought a lot of extra people into the courtyard. The gym, aptly named Limber Up, was very busy. They offered all sort of exercise classes. However, Gill's favourite was the fabulous Lady Mary Vintage shop which had just opened.

Robert

Robert was sorting out books inside the window of Loose Leaves. He had hoped that he could deal exclusively with old and rare books but the economic climate dictated that diversifying was the only way forward. He still had a section dedicated to his old books. He also stocked fiction, nonfiction and even magazines. When people came in to look for these magazines, they were sometimes drawn towards the rare book section. He kept some of them under glass to keep them from being damaged. He needed to find someone who could restore some of the older ones. Maybe Matt Vaughan might be able to help him. He often got some great books thanks to Matt's eagle eye.

He turned on his computer and looked at the website that Clodagh had helped him to set up. She was a joy to be around and they had become really close. The dancing was going well and he had not felt this alive in a long time.

Ann appeared at the door with his daily cuppa and sandwich.

"Hi Robert, I'll leave these in the back for you."

On her way back she looked closely at him.

"You okay, Robert? You look a little pale. Can I do anything for you?" Ann was worried.

"I'm alright, Ann. It was very warm last night and I didn't sleep much. I have a slight headache but I will be fine. You get on back to your business. I will sit and have my tea," he smiled weakly.

"I am going to get you some water from the fridge. Gary is in the Tearoom."

Two minutes later Ann returned, closely followed by Clodagh and Gill. She handed him a large bottle of cold water before returning to her Tearoom, leaving her two friends to take care of him.

"The cavalry has arrived. You go and sit and have your food. Gill will take over the till for a while. I will put away the rest of these books so shoo," Clodagh's expression did not invite argument.

As he sat and picked at his food, Robert realised that he was indeed exhausted. Ever since he had decided to open his bookshop he had worked very long hours. He was almost sixty years old but today he felt closer to ninety.

"Better?" Clodagh pulled out a chair and sat opposite him.

"Yes, thanks. I was just hungry. When you live on your own you sometimes forget about preparing healthy meals and I'm afraid that I'm a great one for the old grazing. I must try to make more of an effort. With the Farmer's Market now being a weekly happening, I will have no excuse. I used to be a dab hand at cooking." He sipped his tea.

"I'm a bit like that myself. Tell you what. Why don't I cook dinner for you tonight and you can do it next week? After all we need to keep our strength up for all this ballroom dancing. I wouldn't want my partner getting sick on me now, just as we are getting really good at it. I have a brand new kitchen that is crying out to be used. What do you say, you free tonight?" she asked.

Robert put down his cup. "You don't have to do that. I wasn't fishing for a dinner invitation. It is a nice idea, if you are sure?" the hopeful look on his face said it all.

Chips in a Bag, Classy Mr Murray

"That's settled then. It will be something simple. About half seven. I'll give you directions before we leave. I had better get back to the shop. See you later so." Clodagh stood up.

"That sounds perfect. Thanks again. I'd better do a bit myself. I think I will try to get someone to help me out here a few hours a week. See you later so."

After she had left, Robert sat for a few more minutes before returning to the till where Gill was putting some books in a carrier bag for a customer.

"This is the man to help you!" Gill pointed to Robert.

"How can I help?" he enquired.

"I was looking at your collection in the cabinet over there. I recently acquired some books from an elderly relative. Some are in need of repair. I was wondering if you did that sort of work yourself. If not, maybe you could point me in the right direction?" the man said.

"Actually, I do have a contact, Matt Vaughan. He will definitely be able to help. Why don't you leave your number and I will get back to you?" Robert took out a card for him to write on.

"That would be great. Thanks." He scribbled his name and number on the card and handed it back to him.

After the customer had left, Gill turned to Robert.

"I should have guessed, what with all those old books, that you would know Matt. He is a good friend of ours. Joe went to school with him," Gill said.

"It's a small world in the antiques business and he is the best and the fairest. I know that there was a place that he used to use himself for restoring books. He said that they were the most professional around. I'll give him a ring today. Thanks so much for all your help. Since coming here, I have gained so many new friends," he smiled.

"I know what you mean. Brandon Lodge seems to have a magic about it. I'm so much happier since I started working here. We are quite the little family. We must look out for each other," Gill said.

Gary & Ann

Gary had looked up when Ann had come back after giving the water to Robert. He had a tea towel thrown over his shoulder.

"Everything okay with Robert? I was a bit worried when I saw all three of you rushing in there," he turned to the oven to check on some scones.

Ann put down the tray.

"He is a bit better now. I got a bit of a shock when I saw him at first. He looked green. He needs to take it easy. I hope that he is eating properly. He lives alone and is often still here when I lock up. Clodagh will sort him out. Those two have become really close since they started that dance thing. I wonder."

Gary put the scones onto a serving dish and placed a glass cover over them.

"Don't you start matchmaking again… at least not for others," he muttered under his breath.

"Those scones look lovely. I didn't realise that you were such a good baker. I will have to up your wages!" she finished the scone that she had sneaked from the pile. "Market research," she quipped and avoided the tea towel that he had thrown at her.

"I make a mean tart as well," he quipped.

"Me too," she blushed when she realised what that must have sounded like.

Gary pretended not to notice her discomfort.

"I will make you a sample Tarte Tatin for your market research. I worked in a top class bakery in Australia. The baker was really good with his hands. Could do magic with a few ingredients! Amy worked there too, only she stayed." He looked for her reaction.

"Is she still there now?" she watched him closely.

Gary poured them both a cup of tea. The Tearoom was quiet for the moment.

"Yeah, she's still there. As I said the guy was good with his hands!"

"I'm sorry Gary. I didn't know. You okay about it?"

"We would have split eventually. She is very happy, even talking about marrying her Australian baker. I'm a free agent," he added hopefully.

"Tell you what, why don't you make that tart and I will be the judge of how good you are with your hands!"

Gary was about to risk putting his arms around her when the door opened and two women entered. They appeared to be arguing.

The younger woman approached the counter as the older one sank heavily into a chair by the bay window.

"Excuse me. Are you Ann?"

"Yes. How can I help you?"

"My mother would like a word if you don't mind." She glanced back to where the other woman appeared to be hunched over the table.

"Is she okay? I'll get some tea."

"My Dad died last night. My name is Jane O'Brien and my mother is Maureen," she spoke quietly.

Ann noticed that Gary had approached the distressed woman and was leading her to the privacy of a small alcove.

"I'm so sorry." She went outside the counter and led Jane to where her mother was sitting.

After the tea was poured and Gary had returned to the counter, Maureen spoke for the first time.

"My daughter does not agree with what I have in mind for my husband's funeral. Jack was a man who enjoyed life and the finer things in life for as long as he could. He wouldn't want long faces and dull food in some impersonal hotel room or pub. He was proud of our home and loved to entertain so that is what I intend to do. Jane thinks that a celebration will be disrespectful but I know what he would have wanted. There will be no funeral homes with incessant hand shaking. He will stay at home until it is time to go to the church. There will be good food and drink available for all. No expense will be spared. This is where you come in. I saw what you provided for Tom Murphy's funeral. I was impressed. I want something similar, on a larger scale. Money will be provided up front for any purchases needed. The wake will be the day after tomorrow. I will provide people to serve the food. You just need to supply it. This is what I would need." She pulled a large sheet of paper out of her handbag and handed it to Ann.

Ann looked at the extensive list. She would need some help to pull it off on time but it could be done.

"Yes, I can do this. I will get on to the suppliers right away. May I get you a pot of tea and a sandwich?"

"Thank you. That would be nice. You okay, love?" her mother gently touched her daughter's arm.

"For God's sake, Mom. This is a funeral, not some fancy birthday celebration. Who cares what people get to eat or drink? Why can't we be left alone?" she started to cry.

Ann slipped away to get the tea and sandwiches as Maureen comforted her daughter.

"All okay there?" Gary asked.

"I hope so. I'll fill you in later. The lunchtime rush will be starting soon. Thanks for your help," she filled a plate with assorted sandwiches as well as a few pastries.

"We make a good team, you and I," Gary added.

Clodagh

Robert hadn't looked well at all. Clodagh hoped that it was just tiredness. She was aware that he was more interested in her than she was in him. She wasn't sure that she wanted a relationship. Robert was a very attractive, available man but she was used to being by herself. Her invitation was made purely on a friend to friend basis but she had seen the look on his face! She knew that his birthday was coming up as Ann was obsessed with horoscopes and would almost insist on knowing your star sign before she served you. She would pick up something nice for dessert in the Tearoom.

Gill

Gill picked up three coffees and returned to the shop. Every time she opened the door, the smell of the yarns and the riot of colour warmed her heart. Clodagh was putting some new stock in wicker baskets which were scattered around the airy room. Several customers sat around the table looking through pattern books and sipping the drinks that they had bought in the Tearoom. At the far end more people looked at the collection of designer bags and accessories which were tastefully housed in glass cabinets.

She handed one to Megan.

"Thanks Gill. Clodagh just came back so if you need to take more time to grab some food..." Megan indicated towards where Clodagh was on the phone.

"No, I'm good. I will just have a quick word with her and help you out here. There is another tour bus due in," Gill said.

"Here you are. What did you think about Robert?" She handed the cup to Clodagh.

"I hope it is just the heat. I invited him for dinner tonight," she blurted out.

"Good for you. A girl has to do what she has to do. It's obvious that he fancies you." Gill was delighted.

"It's not like that. I worry that he is not eating properly."

"Yeah right..." Gill added.

"It is not like that. I am perfectly happy on my own." She sipped her Americano.

"Keep telling yourself that and you will be fine," Gill told her.

"Thanks Gill. I'll bear that in mind. I must ring David and see how he liked his birthday present." She grabbed her coffee and went into the back room.

Clodagh

He answered almost immediately. "Hi Clodagh! You protecting our investment? Thanks for the book. I love it."

"Well, I am glad to hear that. Robert came up with the idea. He has some rare treasures in that shop of his. After all what can you get for the man who has everything! You can cook just like they used to in the kitchens of Brandon Lodge. Looking forward to seeing you and Mike next weekend. You can get all domestic with the new recipes." She noticed Robert was locking up Loose Leaves.

"Must go, I've a dinner to organise for another birthday boy. Talk later."

She waved at Robert.

"See you soon," he shouted across the yard.

Clodagh entered the Tearoom as Ann was tidying up.

"Did you manage to keep me one of your pear tarts? Robert likes them so at least dessert will be edible," she laughed.

Ann reached under the counter and produced a large box.

"I'm glad that you invited him for dinner. He really scared me earlier. Did you manage to persuade him to tell his daughter?" Ann added a pot of whipped cream and a plastic container of coulis to the box.

"Yes. She called in the afternoon when I had popped back in to see him so he didn't have a choice. She had noticed that he had been working too hard so she is taking him away for a few days next week. She has even organised someone to stand in for him. How is your knitted bag coming along?" Clodagh made herself a cup of green tea.

"It's getting there. It should be finished for the weekend. I was planning on working on it tonight but I have been asked to provide food for a funeral buffet so I will have to get started on that. So it's Robert's birthday. Any idea for a present? I bet that he would be happy with just you," she smiled cheekily.

"At it again I see. Maybe you should consider taking a leaf out of my book and cooking a meal for that handsome fellow over there. A blind dog could see that the both of you are crazy about each other," Clodagh retorted.

"Maybe I will. Hope you enjoy your dinner. Any plans for the weekend?" Ann asked in an effort to change the subject.

"I must go to Killarney on Thursday. Claire will be opening her own hair salon at the weekend! David and Mike are coming over for the opening so it should be fun. David was sixty this week so its birthdays all round. Thank God for Gill. She is a natural born manager. I had better get a move on or my guest will arrive before me and I will have to phone for a takeaway! Bye now. See you in the morning. Be good." Clodagh waved at Gary who was clearing the last of the tables.

Margaret Kelleher

Chapter Ten

Danny

Danny was frustrated. It had been over four months since he had started negotiations on the house in Blackstone Village. Barney still didn't know that Danny was acting on his own behalf. Maybe the time had come for him to come clean. Then Barney might soften a bit and drop the price a little more. The asking price was competitive. When he had done all the maths, he was still short quite a bit. Would he be able to get finance to make up the shortfall? Did he even want to? He would have a chat with his Dad. James was usually very good at spotting pitfalls. The Prince of Doom would have nothing on his father! Yet he was very good at clarifying any situations. If this could be done, then his Dad would tell him. The problem was that he was difficult to catch lately.

He had agreed to meet him in Murphy's Bar for lunch. Hopefully he would turn up this time and not cancel at the last minute as he had been doing a lot recently. If he was married to the man, then he would have suspected that he was having an affair! Then there was his mother who was behaving very strangely ever since the weekend of the wedding. There was definitely a subtle change in the relationship between her and Pat.

As he studied the menu in the pub, his mind wandered back to the other problem on his mind, his love life. It had been months since the wedding but he hadn't heard from Beth. He had to assume that she had forgotten all about him and gone back to her life in England. He would have loved to have gotten the chance to get to know her better. He couldn't get Pamela out of his mind either. She kept inviting him to accompany her to different events. He would try to decline nicely but she usually wore him down.

"Please, Danny. I have nobody else to ask. Just as friends!" She would keep going until he agreed. What worried him more was that, after a few too many at a party, they had crossed the line and slept together. That could not happen again. He was not going to lead her to believe that there was more to their relationship.

"Hi son, penny for your thoughts." James pulled out a chair and sat down.

"Not sure that they are worth even that much. You are difficult to get hold of these days. I don't suppose that it has anything to do with that attractive blonde woman that Mam and I saw you with last Friday night in the Valley Hotel?"

"What were you and your mother doing there?" James was clearly uncomfortable.

Danny signalled to the waitress.

"I asked her to look at a property with me in the village. She has a good eye and I trust her judgement. Anyway when we were finished I took her for a drink in the hotel. She had never been there since it opened and she wanted to have a look at it. She used to know Vincent O'Connor, so she was curious about what he had done with the hotel. She was going on about how nice it was when the lift doors opened and you and this woman came out. Ye were so wrapped up in one another that you didn't see us sitting in the foyer," Danny added.

"Thanks. That's lovely." James smiled at the waitress as she placed their order in front of them.

"Anyway that's not why I wanted to see you. I want to ask your advice on a property that I am interested in out in the Valley. Hillside Manor. Do you know it?" Danny speared his steak.

"Indeed I do. That's a huge place. Isn't Barney handling that one? Who's your client?" James enquired.

"I am." Danny waited for his father's reaction.

"I was looking at it online recently. I feel that the asking price is a bit on the high side but it is a big site. Do you have a plan? You usually have one before you run it by me." James asked.

Danny took a folded sheet out of his inside pocket. He smoothed it out before placing it on the table between them.

"You know how McCarthy's are trying to buy up all the property on the street where I live? If I decide to sell to them, then I would get nearly three hundred thousand for my apartment. Then there is nana's house. If Kathryn agrees to sell that, then it would give me another fifty thousand. I'm still short a bit but maybe I could use the office building as collateral. Uncle Conor may not agree. Dad, what do you think?" Danny looked hopefully at his Dad.

James studied the figures on the page in front of him.

"This is well thought out. Well done, son. I am proud of you. There may be an alternative to using the office building as collateral. After you and Kathryn were born, I opened some investment accounts in both your names. They did very well in the boom years and thank God, I was able to redirect them into safer options. They may have lost a little but they have more than is needed to make up the shortfall that you are looking for. Your mother and I were going to give them to each of you as a wedding present. Don't mention this to your sister yet. It can still be a surprise for her. She may decide to use it and I still want to walk her up the aisle in style. I can't see you getting married any time soon so you may as well use it for your dream house."

Danny was speechless.

"Are you serious, Dad?"

James tucked in to his steak.

"Yup, I've definitely given up on getting a wedding out of you!"

"I mean about the money. It would make the world of difference to me. I wouldn't have to take out any loan. If I could persuade Barney to come down a little on the price, everything would be just great. Do you think I should tell him that I want to buy it for myself?"

"Definitely. We have helped each other out in the past. You might be pleasantly surprised. He is very fair in his business dealings. After all he would still be on track for a hefty commission. It's a win-win situation. Are you planning on moving in on your own or is there a significant other? I find it difficult to keep up with you. Are you still seeing the girl that you took to the wedding a few months ago?" James asked.

"I really don't know how to answer that question. When I tell people that we are just friends they look at me like they think I am lying. I don't want to hurt Pamela but we are not a couple," Danny said.

"I'm sure you will work it out." James looked at his watch.

"I hope so. Everyone is telling me to keep away from her but she is not the worst of them." Danny sipped his pint.

"I have a meeting at three. Come by the house this evening. I'll get out the details of the investments and we can get the ball rolling. Give Barney a ring. His daughter is getting married soon so he might need the cash. Let me know how it goes." James finished his drink.

Caroline went to her office to Skype her mother.

"Hi darling, you look really well. I'm delighted to hear from you. I want to know what date the party will be on so I can book my ticket."

"Ah Mom, there is no need for you to come all the way over from New York. I'm going to be fifty, not twelve! I will be going over in the next few weeks and we can celebrate then. I love your hair. That colour suits you. How is Gus?"

"He is well, thank you. Are you sure that you don't want me to come over to Ireland? If you prefer to come here, then I will book a show on Broadway for the three of us." Her mother smiled at the camera. "I must say, this Skype business is marvellous," she added.

"A show sounds lovely. Dad wants to throw a big party here and invite every person that he has ever encountered. I want something low key, just a celebration with my friends. Gill will be fifty as well so we are going to do something together," said Caroline.

"Ah Gill, she is a lovely girl, not like her mother." Caroline could see her mother bristle.

"You just didn't like her because she accused you of having airs and graces! She was very good to me. Anyway you should not speak ill of the dead."

"I know dear, I'm sorry. I hope you consulted Gill this time. You do have a history of planning surprises for others."

"Trust you to bring that one up. I will let you know what I'm doing in a few days. I'm meeting Gill this evening. We will decide together what we want to do. Whatever it will be, you will not be required to endure a six-hour flight. Look I have to go and check on the function room. We have a society wedding here in a few days. The flowers alone will take hours to arrange, not to mind the chocolate fountains – all five of them. We will chat again soon. Bye now." Caroline waited for her mother's wave before logging off.

Her father knocked before entering the room. He kissed the top of her head.

"Busy day today. I was looking for you earlier. The mother of the bride was on again. I told her that everything was under control. You might give her a call back." He walked to the drinks cabinet and poured himself a whiskey. He picked up a second glass.

"I'm driving later," Caroline shook her head.

"You okay, love? You look a bit preoccupied." Her Dad sat on one of the plush couches that were dotted around the huge room.

"Oh, you know... Mom wanted to come over here for my birthday. I have just realised that I am almost fifty, middle-aged but only if I live to be a hundred! What have I got to show for it? Everything I have has come from you. I feel like a spoiled bitch that takes everything for granted. I spent years blaming Mom for leaving us and never trusted anyone enough to marry and have a family. Now it's too late."

"Look Caroline, you are my only child and of course everything I have is yours. You have always worked damned hard in every hotel that we acquired. There would be no weddings in any of them if it were not for your expertise and creativity. The décor is also down to you. Look at how that new painting you bought coordinates perfectly with what was already there. You are a young, beautiful and talented lady. You may not have fifty years left, but you have years ahead of you. I don't know what happened between you and Dylan but you need to speak to him. You two are perfect together. I know it's none of my business, but I'm pretty sure that the guy I saw tripping down the steps a while ago is not the one for you." He patted her arm.

Caroline blushed.

"Thanks, Dad. Maybe I will give him a call. I think that I will keep the birthday celebrations low key. I might just have a meal here with a few friends. I'm meeting Gill tonight. Maybe she and Joe could have one of the suites for a few nights. They went through a rough patch but things are better now. What do you think?" she said.

"Whatever you decide is fine by me. I'm being picked up in a few minutes. Going to Limerick to check on things there. Don't forget to give Antoinette Morley a call back. She will only ring again later. Take it easy. Give my regards to Gill and Joe. See you tomorrow, honey." He kissed the top of her head.

"Bye, Dad. Love you."

After she had spent fifteen minutes on the phone patiently going over all the wedding details and calming the over anxious mother of the bride, Caroline dialled Dylan's number. He picked up immediately.

"Hi Caroline, how are you?"

"I'm good, thanks. Look Dylan, can we meet? I should not have left things like that. It was a shock when you proposed. I thought we were happy as we were." She waited for his answer.

"I shouldn't have sprung it on you like that. I've had plenty of time to think in the last few months. Maybe you were right. It might be better this way. Rumour has it that you have a new man on the go. I may not be in the country but some people seem to deem it necessary to keep me updated on your movements. I am staying in the villa in France with a few friends. Maybe we can chat sometime. Enjoy your birthday. I must run. We are going out to dinner."

"Ready, Dylan?"

Caroline would know that voice anywhere.

Debbie Walsh Hegarty was in France with Dylan! That bitch had been trying to get her hooks into him ever since her husband had run off with his business partner Jack. Well it looked like she had finally succeeded. Caroline knew that she had no one to blame but herself. Suddenly her afternoon lost its glow.

Gill

Thursday morning was damp and cloudy so Gill decided to cheer herself up by sorting out the baby wool section which was just inside the bay window. Brandon Lodge was very busy. The weekly market always brought in extra customers and all the units benefitted. Ann and Gary were now partners in the Tearoom and had to take on extra help in the form of Gary's sister who was in university and so was delighted with the part-time job. Robert had also taken on a new assistant, Maria, who had managed to fit in very well with everyone. Gill had mentioned to Joe that Robert knew Matt and was hoping that he could help him find someone who knew their way around old books. Joe immediately thought of Maria so an interview was arranged.

Gill waved to Maria and smiled to herself. Even though she was unaware of it, Maria had been responsible for giving Gill the kick she needed to get her husband back into her bed. Maybe she would thank her some day for being the other woman, if only in Gill's imagination. Maria was really nice and the job in Loose Leaves really suited her. She had an extensive knowledge and know-how when it came to old and rare books and so that side of the business was taking off. Matt had put a few contacts his way as well so things were looking up. She also seemed to have developed a crush on Robert, though Gill didn't think that he had noticed. He only had eyes for Clodagh. Gill would have loved to ask Clodagh if she felt the same way, but, even though they got on really well, it was early days and she didn't want to overstep any marks. After all, it was none of her business. She didn't know a lot about her employer's life before she returned to Ireland and Clodagh didn't elaborate. Gill knew that Clodagh had a non-romantic connection to David McGovern.

Gill was jolted out of her musings by the arrival of another tour bus. She was looking forward to meeting Caroline at the market after work. Joe had driven her to work that morning as her car needed servicing so she was travelling home with Caroline.

Clodagh was in Killarney for the day but Megan would take over at two. Until then, Gill was on her own. Still as she was doing something she loved, she was quite happy to run the shop. Clodagh had allowed her a section to display her own designs and they were selling well. She had decided to focus on vintage inspired shawls and collars and so far they were selling like hot cakes. The jingling of the bell heralded the arrival of a large group of customers and the morning flew by. Gill was a bit worried about Caroline as she had sounded down when they had spoken earlier. It had something to do with Dylan and France. Still at least it had diverted Caroline's attention away from their upcoming birthday celebrations. God only knew what Caroline would plan if left to her own devices.

James

James studied the folder pertaining to Brandon Lodge. The lighting was state of the art, so much so that even at night the place was lit up. All the units had their own alarm systems and the whole place was monitored twenty-four/seven. Everything was going according to plan. He still hadn't met some of the tenants as Conor had attended that introductory meeting on their behalf. James knew that he needed to meet all the tenants himself. He had met Ann from the restaurant and Robert, the owner of the bookshop, on his last visit. He would drop into the wool shop later and introduce himself to Beth. He would also introduce himself to the tenants of the vintage and hat units.

A few hours later he found himself following a tour bus into the courtyard. After parking at the far end of the complex he made his way to the converted barn from where the cameras were operated. He watched the activity in the courtyard and noticed that one camera seemed to be out of focus, as the images were a little blurred.

He played back the footage from the previous few days. Something was not quite right with the camera. It would have to be checked out. It was pointed to the Cottage Tearoom and Beth's Knits. As he scrolled through the previous day's events, he noticed a car that he recognised park in front of the wool shop. It was the same car that had almost collided with him back in March. He wanted to see who the driver was but, because the images were blurred, all he saw was the back of a woman's head – a woman with red hair. He would have loved to see her face. She walked into the Tearoom so she could work there or maybe she was a regular customer. He would have liked to meet her and offer her a driving lesson…

He rang Eamonn and asked him to have a look at camera six as soon as possible. Locking up, he decided to buy some fresh ingredients for his evening meal. He headed towards the market stalls.

Gill

Gill was tidying up after the afternoon rush. It had been amazing. The tourists had loved the shawls and collars and almost all of Clodagh's felted bags had been sold. She had even managed to persuade a few to make their own Aran jumper, with a modern twist of course. The new yarns were so much more skin friendly than the pure wools. She had made up the kits and given them a good discount. Clodagh had texted to say that she would be late back. She had just finished sorting out the pattern books when Caroline arrived.

"Hi Caroline, just finishing up here. Would you like a coffee while you are waiting?"

"No thanks, I'm okay. There is a painting that I would like you to see before I buy it, so we had better get a move on. Some of the stall owners have started packing up. It looks like rain so you can't really blame them," Caroline sighed.

"You feeling alright? You sound fed up. Just let me serve these last two customers and then I will be all yours." Gill smiled at the woman approaching the counter carrying a large selection of yarn and needles.

"You might be stuck here longer than you think. Looks like there is another customer arriving." Caroline pointed to where a woman was approaching the door.

"That's Maria. She works with Robert in the bookshop. She has taken up knitting and where better to get inspiration?" Gill laughed.

"Hi Gill, I know it is late but I promised the boys that I would knit them a superman sweater each. Would you mind if I looked through the patterns?"

"Hi Maria, I love your hair. It's not your usual colour," Gill said.

"I felt like a change but, to be honest, I think she was a little heavy handed with the red dye! Still it's only hair colour!" Maria shrugged.

"Take as long as you like here. Would you mind keeping an eye on the shop for five minutes while I look at some painting with Caroline?" Gill asked.

"No bother, Gill. All the buses have left so this place should be quiet." Maria picked up some pattern books and started to flick through them.

"I will see you outside when you are ready," Caroline said.

Gill and Caroline made their way to where the paintings were being displayed.

"I don't know, Caroline. It's a bit abstract for my liking. To me it's just a mass of swirls and shapes. The colours are beautiful. I guess it could be a sea, or something else. I don't know if it is suitable or not. You are the one with the degree in Interior Design." Gill stepped back in order to get a better view. It still looked the same as it did close up.

Maria had found a pattern and was choosing yarn and needles. She knew nothing about running a wool shop so she hoped that she wouldn't have to deal with any customers. She glanced up when the bell tinkled and the door opened. God, he was so handsome, had a bit of an Elvis thing going on. She loved Elvis. She felt herself blush.

"Hello, my name is James Murray. I'm in charge of security. You must be Beth. Delighted to meet you at last." He extended his hand. As she was still speechless, she took it.

Just as she was about to put him right, his phone rang.

"Sorry Beth, I have to go. We will chat again soon." Elvis left the building.

She was still standing there when Gill returned.

"You okay, Maria? You look like you have seen a ghost. You should sit down." Gill practically pushed the other woman into a rocking chair.

"I did see a ghost. Elvis was here."

"I will get you a cup of strong tea. I know that this place is rumoured to be haunted, but I don't think that knitting was on Elvis's bucket list!"

James

After James had finished his call, he walked back towards his car. He spotted Caroline and another woman putting a large parcel into the boot of her car. He hurried over just as she was about to get into the driver's side.

"Hi Caroline, you didn't mention that you were coming here. I enjoyed the afternoon. Hope to do it again soon," he finished.

"Oh! Hi James, it was a spur of the moment decision. I must fly. I'll ring you later." She pecked him on the cheek before sitting into the car.

She had driven away before James realised that she hadn't introduced him to her friend. She sounded different, couldn't wait to get away. He wondered if they had reached the end of the road.

Gill & Caroline

"Who was that?" Gill looked at Caroline.

"That was the guy that I met the last time I was here. He is involved with security." She indicated to turn onto the main road.

"Why didn't you introduce me to him? You were all chat about him last week. What has changed?" Gill saw the look of anguish on her friend's face.

"It's Dylan. Dad said that I should contact him. I did. He is in his villa in France, with Debbie Walsh Hegarty! I've been such a fool. I love him. I was only fooling myself. No other man can take his place. What can I do?" She almost rear-ended the car in front of her at the roundabout.

"First thing that you can do is to pull into the garage up here. You need to calm down and we both need to get home in one piece! I'll drive and we will find a solution. Dylan would not touch that one with a fork! There has to be another explanation."

James

James was still in Brandon Lodge. He was waiting to see Eamonn and sort out the rogue camera. He wondered again about Caroline. He was enjoying their relationship, but it was mainly physical. Dating her had shown him that he was not completely dead inside. Boy, did she know her stuff. He would never be able to eat a strawberry again! When he had gone into Beth's Knits earlier, part of him had hoped that Clodagh would have been standing behind the counter. The logo and colour scheme were her, but the very quiet Beth was nothing like her.

Clodagh

Clodagh arrived back just before seven. Ann was in the Tearoom with Gary and waved at her.

"Be there in a minute," Clodagh nodded.

After she checked that the shop had been locked up, Clodagh went into the Tearoom.

"Did I miss anything exciting today?" she asked between bites of the chicken salad that Ann had insisted on feeding her.

"According to Maria, Elvis visited Beth's Knits today," Ann laughed.

"Really. Did he buy anything?" Clodagh stirred her tea.

"Not that I know of. My mother loved Elvis." Ann refilled the cups.

"Why are you two talking about Elvis?" Gary appeared from the kitchen area, a tea towel draped over his shoulder.

"According to Maria, he was in Beth's Knits earlier!" Clodagh told him.

"I doubt that. The only man I saw enter that shop today was James Murray."

Clodagh's cup shattered on the floor.

"Oh my God! I am so sorry. The cup just slipped through my fingers," Clodagh lied.

"You okay, Ms Kenny? You have gone very pale." Gary was concerned.

"Yes, I am fine. I'm sorry about the china cup." She tried to gather her thoughts.

"Here you go." Ann placed a glass of water on the table.

"Thanks Ann. It was probably the heat. I am fine." She tried to sound casual.

"You sure that you are alright?" Ann asked.

"Yes. Thanks for everything. I had better go and lock up before any more celebs call," she joked.

"See you tomorrow. Night."

Ann & Gary

Ann and Gary exchanged looks.

"I think the lady protests too much," Gary told Ann.

"What do you mean?" She was intrigued.

"She dropped the cup when I mentioned James Murray. There is a story there!" he answered.

"Well Sherlock, it will have to wait until later. It is time to lock up for the day." Ann handed him the sweeping brush.

Clodagh

In Beth's Knits, Clodagh waited for David to answer the five missed calls that he had received in the past ten minutes. Eventually his name came up.

"Clodagh? Is something wrong? Are you and Beth alright?" he sounded worried.

"We are fine. I just wanted to ask you about the security company that you hired," she paused.

"What about them? Is there a problem?"

"No, everything is fine. I just wanted to know why you picked that particular company. How did you find James Murray?" She waited for his answer.

"I did some research. That company is highly regarded. There are many glowing reviews about their work. Why do you want to know?" David asked.

"Do you remember when I told about the reason that I went to London?"

"Yes of course I do. It involved a man who had cheated on you… Oh no!" realisation dawned on David.

"I am so sorry, Clodagh. Are you alright?"

"I will be. He only visits now and again. Maybe you could let me know when he is due so I can avoid him. Everyone is delighted with the level of security here so I will just keep out of his way. I have plenty to do in the other outlets so it should not be a problem," she reassured him.

"I will indeed. Eamonn will keep you informed… I promise you," David assured her.

"Thanks David. Talk to you later." She ended the call.

James

James was watching television when Caroline rang. An hour later he was waiting for her in the Valley Hotel. The place was packed. It had been refurbished and was a virtual gold mine. The décor was muted but welcoming. He watched Caroline approach. She was stunningly beautiful. Her sense of style was amazing. Heads turned when she entered the bar. She stopped to chat with some of the patrons as she made her way over to where he was waiting. She certainly knew how to work a room. He would miss her. Since she had practically ignored him at Brandon Lodge, he knew that the writing was on the wall. She had given him back a zest for life that he thought he had lost forever and he would always be grateful to her for that.

"Hi James, thanks for coming. Can I get you anything?" She sat opposite him and signalled to the waiter.

"I'm okay, thanks. This sounded urgent on the phone. I will make this easy. It's not me, it's you!" he joked.

"Something like that. I feel awful. I had been seeing someone for a long time and suddenly realised that he was the one. The fact that I might be way too late is neither here nor there. It would be unfair of me to keep seeing you. You are a lovely man and I'm sure the right woman is out there somewhere." She looked stricken.

"It's okay, Caroline. I'm a big boy. I know that what we had was not serious. I hope that everything works out for you," James drained his glass.

"Thanks, James. I appreciate that."

Chips in a Bag, Classy Mr Murray

Chapter Eleven

Gill & Joe
The August Bank holiday weekend was coming up. Joe and Gill usually spent it quietly at home but this year was going to be different.

Gill had developed a new lease of life since she had started work. She had even started running with Joe in the evenings. He had lost over three stone in weight and all his worries about his non-performance in the bedroom were firmly in the past. Life was good. Their wedding anniversary was at the beginning of August and this year they were really going to celebrate in style. They were aware of Caroline's plan for the double birthday celebration and the fact that Gill had agreed to spend a weekend in the Valley Hotel – the penthouse suite no less! They would definitely enjoy that as the both loved Kerry. Caroline was responsible for the décor in this recently acquired addition to the O'Connor hotel chain. Neither he nor Gill had seen it yet.

She was meeting Caroline for a quick coffee to finalise plans for their upcoming birthdays. Joe was just adding the chicken to the wok when he heard her key in the door. He poured the wine and lit the candles. Her favourite music was already playing quietly in the background.

"Hi Joe, something smells good. I'm really hungry." She kissed him on the cheek.

"I'm glad that madam is hungry. Please sit yourself down and we will get started." He pulled out the chair for her. "How is Caroline doing now? Any news from Dylan?" Joe asked.

"She is alright. He is due back in a few days. That Debbie one is back already. I saw her last week in town. I don't think he would have a relationship with her. She is not his type at all. Hopefully it will work itself out before long more." Gill sipped her wine.

"I'm looking forward to our weekend in that new hotel of hers. Did she tell you of the birthday plans she has made? I don't want you to spend the next two weeks wondering what she has in store for you two!" Joe placed the plate in front of her.

"She didn't tell me all the details but she promised that she wouldn't plan anything I wouldn't like. The weeks will fly by. This is delicious." She forked a large piece of chicken into her mouth.

As they drove up the winding entrance to the hotel, Joe whistled.

"Wow, look at that! It's huge."

They parked in front of the entrance and the doorman was poised to admit them. A porter opened the car door.

"If you will leave your keys with me, sir, I will park your car for you." The young man smiled.

Gill was impressed.

After they had been checked in, accompanied to their suite and had their bed turned down, they were finally alone.

"Wow. This is amazing. We have our own living space, bar and dining room. We could seat twelve people at that table!"

Joe opened the patio and walked outside. "Look here Gill," he called.

She almost melted with pleasure when she saw the outdoor hot tub.

"This is going to be some weekend, Joe. Let's test out the tub before dinner."

"This is so posh," Gill whispered to Joe as they waited to be served in the exclusive dining room.

"Thank God we got dressed up. Look at the waiters. I swear that I saw that diner there slip a tip into the waiter's hand. Fair play to him he didn't even glance at it until he got over to the doorway. Did you notice that when the woman over there dropped her fork, she got a brand new one, even though there are about five on the table already? No wiping it on a piece of kitchen towel here. I could get used to this!"

"Your starter, madam. Pan fried scallops with a citrus and ciabatta salad accompanied by a summer truffle dressing."

Gill was really enjoying herself and Joe was delighted that things had worked out so well. She looked across the table at her handsome husband. She still couldn't believe how their lives had changed in such a few short months.

"You know Joe, that stir-fry that you cooked was every bit as good as those scallops. Here he comes with the main courses. He must think that we are joined at the hip because we have chosen the same mains."

"Here we are. Roast loin and slow cooked flank of lamb with basil and parmesan polenta cake, shallot relish and mint and apple jus." He turned to Joe. "For sir." He placed the plate in front of him.

"Enjoy your meal." He actually seemed to bow as he left.

"We will indeed. We are quite hungry as we were very busy in the hot tub before we came down and we have our eye on the dining table when we go back up!" Gill spoke to the waiter's retreating back as she winked at her husband.

The next morning, they decided to have breakfast on the balcony.

"This is the life. Bless Caroline." They both tucked into pancakes with maple syrup followed by a full Irish. They had worked up quite an appetite.

"What are we going to do today, my lovely wife?" Joe kissed her full on the lips.

Gill looked at the brochure.

"We are going to the spa. They have some lovely treatments listed here and I have booked some already. I am going to have a facial and you are booked in for a hot stone massage. You are always complaining of having back pain so this should sort you out. After that we are both going to relax in the thermal suite. This weekend is all about us. I love you, Joe." She leaned over and kissed him firmly on the lips.

"I love you too, Gill. Nothing will ever come between us again." He patted his flat stomach. "I could get used to this life." Joe smiled at Gill.

"I am so looking forward to this. I just hope that Caroline will keep her promise and not add any surprises for our birthdays. A nice meal is all I want. Turning fifty is not such a big deal anymore. Jesus, did I just say that? A few months ago, I wouldn't have said fifty out loud. That shows just how far I have come!" she smiled at Joe.

"I think that you are safe enough. Since Dylan came back on the scene, she hasn't time to plan any surprises! We will have a great time. Matt is joining us later for a quick drink. He is in Killarney to value some antiques before they are sold at auction. Dan O'Brien drove him down. I'm hoping to build up a small crew of drivers for when I am not able to drive myself. I gave Matt the business plan that we worked out. I hope he will go for it. We are almost here."

Caroline arrived just after Matt.

"Welcome to the hotel. What do you think?" She gestured around the foyer.

"The décor is fab. That painting fitted right in," Gill assured her.

"What about you, Matt? Do you like what I have done with the hotel?" Caroline asked.

"I do indeed but if you ladies don't mind I would like to borrow Joe for a while. You two can talk parties," Matt smiled.

"I'm so glad you are here. I must show you the other dining room upstairs. It is vintage heaven. Remember how we used to plan our ideal rooms. Upstairs Downstairs was our inspiration. Come on." Caroline practically dragged Gill past the huge reception area and down the luxuriously carpeted corridor to the aptly named Downton Abbey Room.

"My idea," Caroline laughed.

"I would never have guessed," Gill replied.

The first thing Gill noticed when Caroline threw open the door was the crystal chandelier.

"Antique Spanish," added Caroline.

"Wow. This is unreal. That floor is fab. I just love it, and those ceiling beams. If I am not mistaken they are birch. Are those genuine bronze casement windows?"

"Yup. Remember how we used to pour over those magazines? I tried to recreate it as closely as possible. Do you like the furniture? It's from the Beauvais Collection."

"It's absolutely fabulous. I love the whole room. All we will be short of will be the clothes to go with the room!" Gill added.

"You think?" Caroline laughed.

"You didn't!" Gill was shocked.

"Of course I did. All the guests will be wearing 1920 fashions."

"Why didn't you say? Joe and I will be the odd ones out. I haven't anything suitable to wear."

"Yes, you have. Accompany me to your suite, madam." Caroline led Gill to the lift.

On the bed was the most beautiful dress that Gill had ever seen. It was a mocha pink silk beaded evening gown. Beside it was a pair of shoes complete with French heels and t-strap.

Joe's outfit consisted of a long, tight-waisted jacket, skinny trousers, brown and white jazz shoes and a felt fedora hat.

"Jesus. He won't believe it. Just as well he lost so much weight or he would never fit into that get up. I had better break it to him gently, over a large brandy!" said Gill.

"No need. He already knows all about it. How do you think I got the sizes correct! He would do anything for you and that includes dressing up like Al Capone." Caroline laughed.

"This is all too much. My present to you seems so small in comparison." Gill handed the Beth's Knits bag to Caroline who opened it immediately. She took out the bag.

"Clodagh designed it especially for you. She based it on a flapper evening bag. She mixed some crystals in with the beads to make it unique. I hope you like it." Gill waited for Caroline's reaction.

"It is beyond beautiful. Imagine being the owner of an exclusive Clodagh Kenny bag. I adore it." She hugged Gill.

"Come on. We birthday girls need a drink before the night's events unfold. Let's join the men in the bar. Dylan will be here in an hour. He wouldn't tell me where he was going today."

The food was delicious. For Caroline it turned out to be a double celebration. Dylan got down on one knee and proposed. He had flown over to London for the ring. Caroline didn't hesitate. She had almost lost him. The wedding was to be on New Year's Eve. Everything would be held in the Valley Hotel.

"Thank God for that." Joe whispered to Gill after the announcement was made.

After the dessert was served, Caroline cornered Gill by the bathrooms.

"I would love if you would be my maid of honour at the wedding. I won't be doing the white dress thing so you can pick out your own outfit. The only favour that I will ask is that we go to New York to shop. Dylan insists on sending us, so I hope that you can get a few days off in the next few weeks."

"Wow. I've never been to New York. I'd love to go. Clodagh is in London at the moment so I am working every day. She will be back next weekend. I could go then if that suits!" Gill was delighted.

"That will be perfect. I'm so excited. Debbie was in France with a group and they were all staying in the villa. I should have invited her here tonight. She opened my eyes to how I felt about Dylan."

"You are so lucky. He is a lovely man. His daughter looks like him and she is really trying to mingle. You will make a great stepmother," Gill added.

"She is almost thirty so I don't think that my mothering skills will be too strained!" Caroline joked.

"You never know. I would love to be your maid of honour but I think it would be a good idea to include his daughter. Why don't you go and ask her now?" Gill accepted a glass of champagne from a passing waiter.

"Good idea. Thanks Gill. You are such a wise owl! That is why I keep you as a best friend. Happy birthday Gill!" Caroline hugged her.

Joe appeared by Gill's side. "You enjoying yourself pet?" he hugged her.

"Yes, I am. Caroline is so happy. She has kind of pulled another stunt. She wants me to go to New York to buy the clothes for her wedding." She looked at her husband.

"Whatever makes you happy Gill, is okay with me. Will you be able to get time off from your job?" he asked.

"I should think that it would be fine. I have been working for the past ten days so I can take time off when Clodagh comes back. Do you really not mind me going?" she asked.

"I will miss you like hell, but as long as you are happy then I am happy. Happy birthday to the most beautiful wife in the world." He kissed her soundly.

"I love that outfit, especially the hat. I've always wanted to take a step on the wild side and sleep with a gangster!" She smiled meaningfully at him.

"If you play your cards right, you might just get that chance," he tilted his hat and winked.

"Well I hope you have a strong back. This dress weighs a ton. There are hundreds of beads on it!" she whispered.

"Let me worry about my back. Would it be rude if we left now?" he joked.

"Probably. Caroline went to a lot of trouble to make this evening perfect. We will have to be the last to leave. Speak of the devil, here she comes with the man of the moment."

"Hi guys. Can you believe this dark horse here?" Caroline waved her hand in front of them. "I so love rubies. They are so me!"

"It really suits you. Well done Dylan. It's about time as well." Gill admired the ring again.

Chapter Twelve

Claire
Claire admired the window display. It was autumn meets Christmas. The beautiful shades of greens, reds, and purples drew people over to the window and usually into the salon to enquire about buying them. She had gotten quite a few new customers this way. Not that she needed them. All her clients had followed her to her new premises. It had been a few months since she had officially opened and now it was October. Clodagh had been brilliant. Being a business woman meant that she had contacts everywhere. At almost forty-eight years old, Claire was finally her own boss.

Her car was in for a service so Tim was picking her up. They were driving to Fossa.

Having parked the car in the car park, they made their way inside.

"I love that painting behind the reception desk, it takes up the whole wall. The waves look so real. What do you think?" Claire asked her husband.

"I can't look at it – it makes me seasick." He pretended to sway.

"Well, since you could never watch Titanic, I can understand that." She took his arm and they walked to the huge window which overlooked the terraced gardens which led down to the lake.

"There are quite a few people sitting out there, so maybe we will as well. I know it is a bit cold but it is very crowded in here." Claire looked around the spacious room but all available seats were occupied, mostly by people enjoying afternoon tea. The tiers of sandwiches, pastries and miniature cakes looked delicious and the aroma of tea wafted towards their nostrils.

"Will you be warm enough?" Tim asked.

"We'll try it out. If it gets too cold, we can go into the bar," she answered.

They found an unoccupied table close to the door and within minutes their order was taken.

Claire pulled her grey chunky wool wrap around her shoulders.

"Would you prefer to eat inside?" Tim looked concerned.

"No, it's lovely here. It is quite mild for October. We will be cooped up long enough for the winter. Let's enjoy the sun while we can."

A few minutes later their food was served. Claire picked up her spoon and dunked it into the deep bowl.

"This stew is delicious. How is your steak?"

"It's perfect." Tim speared a piece and offered it to her to taste.

"That's lovely. Do you want to try mine?" she asked.

"No, you're grand. You know that Clodagh has booked a room here for your birthday dinner next week? It's one of the two identical ones that they have for parties. I'm not sure if it is the North or South one that we will be in," he joked.

"They are both exactly the same. Normally I would rather have a meal at home. It is not as if it is a significant birthday. She persuaded me because our businesses are both doing really well. The hotel in Brandon Lodge is finally ready so the official opening will be taking place in November. All the units are doing great so it should be a good night. Remember how we used to pretend to be the lords and ladies of the manor?" she smiled at the memories.

"Indeed I do, it was easy to amuse us in those days! I wonder if we could still get in that basement window?"

"I think our days of sneaking in broken windows are well behind us. Clodagh said that it had been repaired. She always wanted to own that place and she has almost achieved that." Claire sipped the Irish coffee that Tim had ordered to warm her up. It was beginning to get dark.

"Let's have a drink in the bar. I'm beginning to freeze here. If we are lucky we will get a seat beside the open fire. The boys promised to come out for us. Mark will drive my car home so we can have a few quite drinks to celebrate your birthday. I am very proud of my business woman wife!" Tim leaned over and kissed her on the cheek.

James

"Welcome Mr Murray. Happy birthday. We have two birthday parties in tonight. Yours is in the North Room. I believe that some of your guests have already arrived." The receptionist beckoned to the porter.

"Show Mr Murray to his room. Enjoy your stay."

Celebrating his birthday was the last thing on his mind. At least it was not a surprise, thanks to Conor. Kate and the twins had decided that he was going to have dinner with them. They had booked an overnight stay to ensure that he would not try to escape early. Here he was in a luxury hotel celebrating the fact that he was a middle-aged loner! He hadn't planned for his life to turn out the way it did. Up to this year he had been happy enough with his lot. He loved his children and got on pretty well with Kate.

He had always found his job rewarding but maybe Brandon Lodge had been a mistake. The place had messed with his head. Ever since he had started there, he had become very restless and couldn't get Clodagh out of his mind. She had loved that place. He had even convinced himself that the red-haired mystery woman who had almost run into him was Clodagh. When he had gone into Beth's Knits, the owner had not looked anything like her. He had dreamed of a reunion. What a fecking eejit he was! She was hundreds of miles away, probably living happily ever after. He had betrayed her. She had never answered his letter, presuming that her mother had forwarded it to her in the first place.

He plastered a smile on his face and headed for the function room.

Conor tapped him on the shoulder. "You okay, brother? You seem to be miles away. That food here is supposed to be fantastic."

James smiled and followed Conor into the dining room. He now understood how it felt to be a lamb led to the slaughter.

After the meal was over Conor turned to James.

"The women are already discussing Christmas presents. Let's walk down to the boathouse. There are benches and heaters there. We can sit for a while. They won't even miss us."

"Thanks, Conor. A few minutes out would be nice. I've been looking at that star there. I have made a wish but I can't see it coming true."

"Whatever it was, I hope it comes true. You deserve a break. I suppose it is bad luck to reveal it."

"I wished for a second chance but I know I am not going to get it." James drained his pint.

"Why don't you go on down and I'll get refills." Conor took the empty glasses and headed to the bar.

Clodagh

At the opposite side of the building, Claire was enjoying her birthday dinner with her family. Just as dessert was about to be served, Clodagh excused herself to go to the bathroom. She decided to get a breath of fresh air before returning to the party. A few minutes later Claire found her outside gazing at the stars.

"Are you okay, Sis? You seem quiet this evening." Claire was concerned.

"I'm fine. Just admiring the beautiful sky. It's so clear. I've been travelling a lot lately and then I had to run the shop in Brandon Lodge while Gill went to America with her friend. She earned the break, she is amazing. See that star over there? It is much brighter than the rest. You should make a birthday wish." Clodagh pulled her shawl close around her shoulders.

"I think I have all that I need and it is thanks to you that I have my own salon. How are you? Are you happy with your life?" Claire asked.

"I suppose so. I have all of you as well as Beth, David and Mike. I always wanted to come back to Brandon Lodge and I have achieved that." She sighed.

"Clodagh, for someone who says that she has it all, you don't sound too happy. I hope you don't mind me mentioning the war but there is someone missing from the equation. What would you do if James Murray were to walk up to you right now?"

"I really can't answer that question... I knew that it was a mistake to tell you that he is involved in the security of Brandon Lodge! Anyway it is not going to happen. It's his birthday this week too, so he is probably at home tucking into a nice roast surrounded by his family and friends. We had better get back inside. The others will be wondering where we have gotten to." Clodagh turned to go back inside. Claire stopped her.

"They will be fine for a few minutes. Tim is chatting to the neighbours and the boys are probably texting, downloading, tweeting or all the above! I saw Beth a few minutes ago and she was on her phone. There is a boat house at the other side. We will go down and put the world to rights."

"If you are sure, that sounds nice. You can fill me in on all the news from the salon," Clodagh answered.

As they headed out the door, Beth called out to them.

"Come back here, Aunty Claire. You must blow out all those candles."

"Why don't you go down and I will follow you with a fresh glass of wine and a slice of cake," Claire said.

"And miss the blowing out of the candles. What could be possibly be down there that would make a difference to my life? Come on, Sis, we are the Kenny women!"

Joe

Matt dropped the folder onto the table, signalled to the waitress and sat down opposite Joe.

"You're a dark horse. I've looked over these ideas and, I must admit that you definitely have a damn good set of proposals here, definitely mutually beneficial. My accountant agrees. I believe that we have a deal. All my transportation requirements are now in your capable hands. We can sort out the formalities later." Matt and Joe shook hands.

"Have you made any plans for your birthday this year? I'm off to the States in November for two weeks so I won't be here to celebrate with you." Matt ordered a bottle of champagne to go. "You and Gill enjoy this on me tonight. It can double as an early birthday present and a new business celebration. You can even wear that hat you got in Kerry. Those pictures were very funny. You would have looked well in the twenties!" Matt laughed.

"Bloody Facebook, I suppose. Caroline is obsessed with it and she has Gill at it now. I wouldn't have thought that you would bother with it," Joe answered.

"You never know what you might find on it, like your friend trussed up like Al Capone! I'm sorry that I had to leave early that night." Matt countered.

"Well my birthday will not be anything like the one Caroline planned for her and Gill. We are planning a quiet night in. She is just back from New York. We have been to more luxury hotels in the past few months than we have been in years!" said Joe.

"Well, that can't be a bad thing. You deserve all the good things that come your way. But for you..."

"That's ancient history, Matt. Let's leave it where it belongs. We are both different people." Joe interrupted.

Joe dropped Matt off at his office and decided to walk off his lunch.

He couldn't wait to tell Gill that Matt had agreed to his proposals and that he was finally going to run his own business. He had a number of reliable drivers in mind, men like him who had spent hours sitting on the ranks for little work and less money. Now they would have a regular income. Life was good for both of them. Gill was designing and selling her own stuff and the mountain of unique garments had been turned into cash. She had been able to splash out in New York. She loved Brandon Lodge and had made lots of new friends. She would come home every day and fill him in on their lives. It was like a soap opera. Ann and Gary were perfect for each other but hadn't managed to get together romantically yet. Robert was the bookworm who was proving to be a dark horse. Gill wasn't sure if he was in love with two women or neither. He seemed attracted to both Clodagh and Maria. Gill was working late this evening as the official opening was just a few days away. He would put a casserole in the oven for later. He had been trying to ring her all afternoon but she hadn't picked up. He would try again when he arrived home.

Brandon Lodge

Brandon Lodge was a hive of activity. With only a few days to go to the grand opening in November, everyone was working flat out to ensure that everything would be perfect.

Clodagh and Gill were putting the finishing touches to the window display. Since winter had all but arrived, the side window was filled with ideas for sock making. Beautiful yarn had arrived from America. It was a custom blended sock yarn in one hundred and fifty gram balls, perfect for knee high socks. They had placed a basket full of made up samples in the centre of the display. The colours ranged from earthy browns through to all the colours of fallen leaves and onto more Christmas shades from red to grey and white.

The main window had a more romantic feel to it. Inspired by Louisa Harding yarns, the focal point of the display was a mannequin wearing a scarlet velvet jacket and sequined knitted floor length skirt. Two scarves in hand beaded yarns were knotted around the neck. Four more similar scarves were draped at the foot of the mannequin. Packs of the hand beaded yarn in various colour combinations sat side by side with Sermonette and Nerissa wools. Towards the front of the window sat felted bags and hats by Clodagh herself as well as shawls and wraps which were designed and made up by Gill using a mink and cashmere mix of wool aptly called Moonlight.

The narrower window to the left of the door was devoted to yarns and patterns for babies, children and Christmas toys and accessories. The pinks, peaches, blues and mint greens sat beside the reds and greens of Christmas. Many a proud granny would be drawn to that window for the makings of that unique gift.

Inside the shop, the wools and patterns as well as needles, buttons and anything else necessary to complete any project lay in large baskets dotted around the shop.

Ann and Gary were also perfecting their display. They had pondered over whether to use almost real looking cakes but had decided to opt for the real thing. They would use a combination of iced and decorated Christmas cakes as well as mince pies and puddings. A number of tarts and cupcakes would be put out on the morning of the opening.

Robert watched the work progressing from inside his shop. Clodagh and Gill were deep in conversation as they stood outside discussing the display.

"Time for a well-deserved break, Gill. We are all but done here. We may not have to stay as late as we thought. You should ring Joe and tell him that you will be home soon."

"Actually, I haven't heard from him all day. He must be busy. He was meeting Matt earlier and promised to let me know how they got on. I hope everything went okay. He is a smart business man and I know that Matt will see that. I will give him a ring and meet you for coffee in a few minutes. My phone is in my bag at the back of the shop." Gill turned to go into the wool shop.

Joe hit the switch on the kettle. He would try to ring Gill one more time. She always text or rang before she left work so that he would know at what time to expect her home. The Mallow to Cork road could be quite dangerous. It was now almost five o'clock so she might answer. As he was about to dial he heard a phone beep in the bedroom. It was plugged in to the charger. She had obviously forgotten to take it with her. He breathed a sigh of relief. He unplugged it and looked at the screen. Six missed calls. She would think that he was stalking her! He decided to delete four of them. Two would be more normal. Her phone was new and he was having trouble trying to find the right icons. He managed to access Music, Camera, My files and Settings before landing on Messages. He knew that she deleted them as they came in and was not expecting to find seven in the inbox. She had explained all about the Turkish misunderstanding and he knew that he could trust her but somehow his fingers were moving over the phone.

Ann was pouring the tea when Gill opened the door.
"You okay? You look a bit stressed?" Ann enquired.
"Yeah. I'm fine. I left my phone at home. I usually ring Joe before I leave and he might be worried. He had an important meeting today and I would like to know how it went."
"Use my phone. It's on the shelf under the counter."
"Thanks Ann. I won't be a minute." Gill stepped outside and dialled Joe's number.
"Hi Joe, this is Ann's phone. I left mine at home. How did it go with Matt?"
She listened to Joe's excited voice recounting the day's events.
"That's great. I knew that you could do it. We will celebrate when I get home. Any other news?"
He reassured her that everything was good.
"Love you."
She was smiling when she returned to the Tearoom.
"All good?" Ann was clearing one of the tables.
"All great. Thanks for the phone. When did Robert come in?" Gill asked.
"He arrived in the back way. He asked Clodagh if he could have a word. He seems a bit edgy. I hope that there is nothing wrong with him. Actually they both look a bit stressed." Ann looked worried.
"I will leave them to it so. Just tell Clodagh that I left. See you tomorrow. Thanks again, Ann." Gill waved at Clodagh but the other woman didn't seem to notice.
Robert and Clodagh sat at the table in the alcove as it was the most private space in the Tearoom.
"You alright Robert?" Clodagh noticed that her friend was flushed.
"I'm fine. I need to talk to you about something. It is about the night you cooked for me." He was the colour of a tomato.
"What about it?" She waited for him to continue.

"It is a little sensitive." He looked around the Tearoom. "Will you come to my house tonight and we can talk then?" he added.

"About eight? I have to finish unpacking an order first," she answered.

"Thanks Clodagh. I will see you later. I will put some food together. After all it is my turn to cook." He drained his cup and stood up.

Ann approached Clodagh.

"I need a double strength cappuccino with an extra-large slice of apple pie and cream and a side order of extra apple pie and cream, but please don't ask why!" Clodagh pleaded.

"Your wish is my command." Ann went to get the order.

David

David McGovern was worried. He had been due to fly into Cork three days before the opening but a hitch in another deal that he was brokering, meant that he would not arrive until the night before. When Clodagh had told him that she knew James Murray, his first reaction was to cancel the security contract. Clodagh herself had persuaded him not to. She had not seen James in over thirty years and was quite happy to avoid him. However, there was a distinct possibility that he would attend the opening of the hotel.

A large attendance was expected so a marquee would be erected in front of the hotel itself. It would be equipped with heaters and would be more of an outside room than a tent. Tea and light refreshments would be provided as the Tearoom would not be able to cope with the volume expected.

Robert

"Well I never thought I'd say this but 'Go Dad!' Imagine my conservative, middle-aged father being involved with two women at the same time. You are some dark horse! You are getting more action than I am, and I am not even forty. Which one are you entertaining tonight? Maybe it will be a case of handbags at dawn. At least they will be designer ones. I love it. I can't wait to go home and tell Shane all about it. To think that he was worried that you were spending too much time on your own!" Greta burst out laughing.

Robert put down the paring knife and looked at his daughter. In spite of himself he had to smile. He had been so worried that she would not approve of him dating other women. The fact that he was wrestling with feelings for two women seemed a source of amusement to her. He had hesitated before confiding in her but he didn't have any other female friends. He had considered asking Ann for advice but she had been giving him funny looks lately. She was also very close to Clodagh.

"I know that it looks bad but I'm not good at this dating lark. Clodagh is a very good friend to me. I don't know how she really feels about me. She gets on well with Maria and was delighted when I took her on. I don't know if she realises that I have been to Maria's house for dinner a few times since. I enjoy Clodagh's company and maybe I was attracted to her initially but I don't want to be the cause of any bad feeling between her and Maria. Maria knows that Clodagh and I go dancing regularly and I thought that she was okay with it, but now she wants to come as well." He started to scrape the potatoes again.

"Wow, Dad. How do you plan to waltz with both of them at the same time? You need to put your ducks in a row and quickly. This opening thing is coming up soon. Have you decided how that is going to go? You planning on arriving with a woman on each arm? I'm definitely going. I wouldn't miss this for the world!" Greta finished.

"That will not be a problem, at least I hope not. Clodagh will be going to the opening with Beth and David. Maria is travelling with Gill and her husband. I should be able to dance with both of them during the night." He threw the potatoes into the pot of salted water.

"Yes Dad, but who are you going to save the last dance for?" Greta reached for her coat.

"That's what I'm hoping to find out tonight. With any luck my Beef Wellington will help me to solve my problem! Now I must get on with it."

"Good luck with that one. I hope that Clodagh doesn't take your Beef Wellington and kick you up the backside with it. You know where I am if you need any Sudocream. Enjoy." Greta kissed her Dad.

He hoped that he hadn't overdone it on the meal. It was good manners to give your guest nice food, but he didn't want to give the wrong impression. He wanted to tell Clodagh that he and Maria were a couple. Hopefully she would not be too upset.

Clodagh

Clodagh didn't know if she should dress up or not. This wasn't a date – at least she hoped not.

"What does one wear for a non-date?" she asked her reflection in the full-length mirror.

She couldn't ask Gill or Ann as she had never told them what had happened on the night that she had first cooked for Robert. She knew that they had wondered what exactly her relationship with Robert was. A repeat performance of that night was not on the cards. It had been enjoyable but hadn't lit any fires in her.

Anyway she had seen the way that he and Maria had looked at each other.

Finally deciding that a simple maxi dress was the best option, she teamed it with a purple wrap that would form part of her collection due to be launched at the opening.

Robert heard the car pull up and went to open the door for Clodagh. He checked that the fire in the dining room was fuelled up. It was a typical October night, dark and chilly. He had ensured that the outside lights had been switched on.

"You look lovely. Come on in out of the cold. Looks like frost." Robert welcomed her.

"Hello Robert. Thanks for the invitation. Something smells lovely."

"You are welcome. Let me take your shawl. It is lovely."

"I -" they both started and burst out laughing.

After they had eaten and Clodagh had insisted on helping with the wash up, they sat by the fire drinking coffee

"Are you sure that you won't have a drop of something in that. I will only put in a teaspoon. It will just give it a kick. I have a bottle of Jack Daniels somewhere. Got a present of it for my birthday," Robert asked.

"No, I am not too familiar with the narrow roads around here. I don't want to be picked up for driving under the influence! I nearly caused an accident going into Brandon Lodge a few months ago and it really shook me. I thought that the other driver was going to get out and confront me. How about we discuss the elephant in the room instead! You didn't invite me here for Irish coffee. I will make it easy on you and go first. We are good friends and hopefully that will not change. I like you a lot but…"

"I think I'm in love with Maria so you and I can't be together." Robert burst out. "Please don't be upset, but we are not right for one another."

"Oh! Thank God you just said that!" Clodagh stood up and hugged him.

"You and Maria are so good together. Brandon Lodge is proving to be a success in more ways than one," she continued.

"Yes, indeed. The place for romance. Ann and Gary are still dancing around one another but it is just a matter of time before they sort themselves out. I can see a lot from my window!" he laughed at her startled look.

"There is a wishing seat in the little garden that is behind the last outhouse near the road. It was a mess when I saw it last but David promised that he would have it cleaned up. The story goes that couples who went there together always lived happily ever after! There is definitely magic in the place," Clodagh told him.

"Maybe you could make a wish there," Robert said.

"No. That wouldn't work. Legend has it that both parties would have to be physically present side by side on the seat for the wish to come true. Who does that leave for me? It could be the foreman, but he is happily married with a football team of children. The fellow who runs the gym is young enough to be my grandson. Everyone else is female and I am not that curious yet," she laughed.

"Actually you forgot to mention the fellow from the security company. I don't know him personally but he reminded Maria of some singer or actor. He might be worth a closer look! Have you met him yet?" He refilled their coffee cups, adding just a drop of Jack Daniels to each.

"Funny that you should ask that. Definitely a story for another time. I would prefer to see Beth meet someone nice and settle down," she said.

"It's only right that you would be concerned with your child's welfare. She will be fine. I used to worry about Greta as well. We were very young parents. Having only one child to lavish all your love on can have its own set of problems, as I'm sure you know."

"Beth is not my daughter," Clodagh spoke quietly.

Robert was stunned.

"I didn't know. You don't have to tell me anything unless you want to talk about it."

"Actually I think I would like to share it with someone. I have been very unsettled lately. Maybe it was a mistake to come back here. In London I could pretend that the past never happened. Here it is all around me. Sometimes I feel like I am unravelling since I came back."

Robert stood up. "I'm going to make up the spare room. We are breaking out the big guns. I have this lovely wine chilling in the fridge. We are going to sit here by the fire and enjoy the wine. You can talk and I will listen. That's what friends are for."

Greta drove by on her way to work the following morning as she was dying to know how things went. She saw that Clodagh's car was still there.

"I knew that the man did protest too much," she thought to herself.

Inside the house, Clodagh smiled at herself in the bathroom mirror. She had unburdened herself to Robert and now she felt so much lighter. She could see things more clearly and was no longer bothered by the fact that she could run into James in Brandon Lodge. He was part of her past not her future.

"Coffee and toast okay?" Robert asked.

"Perfect. Thanks so much for listening to me last night. Putting my thoughts into words helped me to see things more clearly." She buttered her toast.

"No bother. That's what friends are for. Excuse me," Robert answered his phone.

Clodagh poured the coffees and popped more bread into the toaster.

Robert finished his call and came back into the kitchen.

"Is it okay if I drop my car off at the garage and travel with you to Brandon Lodge? That was my mechanic on the phone," Robert asked her.

"No problem, I will follow you to the garage. It is the least I can do after bending your ear into the early hours," she laughed.

"If we leave in about ten minutes, then we will miss the rush hour traffic."

Maria

Maria had just parked her car when she saw Clodagh drive in with Robert in the passenger seat. She was just about to wave when she saw Robert reach over and hug Clodagh.

"Damn, I knew that there was more to their relationship than just dancing." Her heart sank.

Beth

The window display in Smithfield's was attracting a lot of attention. Beth had outdone herself. The recreation of Robin Hood meets Maid Marion had been inspirational. The scene was set in Sherwood Forest so the colour palette of browns, greens, purples, blues and golds created a magical path through the forest. Dresses, trousers, jackets, coats and accessories hung on tree branches in the background. People stopped to admire the scene and many of them made their way into the shop to see the latest fashions.

Beth stood inside the door.

"You okay, Beth? You look a bit fed up. Considering what you have done with that display, you should be over the moon. Lucky for us that the usual designer broke her leg. You are a natural at this window display lark." Shirley told her.

"Thanks, Shirley. I used to do it for David and Mike. I am thrilled, just a bit tired. We have been very busy for the last few weeks. Christmas shopping starts earlier every year. My day off is tomorrow but I will be helping with preparations for the opening of Brandon Lodge. Have you any plans for the weekend?" Beth asked her friend.

"Hot date on Friday. New guy from accounts. Hope it lasts until Christmas! I love having a fellow to buy me a pressie. Shallow I know, but I will buy him one as well. It is the season for love. How about you? Any tall, dark and handsome man lurking around Brandon Lodge? You seem to spend a lot of time there and according to you, everyone is falling in love with everyone else! You will have to get your skates on if you want to be hooked up by Christmas." Shirley checked her watch.

"No one there for me. All the men have been snapped up," Beth answered.

"Come on. We are both due a break. Let's grab a coffee and I will fill you in on my new man." Shirley gripped her arm.

Five minutes later both girls had frothing mugs of coffee and toasted sandwiches in front of them

"You seeing anyone?" Shirley asked.

"No. I met this lovely man a few months ago in Killarney. I only spoke with him for a few minutes before his girlfriend arrived to claim him. She was like a lioness. When she saw us chatting she immediately marked her territory. His name was Danny and he said that he was an auctioneer in Killarney. I met her later in the bathroom and she told me that she had lost their baby! He had given me his card but I couldn't ring him after finding that out. He seemed so nice but he must be a complete rat to treat his pregnant girlfriend like that! He was really attractive. I have a thing for curly black hair and beards! Obviously I have no luck in picking eligible men!" Beth answered.

Shirley picked up her phone.

"Eight auctioneers in total and guess what? Only one Danny. His surname is Murray. A twin sister but no brother, I'm afraid," Shirley sighed.

As she resumed putting the finishing touches to the display, Beth wondered what would have happened if Danny had been available. The minute she had seen him, she felt her heart quicken. Maybe she just wanted to have the fantasy of being swept off her feet and living happily ever after. Still, it was not to be as the arrival of Pamela had put paid to her dreams. All the women that meant something to Beth had been badly treated by the men that they had loved. Firstly, there was Aunt Lizzie, who had fallen for some count that she had met in the same hotel that Beth had met Danny in. It had a different name back then but it was definitely the same place. He had promised her the world and had persuaded her to follow him to London. His family had some more suitable wife in mind for him. He bought Lizzie a big house but had married his heiress.

Next was her own mother. Before she died she had created a memory box for Beth. Her father was married and didn't want to know about her. Clodagh had gone to live with Lizzie after some man had broken her heart. All in all, it seemed that the Kenny women were destined to be unlucky in love.

Early next morning, Beth drove carefully towards Brandon Lodge. It was dark and the headlights picked up the glistening pools of frost on the road. She had promised Clodagh that she would be there before nine. She drove through the gates with minutes to spare. Despite the early hour, the complex was busy.

She found a parking place by the wall that divided the complex from the neighbouring farm. She spotted two men in high visibility jackets working on one of the security cameras. Probably a last minute check before the opening. She wasn't close enough to them to see their faces but she remembered Clodagh saying that Maria thought one of the security men looked like Elvis. Ann had even suggested that he would suit Clodagh. Maybe she should pop over and ask him if he had a son or brother that would suit herself!

Clodagh was wrapping a deep plum coloured lace shawl around the top half of a full sized mannequin which she had placed at the entrance to the back room. It contrasted beautifully with the tiered skirt of deep pinks, crimson reds and vibrant purples. The tulle skirt which she had placed under the knitted one fanned out so that the pattern of double moss stitch was clearly visible.

"Wow. That is amazing!" Beth took off her scarf and rubbed her hands together.

"Hi Beth. Thanks for coming so early. Do you really like it?" Clodagh stood back to admire her handiwork.

"I love it. It must have taken weeks to create that skirt. Can I buy it after the opening? It will be perfect for the dinner in London with the gang. They will be so jealous." Beth smiled.

"You don't need to do that. It can be an early Christmas present. Now we have plenty of work to do here. This is the last full day before the opening. Everyone has arrived early," Clodagh told her.

"I know, even the security guys are here. I saw them over by the fence as I drove in." Beth was emptying yarn into a basket and didn't notice Clodagh stiffen.

"Really? I wonder why they are here so early in the morning. Did you get a good look at them?" Clodagh regained her composure.

"No, they were too far away. Why do you ask?" Beth rearranged the coloured yarn so that the display went from red to russet brown.

"No reason." She fiddled with the skirt again.

"I suppose they will both be at the opening. David invited everyone involved in the project. Pity he was delayed. He should fly into Cork about eight tonight and Mike will arrive tomorrow morning. I'm really looking forward to this. It will be lovely to see the hotel in all its glory. You used to talk about it all the time in London. You haven't mentioned it in a while." Beth placed the basket on the table and reached for the box which contained the pattern books.

"I suppose that is because I am back here now. I am looking forward to seeing it. David made me promise not to go into the hotel before he arrived. We were supposed to view it today but now that will have to wait until he arrives. He wanted to try and get it looking as close as possible to how it looked when it first opened," Clodagh sighed.

"You okay?" Beth put down the pattern book and turned to Clodagh.

"I'm fine. Late night last night and maybe a little too much wine." She rubbed her temple.

"Anyone nice?" Beth asked curiously.

"Robert actually, but before you start ordering any hats, it is not what you think," Clodagh said.

"He seems like a very nice man. You get on well so..."

"And he is interested in Maria and that is okay by me. We are just friends. You fancy a tea or coffee?" Clodagh asked.

"Sure. Let's go across to the Tearoom and grab something to eat," Beth said.

As they made their way across the yard, they noticed the two men heading towards them. They were still too far away to identify them.

"Looks like you will get to meet those brothers after all!" Beth linked Clodagh's arm.

Chapter Thirteen

James
"Ah Dad, you can't be serious. I asked you ages ago. You promised that you would go to the dinner and now you are saying that a business dinner takes priority," Kathryn Murray banged the door of the office.

"You know Kathryn, most people bang the door behind them and so I take it that this conversation is not over!" James sighed.

She flopped down on the swivel chair.

"I'm sorry Dad. I know that this is short notice but Anthony's parents changed the weekend that they had decided on to come to Killarney. I know that work is important as well but I need both you and Mam to be there," Kathryn pleaded.

"Of course I will go to this dinner. Maybe Conor can attend the official opening of Brandon Lodge. He is expecting the company to be represented. That contract is worth a lot of money to us."

"Thanks Dad, you are the best. Speaking of Brandon Lodge, do you get any concessions there?" she smiled.

"What do you mean?" He asked.

"Well since Christmas and my birthday are only a few weeks apart I was thinking that you could get me a two in one present. Everyone is talking about Beth's Knits in Brandon Lodge. You could probably get a discount," she continued.

"Could I now?" he responded.

"I'm sure you could. I'm not usually into knitted things but her stuff is unique. She uses real crystals and pearls to decorate the bags. Some are very expensive. I have seen them online and I think there is a place in town that sells them. She is from London and has come to live here with her daughter. That's who the label is named after. Her own name is Cl…"

Their conversation was interrupted when Kathryn's phone rang.

"That was Anthony. He was making sure that everything was arranged for the weekend." She looked hopefully at her father.

"Remind me again why we must meet the king and queen on that night. Could we not do it on Saturday night instead? Then I could go to the opening as well," he asked.

"Stop calling them that, Dad. They are set in their ways. They don't like travelling. They have booked into the hotel for the weekend. His Dad has some golf thing on Saturday. It could go on late so he wants to make sure that he has time to meet all of you. Please Dad?" she pleaded.

"Well I hope the Quayside measures up to their exacting standards. According to your mother they live in some preserved pile somewhere rural and dotted with horses! Her words, not mine!"

"Dad! Stop it. Anthony is their only child and they are a bit protective of him. He is really nice. I love him," she blushed.

"Love him. Well that's a horse of a different colour, so to speak!" They both burst out laughing.

"Look if Conor can't go to the opening, then I will send Danny. He can charm the birds off the trees. Brandon Lodge won't know what hit it!" James promised.

"Thanks Dad. I would be happier if Danny wasn't at the dinner with us. He is an awful messer. He would rent a floozie to hit on Anthony's Dad just to annoy me!" she shuddered.

"Your brother is not that bad. He likes to wind you up. He would never do anything to hurt you. He owes me one or two favours so I will ring him later."

"You're the best Dad in the world. I love you. See you later." She hugged him before leaving the office.

"You want me to represent you in Brandon Lodge? You sure that I'm up to the job?" Danny was dubious.

"It is a social gathering. Good food and drink. Conor has to go to London and I have promised Kathryn that I would be available to meet the in-laws. I was looking forward to going myself. They are having a dance with a live band. All those waltzes, quicksteps and jives. You can dance so you will have a great time! I'm stuck with the posh dinosaurs and I will have to foot the bill." James added.

"No contest there, Dad. Though I would have gone just to keep my beloved sister on her toes! She is so easy to wind up. Pity you can't go to the opening; you could have worn that slime green silk shirt you bought last year! You must have been drunk or colour blind. Ugh!" Danny shuddered.

"I got that as a gift from your mother. I only wore it once!" he countered.

"Mam! Really. You must really have done something to upset her. She usually has great taste in clothes," Danny answered.

"Let's stick to the subject at hand. Will you go on Friday?" James persisted.

"I know that Kathryn has you backed into a corner, and you did help me with my house so how can I refuse! Give me a look at the file so that I will have the answers to any questions that I might get asked."

"Thanks, son. I hope you don't have to change any plans on my account. You can take someone with you if you like. I'm sure it would be okay."

"No, I think I will go solo. Pamela is behaving very strangely. We have gone out a few times but she can't pass a jewellery shop without dropping hints. I come out with a nervous rash. Surely if I loved her I would want to take this to the next level…" Danny shook his head.

"You are nearly thirty-one Danny. You know your own mind. I would love to see you settle down with the right woman. Who knows? The love of your life could be at Brandon Lodge," James quipped.

"Thanks, Dad. I will sort it out. It is not fair to Pamela to keep stringing her along. I will talk to her next week. She is going away on a hen this weekend."

"Good lad. I'm sure it will all work out. Here you go. This should answer all your questions." James handed Danny the file.

"Okay, Dad. I won't let you down. I will be on my best behaviour. After all, I am a successful man about to move into Hillside Manor. It's all about image. Image is everything."

James looked at his son. He reminded him of himself when he was younger. He had the same jet black curly hair, was well over six feet tall and it was easy to see why he was such a hit with the girls. He had charisma by the bucketful. The goatee beard only added to that charm. He was a successful auctioneer and looked the part.

He hoped that he would meet the right person and settle down. So far it hadn't happened.

"Thanks again, Danny. I appreciate it."

"No worries, Dad. Next Friday night at eight o'clock I will present myself at the door of Brandon Lodge ready, willing and able to promote CJ Securities to the best of my ability."

Brandon Lodge

It was finally here. The day of the official opening of Brandon Lodge. It would be the biggest event the locality had seen in years. No expense had been spared in making the place look fabulous.

Everyone involved had been hard at work since daybreak. It was now early evening and the gates would open at four o'clock.

Lights had been strung all along the avenue and the car parks. Lanterns had been hung along the steps leading up to the main door. Caterers had been coming and going all day. The market stalls had been set up under the cover of a huge marquee. Heaters had been strategically placed to make sure that it would not be too cold. Access to the hotel itself was strictly by invitation only but all the events on the grounds were open to the public. These included a local band in the gym and a traditional group in one of the smaller outhouses. A traditional Irish stew was being served in the downstairs kitchen of the hotel which was accessible from the back of the hotel. The ballroom was situated at the front of the hotel. The huge chandeliers glistened.

David

David was thrilled with how the ballroom looked. It was a carbon copy of the way it had looked thirty years previously. He hoped that Clodagh would approve. James Murray was unable to attend, his son would be coming instead. He had always hoped that Clodagh would meet someone and settle down. She was an excellent role model for Beth but she had lost out because she had been cast in the role of mother at a young age. James Murray had mentioned a daughter as well as the son, so he had his own family. David found the other man to be honest and straightforward so he could not imagine why James had treated Clodagh so badly all those years ago.

This would be the first time that Mike would see Brandon Lodge in all its glory. He had flown in on a later flight and would arrive shortly.

Beth

Beth picked up her bag, the final touch to her outfit. It was a purple and black felted evening bag with diamante trim. It had been a present from Clodagh for her thirtieth birthday back in January. She was wearing a diamond choker with matching bracelet and diamond stud earrings. They had belonged to Aunt Lizzie and had been passed down to Clodagh and then to Beth. They were her most precious possession so she rarely wore them. Tonight was a special night so she decided that it would make Aunt Lizzie part of the celebrations. She took one final look at her reflection in the mirror, picked up her jacket and left her apartment. She was to collect Clodagh and didn't want to be late. Gill and Joe were on their way and Maria was travelling with her daughter.

The hotel was a credit to David. Beth had sneaked a look at it the previous day while Clodagh was in Cork meeting a supplier.

Forty minutes later, Beth pulled up outside Clodagh's house.

Inside, Clodagh was gathering her shawl and bag. Beth whistled when she saw her.

"Wow Mom, you look absolutely beautiful. That shawl is unreal; they will sell like hotcakes."

You look fabulous!" She hugged Clodagh.

"Thanks pet. Probably all that dancing with Robert. Hope we will be able to keep it up. Maria may not want to share him. Ann has also been keeping me on my toes. Her menus are so delicious that I don't crave sugar like I used to. You look fabulous as usual. I am so glad that you are wearing Aunt Lizzie's jewellery. It is too beautiful to be kept locked up. She often wore it herself, said it made her feel confident."

"I just don't want to lose it. I feel that the clasp of the bracelet is loose. I will get it checked out tomorrow. Those shoes are incredible. I knew that they were meant for you when I saw them online. Cinderella had nothing on you!" Beth laughed.

"They are lovely. It is a pity that I can't walk in them. They are strictly car to bar shoes. As for Cinderella, I hope I don't fall apart at midnight." Clodagh eased herself into the passenger seat.

"Brandon Lodge awaits us."

Danny

Danny Murray was running late. He had shown a client around a little cottage that had been on his books for ages. He could sense that the man was interested so he worked extra hard to enhance the finer points of the house. It had worked and his commission would be substantial. The downside was that he should have left for Brandon Lodge over an hour ago. He had spilled a coke on his shirt when he had to brake suddenly at the roundabout because some eejit had gone the wrong way around it. Since he knew that his Dad always kept spare shirts and ties in his office, he would have to stop there as it was nearer than his own apartment. He would be murdered if he missed this gig.

In the office, he found a lot of very unsuitable shirts and the matching ties were brutal. He wouldn't want to be laid out in any of them... He poked around in the drawers and found the perfect accessory. A lovely red but very wide tie hidden in the bottom drawer behind a lot of bits and pieces.

"Perfect with this grey silk shirt, and wide enough to cover the small stain. Danny, you look cool man. Brandon Lodge won't know what hit it!"

Gill
Gill stood under the shower and the hot water cascaded over her, easing all her aches and pains. The last few days had been exhausting. Last minute deliveries of materials and finished items. She had her own section in the shop and her designs were selling well. She was delighted with the extra money and Joe was thrilled with the extra space. He was no longer falling over stashes in baskets. Tonight would be the culmination of all the hard work of the past few months. It would be a great night. As she turned off the shower, she heard the front door close.

Joe called out from the hall.

"I'm home. I'll be ready to leave in half an hour."

"Okay love, take your time. We have ages yet," she answered.

Maria
In Maria's house, Laura was waiting patiently for her mother to come downstairs. She must have tried on every stitch that she owned. Finally, she heard footsteps on the stairs. Her mother appeared wearing a vintage inspired grey silk dress with a black lace shawl. She was wearing a diamante slide in her hair.

"Oh my God Mam, that outfit is fabulous."

Robert
Robert fixed his tie in the hall mirror and left the house. He was looking forward to this night.

Clodagh
"Look at it Beth. The lights are magical. It looks like a fairyland. I can't wait to see the inside. I wonder if David and Mike have arrived yet?" Clodagh pulled her shawl closely around her body.

"Only one way to find out. Come on. We will be able to have a look around before the place becomes crowded. We have nearly an hour before it all kicks off." Beth began to walk towards the hotel steps.

"I don't believe it. It looks exactly the same as it used to look all those years ago! How did you do it? I love it!" Clodagh hugged David, and then Mike.

"I'm so glad. I wanted you to feel at home. You used to tell me stories of the good times that you had here," David was delighted with her reaction.

"Thank you both so much. Do you mind if I walk around on my own for a few minutes? I just want to reconnect with it," Clodagh asked.

"Go right ahead. We will wander around and make sure that everything is in place. We open in less than an hour," David answered.

Clodagh walked slowly up the spiral staircase. She could almost hear the music. The huge gilt mirror was exactly where it used to be. She sat on the loveseat beneath it. She was delighted that she had managed to hide her true feelings. David was one of the most romantic people that she knew. In his world love would always triumph. She shivered.

This was all wrong and she was shocked to the core. Tears began to pour down her cheeks and she tried to brush them away. She heard voices downstairs and tried to pull herself together. She heard footsteps and suddenly Robert was beside her.

"Hi Clodagh, are you okay? Mike sent me up. David and Beth are gone on some errand. He thought that you seemed a little distracted. He thought that maybe I could help." He put his arms around her.

"He is a very intuitive man. David wanted to recreate a good memory but this is just a reminder of what went wrong. Thirty years ago I was facing the rest of my life with the man that I loved. Thirty years later I am back here and all alone. I told you why I went to London and why I came back. It won't work Robert. All of this was a mistake. I should have stayed in London. There is no happy ending for me." She collapsed into his arms.

"I can't tell you what to do, but don't make any rash decisions. This has been a huge shock to you and I can understand why. You have to give yourself time to process all of this. Have you ever considered speaking to James? You owe it to yourself to get an explanation."

"I don't think that would be a good idea. You are right about this being a shock. Tonight is not all about me. Lots of people have worked very hard to make Brandon Lodge a success. I will not spoil it for them. Will you promise to save a dance for me later?" she leaned over and kissed Robert on the cheek.

"Of course I will. I will keep an eye on you tonight. If it all gets too much for you, just give me the nod and I will take you home," he promised.

"You are the best friend a girl could ask for. Maria is a lucky woman. If only…"

"I know…" he whispered.

Downstairs, Gill and Joe had arrived, closely followed by Maria and Laura. Ann and Gary had arrived an hour before and were checking out the hotel kitchen. All the other business owners were gathered in the drawing room. There was to be a short meeting and toast before opening time.

Maria noticed Clodagh and Robert walk down the stairs arm in arm. They looked like a couple.

David stood at the head of the table and began to speak.

"I am very glad to finally be standing here. You have all done an excellent job of promoting your businesses. Brandon Lodge is a success and we have not yet reached the first anniversary. That will be an even bigger occasion than this. I just wanted a chance to tell you how much I appreciate your help in making a dream come true. May I propose a toast to Brandon Lodge?" David raised his glass.

"To Brandon Lodge."

Danny

When Danny turned into Brandon Lodge, he whistled. The place was like something from a fairy-tale. Under the powerful lamps the Farmer's Market was in full swing. The place was crowded. He followed the signs for parking and was soon wandering around the various stalls.

Inside the hotel, guests were beginning to arrive. A number of local bands and groups had been hired to play in different rooms. The main band would start up in the ballroom at eleven. Waiters and waitresses constantly walked the rooms with canapes and champagne. A buffet was set out in one of the larger rooms.

Laura and Beth were chatting in the hall.
"I love your jewellery," Laura commented.
"Thanks. They were a gift. I don't wear it too often. I feel that the bracelet is loose," she looked at her wrist. "Oh Jesus! It's gone. I've lost the bracelet." She was horrified.

Danny decided that it was time for him to go into the hotel. He could have walked around for hours but he had a job to do and he was not going to let his father down.

As he walked up the steps, he saw something glitter in the light of the lanterns. Bending down, he picked up the bracelet. It was heavy and he had a hunch that it was valuable. Someone would be glad to get it back.

He produced his invitation and once inside the door he found himself in a large entrance hall. The wood panelled walls were dotted with lanterns but the dominating feature was the huge chandelier suspended from the ceiling. The spiral staircase led up to a large landing. Music was coming from upstairs. He was about to investigate further when he heard a voice that he would have known anywhere.

"Oh Jesus! It's gone. I've lost the bracelet."
"Would this be what you are looking for?" Danny dangled the bracelet at a very startled Beth.

"Oh, thank you so much... Danny! Where did you come from? Why are you here? Where did you find it? It was belonged to Aunt Lizzie and... why are you here?"

Danny leaned against the wall and waited for her to draw breath.

"Well, let me see. I came from Killarney. I am here for the official opening on behalf of CJ Securities. I found the bracelet on the steps outside, and I've already answered the last question. Maybe you should put this bracelet in a safe place. The catch seems to be broken." He handed it to her.

She put it into her bag and regarded him again.

Laura had been watching the exchange with interest. She stretched out her hand.

"My name is Laura. Why don't I get you both a drink while you chat? Champagne okay?"

"Please excuse my manners, Laura. I am Danny Murray and my father and uncle run the security here. Champagne would be lovely. Why don't we go upstairs and find a seat? We have a bit of catching up to do." He took Beth's arm and led her upstairs. They sat underneath a large mirror.

"I don't believe that we have run into each other again. I had hoped to hear from you." He looked at her closely.

"I am speechless. I never expected to see you again. You were with your girlfriend at the wedding. I do not break up relationships." She looked him in the eye.

Laura returned with their drinks.

"I will leave you to it. I must find my mother. It was nice to meet you, Danny Murray. Goodnight, Beth." She smiled at the couple.

"Goodnight, Laura. Enjoy yourself," Beth said.

"Pamela and I are in a casual relationship. We both know that." He took her hand.

"You sure about that? Pamela had a different story to tell. I don't want to be responsible for hurting anyone," she answered.

"I am certain. Pamela will be as relieved as I am." He leaned over and kissed her on the cheek. "Cheeky," she smiled.

Clodagh

Clodagh had walked outside for some air. She had been looking forward to coming back to Brandon Lodge. It had been such a mistake. The recreation of the ballroom had been the nail in the coffin. She would leave Gill run the shop and she herself would return to London. She wouldn't tell anyone for a few weeks. David was so thrilled with his success that she didn't have the heart to spoil it. Mike already guessed, he could always read her like a book. Robert had been so attentive to her that she felt that there could be something between them if she stayed around. Maria really liked him so Clodagh would not complicate things further. Damn you, James Murray! If only…

"You okay Clodagh?" Mike took off his jacket and placed it around her shoulders.

"Yes, I just needed some air. Look at this place. It is almost ten o'clock at night and the market is buzzing!"

"You will miss it then?" he asked.

"You know me so well," she leaned against him.

"Why don't we go down to the kitchen? I would love to try this Irish stew dish," Mike said.

The kitchen was busy but they found a table by the window that had just been vacated.

The waitress placed the steaming bowls in front of them.

"Eat up. You didn't touch any of the food upstairs. I don't want you fainting on me," he urged.

She picked at the food in the bowl.

Mike put down his spoon and looked at her.

"You know what an old romantic David can be? He wants everyone to have their dream, all nine yards of it. When he found Brandon Lodge was for sale, he moved mountains to get it. You used to talk about it so much. He couldn't resist the challenge. That is why tonight is a walk down memory lane for you," he paused.

"I appreciate what he did. I really do. When I found out that James Murray was involved here I had mixed feelings. He is married with at least one child so there is no chance of a happy ending there. I thought I was going to meet him a few days ago in the Tearoom but neither of the two guys were him. I was so disappointed. I had hoped that… well I don't really know what I wanted to happen! He could be here tonight. I am so confused!"

"He won't be here. He rang David earlier. There is a young man representing the firm," Mike reassured her.

"I don't know whether I am glad or sorry," she told him.

"David will be worried about you and looking for me. Are you ready to come back inside? I know this is hard for you but you are a businesswoman as well and your public awaits you. There are people who wish to speak to you," he reminded her.

"Of course you are right, as usual. I will show you how to get to the ballroom without going in the front door. Inside I will smile and pose and answer questions. Tonight is for celebrating. Come along, Mike."

Robert

Robert and Maria were dancing when Clodagh and Mike entered the ballroom. He waved at them. In his arms Maria stiffened.

"You okay?" he enquired.

"Yes, Clodagh looks fantastic tonight. She must be over the moon with how things have turned out," Maria said.

"Looks can be deceiving," he murmured.

"What do you mean?" she looked up at him.

"Oh nothing. This music is lovely. I promised Clodagh a dance later. You don't mind, do you?" he asked.

"Why should I mind? You and Clodagh are just friends. Right?" Maria retorted.

"Of course." He looked away.

Clodagh

After the interviews had been conducted and the photographs taken, Clodagh went to the bathroom and locked herself in a cubicle. It seemed to be the only place where she would not be disturbed. Thank God that most of the guests had left and she would soon be free to go as well. Gill and Joe had left a few minutes beforehand. Ann and Gary were still somewhere in the hotel and she hadn't seen Beth in ages. She had danced with Robert but felt Maria's eyes boring into her back. She would not think about that tonight. She had not seen Maria leave.

Leaving the bathroom, she wandered upstairs. She would find Beth and they could leave.

At the top of the stairs she stopped dead in her tracks. Beth was sitting with a man who was the image of James Murray. It had to be his son. He had his arm around Beth.

"Mom, come and meet Danny," Beth had spotted her and called her over.

When Danny stood up Clodagh was transported back thirty years. He was the image of James, but with a beard. She had to take a deep breath before she approached them.

"Hi Danny, I'm pleased to meet you. My name is Clodagh." It was when she went to shake his hand that she saw it. He was wearing the tie that she had made years ago. It was all too much for her. She reached out and made a grab for it. She was vaguely aware of Robert's voice before she hit the floor.

"Clodagh. Can you hear me?" she opened her eyes and found herself in Robert's arms.

"Thank God you are alright." He kissed her.

Maria turned on her heels and walked down the stairs followed by Laura. Robert didn't seem to notice.

When she had recovered sufficiently, she realised that she was holding the red tie in her hand. There was no sign of Danny Murray.

Beth, David and Mike were around her. Robert wasn't there so maybe she had imagined the kiss.

"Are you alright, Mom? You gave us such a fright. You were talking about a cow! What happened?" Beth was distraught.

"I'm fine, Beth. I didn't eat enough today and the champagne went to my head. I am sorry if I gave you all a fright. I just need a good night's sleep. I will be fine in the morning," she reassured them all.

It was almost two o'clock in the morning when Clodagh was back in her own bedroom. She looked at her reflection in the full-length mirror and the person looking back at her was vastly different from the person who had stood there only hours earlier. She looked much older and her face was drawn.

"Shit. Damn you, James Murray!"

She could not believe that she had pulled that thing from around Danny's neck. He must think that she is a complete lunatic! Thank God he had loosened it or she would have strangled him. He would probably enjoy telling that story to his father.

Then there was the kiss from Robert. What the hell was he playing at? Maria was only feet away from him at the time.

She lay down on the bed without undressing. There was a gentle knock on the door.

"Mom, are you okay? Can I come in?"

"Sure Beth. I'm still awake."

Beth came in with a tray.

"I made some cocoa and toast. You sure you are alright? You gave me such a shock. Danny was a bit taken aback when you grabbed his tie but he recovered well." she giggled.

"I am so sorry about that. We will talk tomorrow and I will explain it all to you. Let's have this before it gets cold and then we can get some rest. It has been a hectic few weeks but at least we have the weekend in the Quayside Hotel to look forward to."

"I have been looking forward to it for ages. I want to find out more about Aunt Lizzie and I don't intend to get lost this time!" Beth smiled.

"That's good to hear. I am hoping for a peaceful weekend. I have had enough drama for a while. I'm wrecked. You should get some rest. See you in the morning," Clodagh yawned.

After she was sure that Clodagh had gone to bed, Beth went downstairs to lock up.

She checked her phone.

Hope your Mom is feeling better. See you very soon. X

Danny

Danny was delighted that he had met Beth again but he couldn't understand why she thought that he and Pamela were engaged not to mention that Pamela claimed that she was pregnant! He would have to get to the bottom of it. Far from getting serious and planning marriage, their relationship had run its course. He needed to have a serious talk with her as soon as she got back from the hen weekend. He wanted to see Beth again but he had promised her that he would sort it out with Pamela.

He rubbed the mark on his neck. He knew that creative people could be a bit odd but Clodagh's behaviour had been positively bizarre! She had almost choked him in a bid to remove the red tie. He would have to explain to his Dad that he had lost it and hopefully discover the story behind it. It had definitely been very important to her for some unknown reason.

He had text his Dad earlier but James had not replied.

David

David poured himself a double brandy. He was relieved that the opening was over. Ever since Clodagh had mentioned that James Murray, he had been worried that something would happen on the night. He had been right to be worried.

Even though James himself was a no show, his son appeared and captivated Beth. He had noticed how she had spent the entire evening with Danny. That could turn out to be another can of worms. Poor Clodagh had been so upset. Not to mention that fool from the bookshop smothering her with a kiss, with his partner just a few steps behind him. Was he trying to put a harem together? Thank God that Clodagh and Beth were going away for a few days.

Robert

Robert paced the floor. He could not believe that he had actually kissed Clodagh. How could he have been so stupid! Maria had stomped off and David looked like he wanted to murder him. He would have a lot of explaining to do, both to Maria and Clodagh. The problem was that he had no idea why he did it.

He poured himself a very large Jack Daniels and sat in the darkened room.

James

James Murray was bored senseless. The food was great but Anthony's parents did nothing but complain from starter to dessert. They were the most opinionated and stuck up pair of snobs that he had ever encountered.

He had excused himself from the table and wandered outside to get some air. He was in no hurry to go back in. He stood outside admiring the moonlit lake with the mountains framing it in the background.

Kathryn joined him.

"You okay, Dad?"

"Just delaying the inevitable. What is your excuse?"

"Anthony is going to ask you for your permission to marry me. I want you to act surprised. Promise?" she said happily.

"Of course, I will, pet. If you are happy, then so am I. You know that the money is there for any kind of wedding you want. We will show the royal couple that the Murray's know how to host one hell of a do!" He hugged her.

"Thanks Dad. I didn't tell Mam yet so don't let on."

"Of course I won't. I hope you will both be very happy. I'm going to give you one piece of advice. Always be honest with one another. A good relationship should be built on trust; believe me I know what I am talking about."

"Dad, were you and Mam ever happy together? You have lived apart for years. Was it because of me and Danny that you broke up?" she looked up at him, her expression unreadable.

"Of course not. You two kept us together. Tonight is not the right night to be raking over the past."

"Come on now, you go in or the two will have beamed themselves back to the country before the big announcement." He pushed her towards the steps.

"You know Dad, sometimes you're a hoot!"

"That's 'owl' me for you. Hoot. Owl." They burst out laughing and Kathryn went back inside. A few minutes later Anthony made his way down the steps towards James.

Chapter Fourteen

Clodagh

Clodagh twisted and turned for hours. Eventually she gave up trying to sleep and got up. Trying not to wake Beth, she tiptoed downstairs to make herself a cup of tea and a sandwich.

Sitting in the kitchen, she tried to make sense of the previous night's events.

Where did Danny get that stupid tie? It had to have come from James. Why would he give it to his son to wear to Brandon Lodge? Did James want her to know that he was happily married? There could be no other explanation.

"You look much better Mom. How are you feeling this morning?" Beth came into the kitchen.

"I'm much better. I really think that a lot of it was that I was hungry. I've already had sandwiches and I could still eat more. Why don't I put on the frying pan and we can talk about last night over a full Irish?" Clodagh smiled.

A few minutes later, they were seated at the marble breakfast bar.

"Look Mom, you don't need to explain anything to me. Danny was fine about it. He even joked that he was quite used to being attacked by adoring women trying to remove his clothes. It has been a stressful few weeks preparing for last night. Just one question. What was wrong with the tie that he was wearing? I would have thought that a hand-knit would have impressed you of all people. I liked it myself, even if it was a bit eighties. The red really suited him," she added dreamily.

Clodagh buttered her toast and bit into it before answering.

"Actually it was my type of thing. Let me show you." She went into the hall and picked up the bag that she had discarded on the hall stand when she had arrived home from the hotel.

She took the tie out of the back pocket and handed it to Beth.

"Turn it over and tell me what you see."

Beth did as she had asked and looked closely at it. At the edge of it was a tiny embroidered rose with C.K. beside it.

"It is one of yours. You made it. I have never seen anything like it in any of your collections and you stopped using that label years ago. How did Danny get hold of it?" Beth was baffled.

"This was a present that I made for my boyfriend when I was a teenager. His name was Richard."

"Where is he now? Why would he give it away?" Beth asked.

"He never got it. He stood me up on my birthday because a cow was having a calf! His friend, James Murray, came to tell me and he put it in his pocket while we danced. I never saw it again until now. James Murray must have given it to his son."

"Danny…" finished Beth.

"Yes. The security company that David hired is run by Conor and James Murray. I didn't recognise the name because, back then, the company was called Dan Murray and Sons." Clodagh refilled both their cups.

"In a nutshell, James was the reason that I went to London. In retrospect it was the best thing that ever happened to me. If I had stayed at home, then I would have never met Aunt Lizzie, your mother, you, David or Mike. I did love him very much but he met someone else and she got pregnant. I know that she had a girl who is obviously your Danny's sister," Clodagh explained.

"Oh my God. Do you want me to avoid Danny? I will if you say so," Beth sounded upset.

"Of course not. I am over James and he is definitely over me. You go right ahead and see who you like. Did you tell him that we will be in Killarney later?"

"Yes, I am supposed to meet him in the town. You are meeting Aunt Claire so I was hoping that you wouldn't mind if I slipped away for a while…" Beth watched Clodagh closely.

"Of course, I don't mind. You go and meet him and have a lovely time. We can meet up later in the hotel," Clodagh smiled.

"As long as you are okay with it. Let's tidy up here and get going." Beth stood up.

Just as she was zipping up her weekend bag, Beth's phone beeped.

Hi beautiful, sexy and most gorgeous woman in the whole world! How long will I have to wait before I get to hold you again? Can't wait xxxxxxxxx

She smiled and texted him back.

In about two hours. Will ring when I arrive x

In her own room Clodagh also got a message.

Hi Clodagh, hope you are feeling much better this morning. I am very sorry for my behaviour last night. I hope I did not offend you too much. Maybe we could meet for a chat when you get back after the weekend.

Clodagh decided not to reply until she had time to figure out what she needed to say.

"Will have to deal with this later," Clodagh spoke out loud.

"Deal with what?" Beth looked worried.

"Just got a message from Robert. He said that he was sorry for last night. It's Maria he should be talking to. I really don't know what got into him!"

"You sure about that? It seems to me that you two keep gravitating towards each other."

"Don't be silly, Beth. He and Maria are really suited to each other," Clodagh assured her.

"I think the lady doth protest too much!" Beth said.

"I wonder what treatments are on offer at the hotel spa this weekend. I intend to look ten years younger by Monday." Clodagh changed the subject.

"Did Claire say where we are to meet her?" Beth picked up her jacket.

"We are to go to her house first."

"You ready to go?"

Ann

Ann slept late on the morning after the opening. The night had been a complete success. The dishes that she had prepared had been very well received and she had made valuable contacts. Her business was growing and so was her relationship with Gary. It was still early days but she was even considering introducing him to Leo in the near future. They were now business partners and it was going well. They were getting more orders for outside catering. Life was looking good! She lingered in bed a while longer as her mother had insisted on keeping Leo overnight. Ann would drop into the Tearoom on her way to pick up Leo as she and Gary had a sixtieth birthday party later that evening. He was meeting her there at ten to sort the food.

Gary was already there when she arrived. He waved and put the kettle on.

"Hi Gary, wasn't last night just great? I think we are on our way." She hugged him.

They were sorting out the list of dishes when they spotted Robert's car approaching. He parked in front of his bookshop but made no attempt to get out of the car.

"Why is he here today? The place is closed. He is just sitting there. I wonder if he is alright. One of us should go out and check on him." Ann was worried.

Gary moved towards the door.

"I'll go. It might have something to do with last night. Clodagh fainted and Robert got such a fright that he kissed her. Maria saw him and stormed off. Pretend you don't know anything about it."

"What do you mean pretend? I don't know anything about it." She spoke to an empty room.

A few minutes passed before Gary returned followed by a very pale Robert.

"Hi Robert, sit down and I will make you some tea and toast. What did you tear into last night to have you looking like this?" She attempted to lighten his mood.

In spite of how he was feeling inside Robert managed to smile.

"Oh, the honesty of youth. Straight to the point! Well to give you the edited version I think that I may have blown my friendship with Clodagh for good. Maria thinks I'm a rat and so I went home and discussed my predicament with Jack. It all made perfect sense after a while." He rubbed his forehead.

"Who is Jack? Never heard you mention him before?" Ann was puzzled.

"Jack Daniels... hence the hangover. The bottle was thankfully half empty before I started the conversation, which was a good thing. I am not much of a drinker really. It doesn't take much to make me drunk. I was as sick as a dog this morning so toast is about all I can take at the moment."

"I'm sure it's not as bad as you think. You were dancing with both of them last night and you all looked happy." She was dying to know about the fainting incident but would have to wait for Robert to bring it up.

He sipped the tea that Gary had poured.

"It was getting late and Maria had gone to find Laura. Clodagh was going upstairs so I followed her to see if she needed a lift home. Beth and the young fellow from the security firm were sitting in that seat under the mirror. Beth called her over and she must have felt faint because next thing I know she was grabbing his tie and down she went. She was muttering about cows and I got an awful fright."

"Poor Clodagh. Was she okay?" Ann put the plate of toast on the table.

"I kissed her. I don't know why. David McGovern had come up the stairs behind me and looked like he wanted to stab me. Maria must have come up as well because she was standing there looking horrified! She took off with Laura and is ignoring my calls. David's partner Mike stepped in and took charge. He took Clodagh and Beth home. So there you have the highlights. I texted Clodagh this morning but she hasn't replied."

"That does sound strange. It was probably just exhaustion. When she's busy, she forgets to eat. It has been stressful for everyone for the last few days. Hopefully things will settle down now. Give her a call later," Ann advised.

"She is going to Killarney today with Beth. I think that they are staying until Tuesday. It might be better if I waited until she came back. I might make a better job of explaining myself face to face. I hope I haven't lost a very good friend," Robert sighed.

"Well, you have a few days to get your ducks in a row," Ann said.

"Wayward ducks are the least of my worries! Something smells lovely. Do you have another booking for tonight?"

"Yes, it's a sixtieth. Want to see the menu? You must be an expert on those," she joked.

"Funny but true. I have attended my fair share lately. Nothing too spicy now," he looked at her list.

"This is impressive. You are doing well. You will soon need more help. Don't wear yourself out."

"I won't. Enjoy your weekend, Robert."

After Robert had left, Gary made coffee.

"You look thoughtful. Care to share?"

"I wonder what got into Clodagh last night. She is not prone to fainting fits, or attacking security men! I hope she is okay."

"She will be fine. Come on, we have a lot to get through before tonight," Gary said.

Kate

Kate was delighted for Kathryn and Anthony. He was a nice lad but his parents were two of the most pompous prats that she had ever encountered. It was the first thing that she and James had agreed on in a long time.

She smiled as she recalled the moment that Anthony had gone down on one knee and proposed, right there in the dining room. Fair play to him. The ring was beautiful but Anthony's parents looked like they were sucking lemons. Kathryn would have her work cut out with those two. They were still at the hotel and another dinner was planned for tonight. Why Anthony had insisted on a second meal was beyond Kate. She had booked a hair appointment and was even going to get gel nails. She would show that woman that Kathryn's family could hob-nob with the best of them!

She was about to leave the house when her daughter burst in.

"Morning, Mam. I am so excited. I will never take this ring off again! It is just fab." She flopped down on the nearest chair.

"Morning to you too. If you keep your hand extended like that, you will have trouble driving your car!" Kate joked.

"I will put it down eventually. Thanks for being so nice last night, especially when Anthony's Mam kept going on about the shops you should buy your clothes in. Your outfit was so much nicer than her one and you are way younger and prettier than she is. The mother of the bride will be the second best looking woman at the wedding!" Kathryn assured her mother.

"Thanks, pet. Maybe she was nervous. Tonight might be much better. Danny will be there so he will keep her on her toes. Did you hear from him this morning? How did last night go?" Kate checked her watch and decided that they had time for tea.

"He rang me earlier to congratulate me. He was all excited. Apparently, he has found the love of his life. Her name is Beth Kenny and she is the daughter of Clodagh Kenny." Kathryn was too busy admiring her ring to notice how pale her mother went.

"I must ring him later. I'm sure he will tell me all about it. Was he talking to your father?"

"Yeah, Dad was talking to Danny last night, just before Anthony proposed. I'm glad he found someone to get him away from that Pamela. Did you know that she is saying that she and Danny are getting married? I've tried talking to him but he can't see any bad in anyone. She is seriously scary. One of the girls in the restaurant told me that Pamela stalked some guy for months and even attacked his girlfriend but I don't know how true that is. Danny wants to bring this new girl tonight as she is in Killarney for the weekend. I am thrilled because if he is trying to impress a new girlfriend then he is less likely to act the maggot in front of Anthony's parents," Kathryn said.

"Shit!" Kate muttered.

"You alright, Mam?"

"Yes, of course. I just burned my finger," she lied.

"Here. Sit down and I will pour the tea. You are probably just overexcited at the thought of your only daughter getting married.

It will be grand. Dad is footing the bill. He told me so last night. Anything I want. We will have a ball planning it. We might even get the wedding planner fellow to help us with everything. You know the guy from Cork... Franc." Kathryn giggled.

"Just because your Dad has promised you unlimited funds for this wedding is no reason to get too carried away! Wedding planner indeed..." Kate tried to act normally.

"I won't Mam... promise. Come on so, time to go and get pampered for round two tonight." Kathryn gave a twirl and her ring glittered in the winter sunshine.

After her daughter had dropped her into town and gone to get her nails done, Kate treated herself to a coffee and thought about Danny. He would be at the Quayside tonight with Clodagh Kenny's daughter. Maybe the girl would not remember their encounter back in April.

She needed to talk to James since he was supposed to know all about Danny and Beth. What he may not know was that Danny and Beth were almost the same age. That could mean either of two things. Clodagh Kenny went to London, met someone and became pregnant within a couple of weeks or Danny was dating his own sister. Jesus, what was she going to do? She would have to talk to James and before tonight. Why the hell was he not answering his bloody phone! She had a hair appointment in thirty minutes and she was damned if she was going to miss it. Tonight she would need all guns blazing if only for damage limitation.

Danny

Danny was updating his website. He had just added a new property to his portfolio and it looked promising. It was a cottage in a prime location, practically within walking distance of the town – if you were seriously into keeping fit... The elderly owner had recently died and the relatives were swarming around it like vultures. They wanted a quick sale so the asking price was very competitive. Danny studied the photographs that he had taken. In the evening sunlight the house looked quite romantic, at least on the outside. The inside was a different matter! The old fellow must have had a menagerie of animals living with him. Still it had huge potential so hopefully it would sell quickly. He pondered the wording that he needed to use in order to get the best price.

This picturesque cottage is located on the outskirts of Killarney town. Built circa 1930 it has old world charm and comes with a two-acre site. The interior has three rooms. A recent extension contains a good sized bedroom and bathroom. It retains some nice old features and is in excellent structural condition with an asking price of 130,000 euros.

When Danny had finished he made himself a coffee and thought about Beth. Thank God his father had asked him to go to Brandon Lodge. He was looking forward to seeing her again in a few hours. She was on her way to Killarney with her mother. He rubbed his neck and hoped that whatever he wore tonight would not lead to a repeat performance. He would also have to come clean to his Dad about the tie. They had arranged to meet so that Danny could fill him in on the previous night.

Claire

Claire folded the last of the towels and made sure that the salon was spotlessly clean. The place was busy and she loved it that way. She was so glad that she had opened her own place. She had a few minutes to spare before her next appointment, a new client, Kate Cashman. A quick cup of tea and a read of one of the latest celeb magazine would be just the thing.

Flicking through the pages she found the horoscopes. She looked at the predictions under Taurus.

Work will mix well with leisure in the week ahead. You might take the opportunity to travel with or entertain someone close to you. Business is good at the moment so take some time out to relax and be pampered.

The usual rubbish again. At least it didn't mention a tall, dark and handsome man coming and sweeping her off her feet. He would have his work cut out for him there. She was a size sixteen and proud of every ounce. Dieting was not a factor in her life. She walked a little and her diet was not unhealthy so she was happy. She had to admit that Clodagh looked fabulous since coming back to Ireland. She had taken up dancing and embraced a healthy lifestyle, thanks to the young girl who ran the Tearoom.

She had just finished her fruit scone when Diana called her. Her client had arrived.

The woman was tall and elegant with greying hair. Claire thought that she was in her mid-sixties.

"Good afternoon, Ms Cashman. Welcome. My name is Claire. Let me take your jacket. Would you like a tea or coffee?" Claire indicated a seat beside her.

"Tea would be lovely, thank you." She sat down and patted her hair nervously.

"Now, what can I do for you today?" Claire placed the tea on the table in front of the mirror.

"I am going to a family dinner tonight and I want to look fabulous. As you can see, I have never coloured my hair. I would like a younger look. My daughter got engaged last night and her mother-in-law to be, who is nearly seventy looked younger than me! What colour do you think would suit me?" Kate sipped her tea and took a piece of the scone that Claire had placed on a plate.

"I will get some magazines and you can get some ideas about what you like. You enjoy your tea and I will be right back." Claire returned some minutes later with some books. Ten minutes later the two women were still discussing colour, style and length.

Two hours later the transformation was complete.

"Wow. You look fantastic. Your husband won't know you. That auburn colour complements your eyes." Claire admired her handiwork.

"I can't thank you enough. If I could get a nice outfit to go with it, life would be perfect," Kate smiled.

"No problem, I am going to the Quayside tonight and I discovered this fabulous boutique hidden up the alley by the new ice cream shop. You should drop in. You might find something there," Claire added.

"Well if I do, you will see it tonight. I will be at the very same hotel! Is it a family do?" Kate asked.

"My sister and niece are visiting from Cork. Clodagh recently opened a new shop and she and Beth are taking a well-earned weekend off. We will all probably end up in the bar later. The music should be good."

"Your sister. Is her surname Kenny?" Kate looked a little taken aback.

"Yes, that's her. Have you heard of her? She trades under Beth's Knits."

"My daughter mentioned her new place. She loves her bags," Kate recovered quickly and pulled out her wallet. "You have done a fantastic job of my hair. I will tell all my friends. I will pop into that boutique. Thanks."

"You are quite welcome. Enjoy your night." Claire handed Kate her card.

Just as Kate was about to leave, she turned around.

"Did your sister keep her maiden name after she married?"

"She isn't married. Why do you ask?" Claire replied.

"No reason. Thanks again."

As Claire tidied up she mused that people sometimes ask the strangest of questions.

Kate

As she was making her way to the boutique, Kate's phone rang.

"Hi Kathryn, I will meet you in Kelly's in about an hour. I have a few things to do first." They chatted for a few minutes.

As she walked along, she wondered if she would ever be free of Clodagh Kenny, though her sister was really nice. It was bad enough that Danny would be there with Beth Kenny, but to have Clodagh as well! It would definitely be an interesting night. She wondered if James knew all of this already and that was the reason that he was ignoring her calls. Well, he could go to hell. She had tried to contact him.

James

James had a hangover. He had slept longer than usual and woken up with a headache. The surprise engagement announcement had been celebrated with a very large bottle of champagne being opened, followed by numerous bottles of wine. By the time the taxis had arrived, his hangover had started. Luckily, he didn't have to be anywhere until lunchtime when he was due to meet Danny. There was another gathering in the hotel later so he needed to sort himself out. He would have to pretend to enjoy the company of Anthony's parents and foot the bill for dinner.

Danny was already in the office when James arrived.

"You're early. That's one for the books," he joked.

"I'm too happy to be in bed, Dad. I found my soulmate last night. Beth is absolutely gorgeous and I'm in love. She will be at the hotel later and I will introduce you to her."

"That's great. Now tell me how the function went. I hope you introduced yourself to David McGovern," James massaged his temples.

"The English dude. He was very nice. Introduced me to his partner, Mike. We all chatted for a while and had our picture taken for some magazine. I had already met Beth and she wanted to introduce me to some of her friends and to Clodagh Kenny. I know that creative people can be a bit crazy but she nearly choked me trying to pull that red tie off me. It was only the old knitted thing that you had stuffed in the drawer and she is supposed to be a famous knitting designer! Jesus, it was scary. When it comes to over-reacting, that Clodagh was seriously in overkill."

Checking his watch, James wondered if he had time for a nap as his head was splitting. What the hell did some knitted tie and Clodagh have to do with anything. Suddenly the mist cleared.

"What did you say? What tie are you talking about? What has Clodagh got to do with Brandon Lodge and Beth? Where did you get it? Where is it now?" His eyes darted to the drawer. "Tell me what happened. Now!"

Danny nearly jumped out of his skin.

"Jesus, Dad. Calm down. What are you doing?"

James had emptied the drawer onto the table and was rifling through the contents.

"Where is it, Danny? What did you do with the tie?"

"For feck sake, Dad. Are you alright? Will you please sit down? You are scaring the crap out of me." Danny considered calling an ambulance as James slumped onto a chair.

"I only meant to borrow it for the night. I was running late and had spilled something on my shirt. I wore it to the opening and when Clodagh saw it, she grabbed me by the neck. I had to pull it over my head and let her have it or I would not have lived to tell the tale." He attempted a joke.

"So, you lost it," James sighed.

"Well, I wouldn't say lost exactly. I don't have it in my possession but I know who has it and the good news is she will be at the hotel tonight. I will ask her for it back. Problem solved. I will also introduce you to the girl of my dreams, who just happens to be her daughter. How cool is that."

At this revelation, James turned an even paler shade of grey. Danny picked up his phone.

"Her daughter? You are in love with Clodagh Kenny's daughter and you think that this should cheer me up! Sweet mother of Jesus, let me wake up now!"

Danny was seriously freaked out. He had never seen his Dad like this before.

"Please, Dad. Please calm down. I will fix it. I promise." Danny went to the drinks cabinet and poured a generous whiskey which he handed to his father.

James swallowed it in one gulp and the colour began to come back to his face. He stood up and pushed his chair back.

"Look son, I know that I am not making much sense to you but I'm not going to explain it to you today. I am going to go home and have a rest before tonight. My car is still at the Quayside so I will take a taxi there later. I would appreciate it if you kept our conversation between us for the moment. Does your mother know who Beth is?" James asked.

"I haven't spoken to Mam today. I will see her tonight. You sure that you are alright? I'll drop you home. I could ring Kathryn if you like. I would stay with you but I promised Beth…" he trailed off.

"There is no need to call anyone. I will take the lift home. I'll be sure not to drink any champagne tonight."

Danny

After he had dropped James off, Danny went to his apartment and had a quick shower. He was meting Beth in an hour. He had a feeling that there was more to the story than a tie. Why did his Dad ask if his mother knew Beth? It didn't make any sense to him.

His phone beeped. It was a message from Pamela.

Hi darling, I know that it is only November but have you any thoughts on what you would like for Christmas? Hen going well. Shopping at the moment. Some lovely jewellery shops up here. We should come for a weekend before Christmas. Hope you made millions for your Dad last night! See you soon XXXX

Oh God. This was not going to be easy. He would have to sit her down and tell her that it was all over between them. He had been trying over the past few weeks to let her down gently but she was just ignoring the suggestions. He had so much to deal with that he decided to put her off until he could formulate a plan.

Busy today. Meeting Dad. Will take ages. Family thing tonight. Sister finally off shelf. Caught some rich fellow from the country. Must be nice to his parents. Talk soon.

He felt a twinge of guilt as he pressed send.

Kate

As she got out of her car at home, Kate was surprised when she heard a wolf whistle. Pat was walking up the yard.

"I hope you don't mind me saying, but you look great. I heard about Kathryn. I'm so pleased for her. I hear that there is another dinner tonight. You will knock them dead. Maybe you would consider going out for a bite to eat with me sometime?"

"That would be lovely," she surprised herself by saying.

James

James tossed and turned. Finally, he got up. He looked at the drinks cabinet.

Margaret Kelleher

Chapter Fifteen

Clodagh
Clodagh wrapped her navy and white scarf tightly around her neck before skidding down the college steps and onto the icy street.

"Oops, sorry!" *She had almost collided with a couple who were cautiously picking their steps along the pathway.*

"Slow down. You could have knocked my mother off her feet." *The young man glared at her.*

"I'm sorry. I really am. I have just finished my first term here and I was so excited that I forgot about the ice." *She smiled sheepishly.*

"It's okay, dear. David is a little too protective of his mother. Is that an Irish accent I hear? My grandmother was from Galway." *The woman smiled.*

"Yes, I'm from Cork. My name is Clodagh." *She extended her hand.*

"I'm Mary McGovern and this is my son David. We are just off to do some shopping. Buying presents can be a chore at my age. That scarf is beautiful. My sister would love something like that. She is always looking for new labels and she loves a vintage twist. I am right in thinking that it is a twenties influenced scarf? Your Flapper hat reminds me of one I used to have. I wonder if it comes in shades of pink. I know it's from Harrods. Did you purchase it recently?"*

Clodagh laughed. "No. I have never been in there. The nearest I have ever been to Harrods is when I visited The Little Yarn Store which is just around the corner from it. I love their stuff but it is so expensive. I made this myself. It didn't take very long at all. I used chunky wool and big needles. I had lots of bits of wool left from other projects so I used them up. It can be made with any type of yarn. It is knitted sideways so I just made it the width that I needed. I live with my great-aunt and a second cousin so we spend a lot of our evenings knitting. I could make one for your sister, as an apology for trying to run you down!" *She finally drew breath.*

Snowflakes began to float silently all around them and David pulled up the collar of his Crombie coat.

Chips in a Bag, Classy Mr Murray

"Look ladies, why don't you two continue this conversation in a warmer setting? There is a hotel down here which provides excellent food. You can discuss lumpy wools and big needles all you want. I'm freezing here and frankly a little bored." David shivered.

"Are you in a rush, dear? I would love a scarf but I insist on paying for it myself. My sister has expensive tastes and that little shop you suggested sounds like just the place to buy the yarn. We will drop you home afterwards, or get you a taxi, whichever you decide." Mary shivered slightly and Clodagh felt guilty.

"No, I'm not in a hurry at all. I can walk home afterwards. I live close by."

"All set so." David linked both women and they made their way to the hotel.

When Clodagh arrived home, Aunt Lizzie was dozing in her armchair and Elizabeth was ripping back her knitting. She looked up when Clodagh entered the room.

"Oh, thank God you are home. This baby will be born before I get this sleeve finished. Please explain this part again. I'm just not getting it and I'm fed up and cranky!"

Clodagh hung up her jacket and put the bag of yarn on the floor. Elizabeth spotted The Little Yarn Store bag.

"When did you rob a bank and buy wool in there?" she asked.

"I will put the kettle on and make you a cup of tea. Then I will sort out the pattern. After that I will tell you about that bag." She promised.

As they sipped their tea, Clodagh recounted the events of the afternoon.

"I have been invited to their house for dinner on Tuesday. She said that I could bring you and Aunt Lizzie with me, just in case you would be worried about me going to a strange house. I should have the scarf finished by then. I must show you the wool she picked out. It is cashmere and cost a fortune. When I told her that you were pregnant she insisted on buying some beautiful baby wool. She got some in pink and in blue. You can make it when you have finished this one. You chose the colour. It will be beautiful." Clodagh hugged the heavily pregnant girl.

"Well, I am going to make the pink one. This baby will definitely be a girl. I can feel it in my waters as Aunt Lizzie would say." Both girls burst out laughing.

"Who is taking my name in vain?" Aunt Lizzie sat up in her chair. "I have kept you some dinner. It is in the oven. Lovely Irish stew. Perfect for a day like today. You got a letter from your mother, I left it on the mantelpiece. Eat your dinner while it is hot. You are on holidays now and I know that your family are looking forward to having you home for Christmas. I know that I said I would go with you but I must look after this lassie here. I heard you, missy. Just remember that mocking is catching."

Clodagh showed them the yarn that she had been given by Mary McGovern. Elizabeth fingered the delicate yarn.

"It's so soft and delicate. I can't wait to use it."

"Aunt Lizzie, I must tell you about the people I met today." Clodagh put her dinner plate on the table. "I think I got my first commission. I'm on my way to becoming a famous designer." She waved her fork in the air.

"I don't doubt it for a second, lass. What was this young man like? Did you like him?"

"He is very nice. He is about thirty which is way older than me. His mother is very nice, really posh but in a good way. I can't wait to see their house. It is one of the redbrick ones over by the park."

Elizabeth put down her knitting and looked dreamily at Clodagh.

"A big house and a few servants. Lovely. So what if he is a bit older than you."

"Been there. Done that. Anyway I don't think that he is interested in me or in any other girl. I certainly am not interested in him or in any other fellow ever again." Clodagh was adamant.

Lizzie got up and made a fresh pot of tea.

"Forever is a very long time and you are very young. Enjoy yourself. Men are not all bad even if the three of us had bad experiences. Eat your dinner and read your letter. There is bread and butter pudding with custard for afters."

"I will get fat on all the goodies that you make!" Clodagh patted her stomach.

"Nonsense girl, a little bit of meat on your bones won't do you any harm. No man likes a bag of bones, too pointy and not cuddly enough!"

"I wouldn't bet the farm on that, Aunty," Clodagh whispered.
"What did you say? My hearing is not what it used to be."
"Nothing important, Aunty. I will save dessert for later. I will read the letter first." Clodagh picked up the letter.
"Wow. It is even bigger than usual. Mam must have lots of news this time."
"We will leave you to it. I'm showing her nibs here how to make the perfect Christmas cake. It had been soaking in Irish whiskey since yesterday. Come on, Elizabeth."

Clodagh curled up on the armchair and tore open the envelope. As she pulled out the handwritten sheets, another envelope fell out. Clodagh gasped as she recognised the handwriting. James had an unusual way of curling his letters. She placed the envelope on the coffee table, as far away from her as she could.

She began to read her mother's letter.

Dear Clodagh,
Dad sends his love. He keeps saying that he will write, but you know what he is like. He still says a prayer for you every night. Anyway enough of that. Claire still wants to leave school and go and work at the hairdressers. I would prefer if she stayed in school. Your father leaves it to me as usual. Maybe she will listen to you, when you get home for Christmas. She is stubborn, a typical Kenny! Speaking of stubborn Kenny women, how is Lizzie? Some of the clan were not too impressed when she took in Elizabeth. Hopefully the poor girl is doing okay. She will have her hands full when the baby comes along.

Mary Murphy's daughter is back home again. She had been missing for most of the year, supposedly had a great job in a hotel in Dublin. Jen O'Connell brought her baby home from the hospital last week. When she was in town pushing the pram, she bumped into Mary on the street, Mary told her that she should be ashamed of herself, parading around with a child and no ring. Jen was always a bit brazen so she asked Mary where her grandson was since her daughter was in the bed next to her in the hospital! Mary hasn't been in town since. Her twitching curtains are very still this week. Her cough has been well and truly softened for her. She was always a spiteful busybody.

Thank God I have two good girls. I know that Dad would be very disappointed if that happened to either of you.

Looking forward to seeing you soon.

I'm very glad that you are enjoying your new college. It was very good of Lizzie to pay for it. It's a shame that she never had any children of her own, she likes having young people around her.

I'm still knitting the Aran jumpers and I had to turn two coats this week for the Roche twins, so the extra money will be handy for Christmas.

I suppose that you noticed the other letter that I sent with this one. I had started to write this letter last Monday. James called on Tuesday. Luckily I was on my own or he wouldn't have gotten up the steps.

I was surprised to see him, but I had just taken a tart out of the oven (he must have smelled it) and some of the neighbours were out pretending to clean the windows for Christmas so I had to let James in. That nosey old wagon in number eight has been wondering about why you haven't been around for the past few months. Can't wait to see you.

Anyway to get back to James. He called and I let him in. I only gave him a very small slice of tart so that he knew I was cross with him.

He asked me how you were getting on and I told him that you were having a great time, out every night with your new friends. Told him that you had even mentioned a new boyfriend. May God forgive me for telling lies! He asked me for your address but I said that you already knew his one and would write to him if you wanted to. He then asked me to send a letter to you. I said that I would and he brought it to me on Wednesday. He hoped that you would read it and maybe answer it.

I'm not very happy about it but I gave him my word. That's all my news for now. I will see you very soon.

The turkeys must be killed and plucked soon so I will be very busy. I will finish now. Dad will be in soon for his dinner.

God bless,
Love Mam, Dad and Claire X
P.S. Sheila from the wool shop sends her love. She said to tell you to hurry home as she has lost her best customer.

Clodagh folded the letter and put it back into the envelope but left the unopened letter on the table. Her aunt came into the room holding a steaming bowl of dessert. She placed it on the table.

"Any news from home? You look a bit put out."

"I'm fine Aunty, just tired. I stayed up very late for the past few nights finishing my projects. Some of them are due in the beginning of January and I wanted to hand them in before I went home. I'm all done now so I will go to bed early tonight. No news, just the usual small town gossip! Mam can't wait to have me home. I think that the local busybodies have me pregnant and hiding out here." *Clodagh yawned.*

"I'm sure she really misses you. Is that another letter on the table?" *Lizzie sat down by the fire.*

"Yes, it's from James – the fellow that I was going out with."

"Ah, the reason that you came over here. I should thank him for sending you to me. Are you going to open it, or die wondering what he has to say?" *Aunt Lizzie picked up her knitting.*

"Straight to the point, as usual. I don't know if I want to open it. I have managed without him up to now, but if I open that letter..." *she paused.* "I think I might sleep on it. I might open it tomorrow."

"Do that pet. Eat your dessert. Elizabeth is gone to bed. I'm a bit worried about her. She is too young to be that tired. I've a bad feeling about it. I will take her back to the doctor tomorrow. Thank God that you are here. I am not as young as I'd like to be in order to help raise a small baby. I will make us both some cocoa and then we will go to bed," *Lizzie said.*

"No, I will do it. You sit there by the fire. Elizabeth will be fine and so will her baby. We will manage between the three of us." *Clodagh stood up.*

"If it was addressed to you, would you open it, Aunty?" Clodagh asked as they sipped their drinks.

"I can't answer that for you. This one has to be your decision. I love having you here. You are getting on great at college and I know that Elizabeth would be lost without your help. It was lonely here until you both came along. Today you met some new people because of a scarf that you designed yourself. That's fate and who knows where it will lead. I believe in fate. What's meant for you will not pass you by. A few months ago you thought that you knew exactly where your life was going and none of this featured in your plans. You might be meant to be here. That letter could change your path again. Is that what you want? You should listen to your heart and not to the rantings of an old woman. I made my decisions too but those stories are for another day. Before you go to bed tonight, pick up that letter and do what your gut instincts tell you. Either read it or burn it. Otherwise you will only toss and turn all night. Goodnight pet, see you in the morning."

"Goodnight, Aunt Lizzie. I will lock up in a few minutes. I might just cast on that scarf for Mary McGovern. Knitting will relax me. Then I will decide."

"That is great. You will feel much better once you have decided." Lizzie hugged Clodagh and went to bed.

Two hours later, having almost finished the scarf, Clodagh picked up the letter, thought for a moment, then threw it on the fire.

She felt better than she had since she had arrived in London.

"Thanks, Aunty," she whispered.

She locked up and went to bed.

The door of Mary McGovern's house was opened by a very handsome man.

"Hi, my name is Clodagh and this is Elizabeth. Mrs McGovern is expecting us."

"Ah yes. The beautiful Irish girl from the college, and her equally beautiful friend. Please come in and let me take your coats. It's damned chilly out there this evening."

Clodagh looked around the hall. It was bigger than her house at home!

"Oh my word. Where are my manners? My name is Richard McGovern the Third, at your service," he bowed.

"My mother is in the drawing room. This way please." Richard led the way.

A huge Christmas tree twinkled in the bay window overlooking the street. Mary McGovern was seated in an opulent armchair beside a roaring fire.

She stood up to greet the girls.

"Please come in and make yourselves comfortable. Would you like a pre-dinner drink?"

"No thank you, we are okay. My aunt could not come here tonight so she sends her apologies and this porter cake." Clodagh placed the tin on the table.

"Thank you so much." Mary turned to Elizabeth.

"How are you feeling, my dear?"

"I'm a bit tired at the moment. The doctor took some more blood tests last week. I should have the results soon. Thank you so much for the beautiful yarn."

"You are quite welcome. If there is anything else that I can do, please let me know." Mary rang a little bell that was on the table beside her.

"I have finished the scarf. I hope it is okay. You bought so much yarn that I made these gloves as well. I hope that they will suit your sister." Clodagh placed the items on the table next to Mary McGovern.

Mary looked at the scarf and gloves. They were perfect. Clodagh had even hand sewn lots of tiny crystal beads into the scarf. They were much nicer than anything that could be bought in Harrods. Her sister Jane would be thrilled. If there was anything that Lady Jane Jones loved, it was everyone else trying to keep up with her! She loved originals.

"These are absolutely wonderful. You are a very talented young lady." She slipped on the gloves. "I am so glad that we ran into each other, literally!" she smiled.

"They were inspired by the fashions of the nineteen twenties. I love the flapper hats of that time. I have made a few since I came over here. Aunt Lizzie was a tutor in the college that I attend and she loved that era as well. She has lots of books and samples so I got interested." Clodagh couldn't stop herself talking.

"I am looking forward to meeting her. Ah, here are the boys."

David came into the room, closely followed by Richard carrying a tray of drinks.

"A divine little mulled wine that I made myself. Just right for the season that is in it. Richard has even agreed to try it. How are you, Clodagh? Run into any more unsuspecting pedestrians in the past few days?" David grinned wickedly.

"Leave her alone, David." Mary rebuked him.

"Delighted to meet you, Elizabeth. Clodagh told us all about you. I knew you were coming so I made a special non-alcoholic version for you, all the taste but none of the hangover." He handed her the glass.

"Thank you so much. That was nice of you." She sipped the wine.

David picked up the scarf that Clodagh had made. He wound it round his neck and pranced up and down the room, hands on hips.

"Take that off this minute, David. It's pink."

"I like pink, it's my favourite colour."

"I rest my case!" muttered Richard as he filled the other glasses.

"Ah stop joking, David. You should have grown out of that by now," His mother admonished him.

There was a knock at the door.

"Dinner is served, madam."

Richard linked both Clodagh and Elizabeth and followed Mary and David into the dining room.

The food was beautiful.

Clodagh and Elizabeth kept exchanging glances. They had never been in a house like it before. The table was big enough to seat everyone who lived in Clodagh's estate back home.

After dinner they all went back to the drawing for coffee and some of Aunty's porter cake.

David stood up and put his cup and plate on the coffee table.

"I hope that you will excuse me but I have a prior engagement. It has been a real pleasure to meet you again, Clodagh, and to meet you, Elizabeth. May I wish you all the luck in the world with your baby. I look forward to meeting your aunt." He turned to his mother and kissed her on the cheek.

"I won't be late. Sleep well. I will see you at breakfast."

Chips in a Bag, Classy Mr Murray

After David had left Richard excused himself to do some work in his office. Mary, Clodagh and Elizabeth chatted for a while. At about eleven o'clock, Richard dropped both girls home.

Chapter Sixteen

Gill

Gill arrived early on the Monday following the opening. Clodagh and Beth were not due back from Killarney until Tuesday. As she made her way towards Beth's Knits, she waved at Robert who was just opening up his bookshop.

Before unlocking the door, she stood back to admire her part of the window display. She had concentrated on a red, black and purple theme. In between the completed bags, scarves and wraps she had placed the yarns and needles needed to complete each pattern.

She has been delighted the previous week when Clodagh had trusted her with decorating the window at the side of the cottage for the opening.

Ann had spotted her and arrived with a coffee.

"This will warm you up. The window looks great. Everyone has worked really hard for the past few months. Have you spoken to Robert yet? Thank God he looks a bit better today than he did on Saturday."

"I just waved at him. Is he okay?" Gill asked.

"He was in a bit of a state on Saturday. Had a hangover. Apparently, he kissed Clodagh on Friday night and annoyed Maria!"

"You are joking me! How did I miss that? Shhh! Here he comes. You can fill me in later," Gill whispered.

At about eleven o'clock Clodagh arrived. The shop was busy so Gill didn't see her until she stood next to her. Clodagh looked terrible.

"Are you alright? I thought that you were staying in Killarney until tomorrow."

To Gill's dismay, Clodagh's eyes filled with tears.

"Go into the back and I will follow you in. Whatever is wrong, we will fix it." Gill gently pushed her boss and friend into the alcove. She then texted Ann and soon the young woman arrived with coffee and cakes.

Gill served the remaining customers and put up the 'Closed' sign on the door.

As Clodagh stirred her coffee she composed herself.

"I'm sorry about that, Gill. It has been a funny few days since the opening. The ballroom looked like it had when I used to come here thirty years ago. The music, the dancing. It seemed like I was walking back in time. When Danny Murray stood up wearing something that I had made years ago, I just lost it. I don't know if you heard what happened next, but I nearly strangled the poor fellow. It was supposed to be a tie but back in the eighties ties were nearly as wide as a scarf. The last time I saw it was when James stuffed it into his pocket thirty years ago. After I grabbed it from Danny, I fainted. When I came to, Robert somehow appeared and kissed me with Maria looking on. Mike took control of the situation and took Beth and me home." Clodagh took a deep breath.

"Then I found out that Beth had met this Danny back in April and now they are 'in love.' As you know we went to Killarney for the weekend. If I thought that things were bad before I left home, it was nothing compared to what unfolded when we got there!" She drained her cup.

"Then there's Robert. I have no idea what is going on with him. I am so confused. The icing on the cake, was the reappearance of the one and only James Murray, the love of my life and the bastard that broke my heart. So, that in a rather large nutshell, is where my life is!" Clodagh looked at Gill.

"Oh my God, you poor thing. No wonder you are so upset. Why don't I stay with you tonight? We will have a quiet night in. You can talk about it if you want to or we will just relax. Joe is on some walking thing in Clare so I would have been going back to an empty house anyway." Gill picked up the empty cups.

"Thanks, Gill. I would really like that. However, I think that we need wine and chocolate. I need to get this off my chest. Another opinion would be really helpful." She attempted a smile.

"That's settled then. I will open up the shop again. It should be quiet enough today. Most of our customers took advantage of the discount at the weekend. We sold out of lots of our yarns and kits. People are starting early for Christmas. You relax there for a while. Since you are not supposed to be working today, you should go home and chill out."

"I'm okay now. I might go for a walk. I haven't really had time to see all of Brandon Lodge since I arrived. After all, I missed the fact that James Murray was a frequent visitor here. Maybe if I had taken more notice of my surroundings, I might at least have seen the signs advertising his company," Clodagh laughed.

"Is everything okay here? Would you like more coffee or cake or anything?" Ann stuck her head around the door.

"No, thanks. We are fine. I will fill you in later. Thanks again, Ann. I have such good friends here." Clodagh smiled.

Clodagh

Clodagh walked slowly around Brandon Lodge, remembering details of each of the buildings. She had spent so much time here as a child as her grandmother had lived practically next door to the hotel. As she walked towards the perimeter, she remembered the wishing chair that was in the little garden by the outer wall. They used to call it the secret garden. She was headed towards where she thought it used to be when her phone rang.

"Hi Mom, I just arrived at the apartment. Danny is very sorry about how the weekend turned out. He said that James never drinks like that. We both hope that things can be sorted out. I know you said that you didn't mind me seeing Danny but if you do, then..."

"It's okay, Beth. You and Danny have nothing to do with any of this," Clodagh interrupted.

"You sure? Do you want me to come and stay with you tonight? We could spend the evening together."

Chips in a Bag, Classy Mr Murray

"No, Gill is staying with me. Joe is away so we are going to drink some of David's expensive French wine. Ann is preparing some food for us and I still have the chocolates that Mike brought with him. We will have our knitting projects as well. Don't worry about me. I can handle James Murray. I will admit that it was a bit of a shock when I realised that Danny was his son. I'll get over it. I'm very happy that you have found someone that you really like. You didn't have to come back today. You could have spent more time in Killarney."

"I wanted to make sure that you were doing okay. Danny has arranged to meet Pamela this evening. He wants to tell her himself about us."

"I hope it all works out. I'll talk to you later. Bye, pet."

"Bye, Mom. Love you."

Just as she was about to give up, Clodagh noticed that the rusted gate that led to the garden had been replaced. She pushed open the shiny black gate and was delighted that the garden had been given a makeover. The wooden seat had been stripped down and re-varnished. She stood still and let memories of better times wash over her. The seat had been created by shaping a fallen tree trunk. Leaf shapes had been carved onto the seat backs. She sat down and closed her eyes. She needed to sort everything out in her head. At the moment it was just a muddle of thoughts and events going round and round. Talking with Gill would hopefully make everything clearer. She would go home and grab a few hours' sleep and then come back in the evening to collect Gill. She left the garden and made her way back to the wool shop. Gill was restocking the shelves and a few customers were browsing through the pattern books.

"You feeling any better?" Gill asked.

"Yes, the walk helped. I am going to slip off home for a while. You can leave your car here tonight. I'll collect you later." Clodagh answered.

"Okay, I will see you in a while. Robert is heading this way so if you want to avoid him then maybe you should slip out the back way," Gill told her.

"Oh Jesus wept! I can't face him now. I will see you later." Clodagh hurried through the shop and down the corridor that led past the Tearoom and out into the side area. She reached her car just as Robert stepped into the wool shop.

Gill

"Hi Robert, are you planning on taking up knitting?" Gill joked.

"No. Is Clodagh here? I thought I saw her coming in a few minutes ago." He looked around.

"No, she just left. She wanted to see Ann about something so she went out the back way." Gill hated lying to him.

"I will catch her later so. I thought that she was away until tomorrow." He turned to leave.

"Robert!" Gill called after him.

"It's okay, Gill. I'll see her later."

"Are you feeling alright? You are a bit pale. Can I get you anything?" Gill was worried.

"I'm fine... just a bit of a headache. I will close up early and head home."

"You take care of yourself. Why don't you let Maria hold the fort and go home now?" she said.

"She is not here today but it's quiet anyway so I will be fine. See you later." Robert closed the door gently behind him.

As she watched his stooped figure cross the yard, Gill wondered what had caused him to age in the past few days. The already grey skies suddenly opened up and unleashed a torrent of hailstones which hopped off the ground and sympathised with the mood which had emanated from Robert.

The bell tinkled and Gill saw a grey coated figure reverse in the door shaking an umbrella before turning and dumping it into the bin provided.

"God, this bloody weather is so changeable. My name is Millie Mackessy. My hat shop will be up and running in a few days. I met Clodagh a few days ago and I'm trying to get to see as many people as possible." She pulled a plum cloche hat from her head, tossed back her blonde hair and held out her hand to Gill.

"I am Gill. Delighted to meet you. I love hats so I could become one of your best customers."

"That's great news. I'm afraid that I know very little about yarn but my mother would not go anywhere without at least one project. She will love browsing around here. She always says that her troubles flow out of her hands as she knits." Millie couldn't resist touching the array of yarns in the basket on the table.

"A woman after my own heart then. Would you like a coffee or tea? We have a little kitchenette back here. Ann's baking is far too tempting to be dropping over too often!" Gill explained.

"No, thanks. I have to collect some supplies in the city. Next time?"

"No problem, Millie. It will be lovely to have another business here. Clodagh will be sorry that she missed you but you can catch up with her again next time."

"I look forward to that. See you again soon." Millie picked up her umbrella.

"At least the hailstones have stopped." Gill walked to the door.

"It is very dark, even for November. See you soon Gill." Millie ran for her car.

Clodagh

Clodagh woke to the sound of banging. She was out of bed and halfway down the stairs before she realised that it was rain on the window that woken her.

"Jesus wept!" She flopped down onto the stairs. She knew that she would not be able to go back to sleep so she made her way to the kitchen and made herself a very strong cup of coffee.

Clodagh spent the next two hours cleaning the house. When she had disinfected the last surface and polished the last floor, she prepared the guest room for Gill and set out the crisps, nuts and chocolates on the dining room table. She was tempted to open one of the bottles of wine but, as she had to collect Gill in under an hour, she opted for another strong coffee instead.

It was difficult to keep the windscreen clear as Clodagh drove into Brandon Lodge to collect Gill. Most of the businesses were closed but the powerful security lights gave the place an illusion of daylight. She parked as close to Beth's Knits as she could.

Gill quickly locked up and ran to the car.

"God but this weather is terrible. Joe rang me a while ago. The rain was so heavy that their walk was cut short. They are all in front of a log fire in the hotel drinking hot whiskeys. So much for a healthy weekend! I wouldn't mind a bit of that myself." Gill laughed.

"Well your wish is my command. I put on the stove about an hour ago and you can have as many hot whiskeys as you desire." Clodagh drove out the gate, indicated and pulled out onto the road.

"I think I will stick to a few glasses of vino. Spirits are not my friends! I could tell you a story or two… if only I could remember them…" said Gill.

"I hear you," Clodagh laughed.

Gill poured the wine and opened the crisps and chocolates.

"You sure you want to talk about this? You were very quiet over dinner. I don't mind if you prefer not to go into it." She handed the glass of wine to Clodagh.

"I think I need to say it all out loud. I would appreciate your opinion."

"Okay so." Gill sipped her wine as Clodagh poked through the chocolates until she found her favourites.

"I met James Murray in Brandon Lodge when I was seventeen. It was actually on my birthday. He was a friend of my then boyfriend, Richard. James was with a large group who were celebrating some party and we hit it off straight away. We were together almost two years. We thought that we would last forever… We had even picked out an engagement ring. We were sitting in the car listening to music when he told me." She paused to pick out another chocolate. "It turned out that he had been sleeping with a girl who was part of his group of friends. To be fair, we had broken up for a little while and I suppose he was entitled to do as he pleased. She was pregnant and he was sorry."

"That must have been a terrible shock," Gill said quietly.

"He kept trying to contact me for the next few months. I had to ignore him, he was going to be a father. I heard that they had gotten married so I decided to go to London. My Aunt Lizzie was a tutor in the London College of Art and Design so she got me a place there. James went to see my mother and asked her for my address. When she refused, he asked her to forward a letter from him. He told her that it would explain everything."

"Did it?"

"I've no idea. I threw it on the fire." Clodagh sipped her drink.

"Really? I would definitely have opened it," Gill admitted.

"I was seriously tempted, but Aunt Lizzie advised me to do what my gut instinct told me to, so I did. Opening it would have forced me to reconsider the decisions that I had already made. I had come to terms with it and had made a new life. I had just met David and his family. Elizabeth needed me as well. I haven't regretted it. I never expected to see James again, and definitely didn't think that his son and Beth would become a couple! I had heard that he had a daughter but in fact, Danny is her half twin."

"You don't seem too upset about the prospect of a long-term relationship between them." Gill picked up a chocolate.

"What can I do about it? It is not like they are related. Anyway they just met. Maybe it will run its course and fizzle out. It was a weird experience. Danny was very wary of me, he kept his distance until he was certain that I was not going to remove any of his clothes!"

"What if their relationship becomes serious? You will have to consider that you could be related to James in a way you hadn't planned." Gill watched her friend closely.

"Well, I will cross that bridge when I come to it." Clodagh picked up her phone. One new message.

Clodagh sighed.

"You okay?"

"It's a message from James. He wants to meet me to explain. Story of our relationship really." She turned on the kettle.

Gill got out cups and waited for the water to boil.

"How did he get your number?" She mixed the cocoa.

"I didn't give it to him, but I have a fair idea who did!"

"The happy couple," they said in unison.

Clodagh went to the drinks cabinet and found what she was looking for.

"Here, this calls for more than cocoa." She handed Gill the cup.

"Good God! How much brandy did you put in?" Gill spluttered.

"This story calls for lots of alcohol," Clodagh laughed. "Claire and I had dinner in the hotel while Beth met Danny in town. She was going to join us for drinks later on. What we didn't know was that the Murray clan had some sort of gathering that weekend. After dinner we went into the bar for a few drinks and to wait for Beth and her beau. Claire had nipped to the loo when they arrived. As I said, I think he was a bit wary of me after the previous night's performance! He looks so like James did when I met him, except for the glasses. It was like a walk into my past. All that it was missing was my mother brandishing an apple tart! Next thing was that Danny's sister came over to our table."

"I'm Kathryn, twin sister to this lovely fellow here. He doesn't seem to want to introduce me so I decided to do it myself. I am delighted to meet you all, especially you Mrs Kenny. I love your stuff. I just got engaged so I am very interested in your bridal shrug line."

Clodagh shook her hand.

"Thank you. Please feel free to get in touch when you have decided on the type of wedding you will have. I must say that you and Danny look very alike."

"Except her beard is darker than mine!" Danny interrupted.

Kathryn glared at him.

"Would you like to join us?" Clodagh invited.

"Thanks, but I'm with my mother and my boyfriend and his parents. My Dad should have been here ages ago. I rang him but he didn't pick up. You were with him earlier Danny. Did he say anything to you about being late?"

Danny looked uncomfortable so Clodagh decided to interrupt.

"You just got engaged. That's lovely. May I see your ring? It's beautiful. I hope you will both be very happy."

"Thank you. Would you mind if I brought my mother over to meet you?"

"Jesus, Sis! Why don't you get all the neighbours while you are at it! Look, congratulations on your engagement, but would you mind going back to your in-laws?"

Kathryn glared at her brother and, for a moment, Clodagh thought that they would start an argument.

Beth put her hand on Danny's arm.

"Here comes my Aunt Claire. I'd like you both to meet her."

Claire was approaching the table but she was not alone. She stopped at a nearby table to chat to someone. The woman who was with her began to introduce Claire to the people at the table.

"That's my mother with your sister. You may as well meet her since she knows your sister already!" she smirked at Danny.

When Kathryn's mother reached Clodagh, she didn't look very happy at all.

"Wow! It's Kate, from April. What a small world. So lovely to see you again." Beth hugged her as Danny and Kathryn looked confused.

Clodagh walked over and sat next to Gill on the couch.

"I wasn't too pleased to be officially meeting the woman that had stolen my life, but since I couldn't pretend that I didn't recognise her, I had to shake her hand. She had changed a lot in the past thirty years so I wouldn't have known her back in April. She went back to her own table with Kathryn. I excused myself to go to the bathroom. I just wanted to get away from all of them for a few minutes."

I sat in the foyer to pull myself together. The front door opened and in came James. Most of the chairs were empty and I was sitting between him and the bar. He seemed to be drunk which surprised me. He walked passed me, stopped and turned around."

"You been stood up again, pretty girl? The first time I saw you, you were also sitting in front of a mirror. I've never loved anyone like I loved and still, love you. How have you been?" he slurred.

"He said the exact words that he had used thirty years before. It was a step too far." Clodagh drained her glass and spluttered as the liquid hit her throat.

"What happened then?" Gill asked quietly.

"I always thought that I could handle any situation. I prided myself on being cool. I couldn't help it. I slapped him. It was so out of character of me but I had attacked a second Murray in under twenty-four hours!"

"Wow! How did he react to that?"

Clodagh looked sheepish. "He almost fell over, though I suspect that it was the alcohol, rather than the wallop, was more responsible for that. I grabbed him by the arm and pushed him down onto the couch. Thankfully it was the most secluded corner of the foyer, so I don't think that anyone noticed. We sat in silence for a few minutes. Eventually he spoke."

"I'm so sorry, Clodagh. I never thought that we would meet again. I didn't recognise the name of your shop in Brandon Lodge. I called in there once and assumed that the woman who worked there was the owner," he said

Gill stood up and staggered a little towards the kitchen.

"I think, Clodagh Kenny that you are talking about James Murray with more than a hint of pity in your voice. Maybe you and he will get a happy ending after all!"

"Afraid not Gill, because then his wife arrived and all hell broke loose."

Danny & Pamela

Danny had a feeling that Pamela would not react well to the news that Beth was back in his life. They had always agreed that their relationship was a stopgap until one of them met someone that they wanted to be with. Deep down he knew that Pamela hoped for more than he was prepared to give. He hated the thought of hurting her but she would be hurt even more if she heard it from Angela or one of the others. She was away for the weekend so hopefully he would get to tell her himself. He had arranged to pick her up from the train station at seven o'clock. Danny waited in the car.

Just before the train pulled into the station Pamela checked her phone. One missed call from Angela and a message from Danny telling her that he was waiting in the car park. She rang Angela back but it went to voicemail.

She would ring her later. She couldn't wait to tell Danny all about the hen party. Her cousin Helen was getting married in a few weeks' time and she hoped that maybe Danny would enjoy the wedding so much that he would even consider getting engaged. He was a little commitment phobic but she was certain that she could change that. The beautiful house that he wanted to buy would make the perfect family home for them.

The train pulled in on time and Pamela dragged her case to the carpark. She spotted Danny's Jaguar and pulled open the passenger door.

"Hi Danny! Thanks for picking me up. It was a great weekend." She threw her arms around him and hugged him.

"Hi Pamela, glad you had a nice time. Would you like to go for a drink or straight home? I need to talk to you about something. It's important." He started the engine.

"I've had enough drink to sink a small ship so why don't we just make coffee in your place. I could stay tonight. I'm not working tomorrow. Off until Wednesday." She smiled at him.

"Actually I'm staying at the farm with my mother tonight. She wants me to look over the accounts for her and tonight suits us both. I told her that I would be there before nine."

"Oh, okay. My place it is. We still have nearly two hours." She trailed her hand up his leg.

"Jesus, Pamela. I'm trying to drive." Danny said crossly.

"You never minded before," she retorted.

"It's raining and the roads are slippery. You want to get home in one piece." His tone softened. They travelled in silence for a few minutes.

"Here we are. You go on in. I must make a call. I'll bring in your case." He turned off the engine and waited for Pamela to leave the car. He watched her walk up the steps, open the front door and switch on the light.

He had promised Beth that he would let her know how things went with Pamela, but he needed to hear her voice.

She answered immediately.

"Hi Danny, how did it go with Pamela? I really hate the thought of her being hurt. I hope she understood."

"I haven't told her yet. She is so happy after her weekend. I am dreading telling her but we had run our course before I met you again. I will ring you later tonight. Miss you already. I have never felt this way before. I can't wait to see you again."

"Neither can I. Good luck. Talk later then." Beth hung up.

Pamela had made coffee and a sandwich by the time he walked into the apartment.

"Here you are. Thank God I had the heating on timer. It's bloody freezing tonight. You must tell me all about your weekend. How did the gig go on Friday night? I'm delighted for Kathryn and Anthony. Are they getting married soon? Between my cousin and your sister, we will have a busy time with weddings. I presume we will be invited to Angela's one as well. God, we will have to invite… Are you okay Danny? You look worried," she continued.

"Pamela, I need to tell you something. Please sit down." he pleaded.

She knew that he thought that it was over.

Chapter Seventeen

Kate
"Hi Kate, can I come in?"

"Please come back later, Pat. I've a bit of a headache," she lied.

"I've been doing that for three days. I am not leaving until you let me in. This time I came prepared. I have sandwiches and a flask," he joked.

He heard the key being turned.

"Hope you don't think I am speaking out of turn here Kate but I've never lied to you and I am not going to start now. I've been sent in to gauge the atmosphere. Your children are waiting for my call. All a bit mysterious. To tell you the truth I am a bit worried about you myself. You were so happy on Saturday and now you are hiding out in your kitchen in your nightwear." His comfort zone had just been shattered and in spite of herself, Kate laughed.

"You are such a gentleman, Pat, always have been. You would be shocked if you knew the truth about me. I suppose I knew that what I did would come back to haunt me some day."

"Whatever happened is over and you are much too strong to be sitting here worrying about things that cannot be changed. I'm risking my job here but you need to get your act together and face the music. Clear the air and move on. You dealt with your old man, you can sort this one out as well."

Kate was gobsmacked. She watched him as he put some bread in the toaster. She twisted her 'wedding' ring but remained silent as he buttered the toast.

"You have no idea what a fool I've been. I made a holy show of myself and embarrassed both my children in front of people that were very important to them. As for James…"

"To hell with James. That man has been nothing but a thorn in all our sides for the past thirty years. The only good to come out of that relationship was the birth of Danny and Kathryn. James Murray never deserved you. If it hadn't been for him..." He picked up the teapot and banged it down on the table.

He pulled out the chair opposite her and sat down.

"I do know what happened on Saturday night. Danny and Kathryn are worried about you but I told them to give you a little time to sort yourself out. You are a sensible woman."

"If you only knew how stupid and spiteful I really am," she sobbed.

Pat went to the cupboard and took down the bottle of whiskey. He poured a little into each cup.

"Come on Kate, drink up and then tell me your side of the story. Talking about it will make things clearer. Start at the beginning."

She sipped her drink and began to talk.

"It all started back in April when Danny was at a wedding in the hotel and met a girl that he liked. He told me all about her on the day after the wedding. He really wanted to see her again. I was pleased for him, until I realised who she was... Clodagh Kenny's daughter," she paused.

"How did you discover that? You were not at that wedding," Pat asked.

"I met her the following day," Kate told Pat the story.

"You see, I never told Danny about it. I didn't want any connection with that family. It worked until Saturday night. The mortification began when I was introduced to Clodagh and Beth Kenny. They both recognised me from April and Beth was so pleased that she started telling everyone how I had saved her life!

Her mother just stood there in silence. It must have been her worst nightmare come true. I escaped back to my own table as quickly as I could. To steady my nerves, I gulped back a large glass of wine and it went straight to my head. We had been trying to contact James all evening but he wasn't answering his phone. Anthony's parents were driving me mad so I had another glass for good measure. I'm not much of a drinker so you can imagine what my humour was like by the time I was on my third glass of wine.

When Anthony's mother complained to the waiter about the temperature of the wine, I had to excuse myself before I stuffed her head into the ice bucket. I was going to ring James again, as he was an hour and a half late. I needed to use the bathroom but I had seen Clodagh leave the bar a few minutes before so I didn't want to bump into her." She paused to finish her tea.

"While I was walking across the hall, I heard James talking. He was sitting with Clodagh. They couldn't see me but I could hear every word. The two of them together, just like old times."

She shivered and Pat took a jacket and placed it around her shoulders.

"You don't have to tell me this Kate. I'm here to make sure you are alright. If this is torturing you, then let it be. It must have been a shock to you, so whatever happened, don't be too hard on yourself. I'm sure he deserved it," Pat assured her.

"You don't like James very much, do you Pat?" Kate smiled.

"I would trust him to safeguard my property. As a father he is not too bad but he loves those two and would die for them. I hate what he does to you. You deserve so much better than him. I always hoped that, if circumstances had been different, that you and I... But that discussion is for another day."

"Look Pat, I said earlier that you would not like me much if you knew the truth. James is not who you think he is at all. The truth is that I ruined his chances of happiness and I did it on purpose. I knew that he loved her, she was all he spoke of. I caught him at a vulnerable moment and took advantage. I slept with him because I thought I was already pregnant and I needed a father." She noted the shock on Pat's face.

"It turned out that I wasn't pregnant. I slept with James with the intention of passing the child off as his. The irony was that I did get pregnant that night and James was the father. When I heard that Clodagh had gone to London, I thought that I could live with the guilt, but I couldn't, especially when I discovered that

I was having twins. I got it into my head that something would go wrong if I didn't tell the truth. James was shocked. I told him that he was free to go to her. I know he wrote to her but I don't know if she ever answered. He stood by me. He is a special person. So you see Pat, I am the villain here, not him. I ruined his life. Any more of that tea going? It is cold in here. I have the fire on in the other room – that is if you still want to speak to me." She looked at him hopefully.

"Of course I do. It is not my place to judge anyone. You were young and in a terrible situation. Your father was an evil bastard. You go on in and I will make more tea."

A few minutes later Kate continued with her story.

"As I stood behind the partition, I could hear every word. I could sense that he had been drinking, which to be fair to him, is out of character. He said. 'You have been stood up again, pretty girl. I've never loved anyone like I loved, still love you. How have you been?'

"Oh Kate. I'm sorry. You sure you want to go on?" Pat was concerned.

"It was actually quite funny. I had to hear her answer, but all I heard was the sound of a slap. He almost fell but she must have grabbed him. I really needed to use the bathroom but I was rooted to the spot until I saw Anthony's mother tottering towards us. I dashed into the function room behind me and waited for a few minutes," she paused.

"When I came out I resumed my eavesdropping. He was telling her how he would have followed her to London. It was so sad, it broke my heart. I remembered a line of the letter that he had written to her. 'I would give anything to have you in my life. You are my life.'"

I didn't even realise that I had spoken out loud. James paled and I knew I'd gone too far.

"I don't understand. Why would those words have such an effect on him?" Pat asked.

"Those words came from the letter that he had written to her. I was in the office a few days after I told him the truth. James wasn't there and his father was very vague about where he had gone. When I was alone for a few minutes, I started tidying the desk and found the open envelope with her name on it. There was no address. I wanted to see what he had written so I quickly made a copy before his Dad came back in. He loved her and only her. I never stood a chance."

"He loved you too. You got married."

"We never married, Pat. I would gladly have taken his name. This ring is just a ring. It's only a symbol of my stupidity and of what a horrible person I was. Now that he knows that I read the letter, James will probably never speak to me again. Danny knows that I kept Beth from him and Kathryn thinks I embarrassed her in front of her in-laws. All in all, I've made a proper pig's ear of the whole thing."

"I'm sure it will be alright. What did you do with the letter?"

"I still have it. Why do you ask?" She looked puzzled.

"Maybe it is time to get rid of it and move on with your life. It was written by a young man facing fatherhood. You said yourself that you offered him a way out. To his credit, he didn't take it. Though you may have to tell the children the truth about your non-marriage, it will save any confusion later," he smiled.

"You are right. They should know. Though I don't know what you mean by confusion. It's not like I will be getting married anytime soon," she attempted a smile.

"Well you might. That is if you would ever consider someone who has had feelings for you for years. If I had known all this before, I would have declared my intentions a long time ago," he blushed.

A week had passed since the events at the Quayside. Kate had spoken to Kathryn and Danny. They had been shocked by the fact that their parents had never married. She didn't go into the details, she felt that it was up to James to tell them his side of the story. She hadn't spoken to him. He had gone to a conference in London with Conor. He was probably avoiding her and she couldn't really blame him. Conor had texted her on Wednesday and told her that they were staying longer than planned. They would not be back until Monday. Her planned conversation with James would have to wait.

Danny

Danny should have been on cloud nine but he still felt very guilty about Pamela. He had been amazed at her reaction. She had burst into tears and begged him not to leave her. He had tried to remind her that they had agreed that their relationship was never meant to be serious or permanent but she was having none of it. She had totally overreacted when he had mentioned Beth and had thrown a plate at him. Thankfully it had missed. He had been so worried that he had called Angela and she had promised to go over to the apartment.

He had learned a lot over the past week. The fact that his parents had never married didn't affect him as much as it would have a few years earlier. It had actually explained a lot. He knew that there was a lot more to the story than he had been told and Clodagh Kenny had a huge part to play in it. It explained why his mother hadn't told him about meeting Beth back in April. She had actually thought that Beth could have been his sister! Once that had been sorted out, she had been okay with him seeing Beth.

His father was another matter. He had been very upset and had acted completely out of character. Danny knew that James and Conor were still in London and he wondered if he should ring him.

"Danny Murray. How may I help you?"

"Hi Danny, Barney here. Your offer on Hillside Manor has been accepted. We can meet to tie up any loose ends in the next few days. Good luck with your new home and I hope that you will be very happy there."

"Thanks so much, Barney. I am free whenever you are. Let me know when suits you."

"Will do, Danny. Talk soon."

He put down the phone and punched the air.

He had been right to take his father's advice. Barney Smith had accepted his offer and Hillside Manor was finally his, and for a lot less than the asking price. He couldn't wait to tell his Dad and Beth.

He dialled his father's number. James was thrilled with the news and promised to meet him the following evening to celebrate. Beth was back at work so he decided to wait until later to give her the good news.

He was about to lock up when he saw Pamela walking up the steps to his office.

"Hi Danny, may I come in for a few minutes?" She looked unsure.

"Yes, of course. Are you okay? You look a bit pale. Can I get you a cup of tea or coffee?"

"No, thanks. I am fine. I hoped that we could talk about us. I realise that maybe I was getting a little ahead of myself, dragging you past every jewellery shop in Killarney. I just hoped that we could be a proper couple. I love you, Danny. I'm sorry for being so possessive. I will change if you will give me another chance. I know that we agreed that our relationship was not supposed to be serious. It was fine in the beginning but then I fell in love with you," she appealed to him.

"Look Pamela. I know that I hurt you and I am so sorry, but it will never work. I have met someone else. I'm so sorry. You are a great person and I know that you will meet someone that will truly deserve you."

"I know that I scared you, Danny. I shouldn't have thrown the plate at you. I didn't mean to," she pleaded.

"I deserved some anger from you but you went mental. Frankly, you scared me. It is not the first time that you've lost it. You need to find a safer outlet for your anger."

She grabbed the edge of the desk in an effort to control herself.

"You are right, Danny. I do get angry sometimes, but I had just been dumped by the man I had expected to spend the rest of my life with, so cut me some slack. I know that you think that you are in love with that Beth, but it's me that you really love. I will prove it to you if you give me another chance." She moved towards him.

"Whoa, wait a minute, Pamela. Think this through. I'm really sorry but I am not in love with you. I never meant to hurt you but we were never right for each other. We had good times together but we both knew that it would not last forever. Please accept that and we can move on with our lives."

"You mean so that you and Miss Goody Two Shoes can live happily ever after in Hillside Manor. That should have been our house!" she snarled.

Danny was shocked. "What do you know about Hillside Manor?"

She paled slightly. After all she had been told that in confidence by Angela who worked with her father Barney.

"You told me ages ago that you wanted to buy it and I presumed that you did," she recovered quickly.

Danny wasn't convinced. He would ring Barney back as soon as Pamela left and find out if he had told his daughter. Until the deal was signed, sealed and delivered, he didn't want anyone outside his family knowing anything about it.

"Look Pamela, let's just leave this conversation here. I have to meet a client in about thirty minutes so I have to get the paperwork sorted out before then." He began to shuffle papers on his desk.

"Ok, as long as you agree to come over to my place later so we can talk some more," she added hopefully.

He walked around the table and placed his hands gently on her shoulders.

"Look Pamela, I don't want to hurt you, but it is over. I don't know how many more ways that I can say this. We are not a couple anymore. It is over. It is finished. There is no more us. Please don't do this." He finished gently.

She turned towards the door, but paused and turned back towards him.

"I hoped that it wouldn't come to this. It will never be over between us, Danny, not as long as I am the mother of your unborn child. I will be waiting for you later. Be there or I will have to tell your precious Beth just what a rat you are!" she slammed the door as she left.

Pamela

Back in her apartment Pamela was tempted to fill a very large glass with gin and swallow it back. When Danny would turn up later, and she was certain that he would, then her smelling of drink would make him suspicious.

He would find out just what Pamela was capable of in order to get what she wanted and that English bitch could go to hell.

She needed to back up her claims with some facts. She dialled Angela's number. As she waited for her friend to answer, she turned on Google and typed in Clodagh Kenny.

James

James was back in the office. He had a lot to catch up on. Conor had persuaded him to stay in London for a few days in order to let the dust settle. He didn't feel any better about his performance the previous week. He had made a right ass of himself. He hadn't heard from Clodagh and he couldn't really blame her. He would give her a few more days to reply to his message, then he would have to go and see her... Sober and sorry. He would beg her to hear him out and if she wanted nothing more to do with him, then he would respect her decision.

Kate was a different matter. She had betrayed his trust by reading the letter that he had written to Clodagh. If that wasn't bad enough, she had quoted it at the hotel. Clodagh would think that he had shared its contents with Kate. The letter had only been in the drawer overnight while he found up the courage to visit Clodagh's mother and beg her for the address. He could not forgive Kate for that.

She had texted him a few times begging him to let her explain but so far he hadn't replied. Until he could figure out a way to move forward from this, then he couldn't face her. On the one hand he was very angry that she had looked at something so private and on the other he was deeply ashamed of how his words must have made her feel. She was an excellent mother to Danny and Kathryn and he respected her a lot. They had become friends over the years but he couldn't love her in the way she had wanted him to. His heart had been given away in Brandon Lodge the night that he had first set eyes on Clodagh Kenny. Kate had tricked him and it had taken him years to come to terms with it. He knew that she had to get away from her father or he would have killed her. Maybe he should meet her. He had no more to lose now and they would have to present a united front for Kathryn's wedding in March.

On a lighter note he had been delighted with the call from Danny about Hillside Manor. He was pleased for his son but relieved that Danny had not mentioned Beth Kenny. He now knew that she was not Clodagh's daughter and consequently not his and so he had no reason to object to their relationship. In fact, the longer it continued, the more chance James had of winning back Clodagh.

Kathryn dropped into the office on her way home from work. She hugged him and told him that he was the best father in the world and that she loved him. He had felt his eyes smarting. He was very proud of both of his children and wanted the best for them. He knew that times had changed and that what had happened to him and Kate would never happen to them. Young people were much more careful now so he had nothing to worry about.

Chapter Eighteen

Joe
"Jesus Joe. If I didn't know the car, then I wouldn't have recognised you. You look like a pull through for a rifle! Is that wife of yours starving you or what? Imagine it's nearly December. Another year over!" Matt settled himself in the back seat.

"I know. Time goes faster each year. How are you doing without the smokes?" Joe pulled out of the airport taxi rank.

"So-so," Matt shifted uncomfortably.

"You mean you haven't managed to stay off them," Joe looked in the rear-view mirror.

"I'm doing really well. It's the social occasions that get to me. I've had a few but I'm really trying not to smoke. Since that scare I realise how much I like living."

"Why don't you come back to our house for a bite to eat? Gill left a stew in the oven." Joe asked.

"That sounds great. The food on the plane was awful... the box it came in looked more appealing." Matt answered.

The aroma of spices, fruit and whiskey hit them as they entered the house.

"I see the Christmas cake marathon has started!" Matt inhaled deeply.

"Yeah, it definitely smells like Christmas. Those cake ingredients have been soaking there for the past few days. Gill keeps adding whiskey and rum. I can't wait for the finished product." Joe took off his jacket and headed for the kitchen.

"Talking of Christmas?" Matt followed Joe and began to set the table.

"Oh poor little rich guy. You know the invitation stands. You will have dinner with us as usual." Joe lifted the dish from the oven and placed it on the counter.

"Thanks, Joe. I'll bring the wine and dessert. I still make a mean Bailey's cheesecake. By the way I want to show you the paperwork for that job in Galway. It's in my office at home. Are you free tomorrow night? We could take care of business first and make a night of it." Matt took the steaming plate from Joe.

"I don't see why not. We can go for a few drinks and a bite to eat. Will I meet you somewhere in town?" Joe sat opposite Matt and picked up his fork.

"No, I will pick you up. I haven't seen Gill for a while. I would love to see some of the toy bears that she has been making for the fundraiser. She told me about it last week when I bumped into her in town. She might even make me one if I throw in a few bob for the school. This stew is fabulous. Is Gill working late again?" Matt asked.

"No, she is actually out with Caroline. Something wedding related. I will let her know that you are coming. She is really enjoying making those bears and David McGovern is delighted that Brandon Lodge is getting involved with the local community. Want more stew?"

"No, thanks. This is fine. I hate to eat and run but I have a meeting at eight this evening. A house clearance. It's always sad when houses have to be sold. I knew this woman. She has a library of books like none that I have ever seen before. I must give Robert a ring. He knows more about books than I do. Paintings and furniture are more my thing." Matt stood up, rinsed his plate and put it into the dishwasher.

"Leave the rest, I am in for the night. Ring me tomorrow and let me know what time I should expect you." Joe stood up.

"Thanks Joe. See you tomorrow." Matt retrieved his jacket from the bannister at the end of the stairs.

"Night, Matt."

After Matt had left Joe settled down in front of the television with the evening paper. He was woken by the sound of the front door closing.

"Oh hi love. I must have fallen asleep. What time is it?" He stretched and picked up the newspaper that had fallen on the floor.

"It's half ten. Caroline is up to ninety about colour schemes and place settings. I swear that she is turning into bridezilla!" She flopped down beside him and kicked off her heels.

"It won't be long now. In a few weeks it will be New Year's Eve. Matt was here earlier. I shared the stew with him. He was delighted with it. I am meeting him here tomorrow evening. He wants to donate to your teddy fundraiser." Joe told her.

"That's great. Every bit helps. A few more of the units are getting in on the act as well. Do you remember me telling you about Millie, the milliner? Well she is donating a fabulous hat to the raffle. She is also planning on running a few courses in the New Year. I might join. I think I would like to try my hand at hat making. If only I could fix things for Clodagh and Beth, then life would be wonderful!" she sighed.

"Things still not sorted then?" Joe asked.

"No. Clodagh is worried about Beth. She is still threatening to go to Australia. One of her college friends was doing very well out there and Beth could stay with her. The whole situation is a repeat of what had happened to Clodagh herself thirty years before. The fact that it was all caused by another Murray was the nail in the coffin," Gill said.

"Poor Clodagh. I really hope that things work out for all of them. Danny seemed like a nice lad when I met him that evening when they called here. I have a feeling that they will be fine. You are a good friend to Clodagh so just keep listening to her," he advised.

"It is hard to see her suffering. I hope she doesn't leave Brandon Lodge," she answered.

"Do you think she might? Tea?" Joe stood up.

"Yeah. Thanks. I don't know but I think that she is considering it. On top of that I discovered that Caroline is a character in the whole saga!"

"What do you mean?" Joe was intrigued.

"Well, the man that she had been dating was none other than the same James Murray. It also turns out that he and Kate Cashman had never actually been married. She has just become engaged to someone else. You really couldn't make it up. Caroline's involvement really put the tin hat on the whole drama," Gill said.

"Wow. It does seem to be a complicated story," Joe laughed.

"If you read it in a book, you wouldn't believe it. I think I might pass on the tea. I am shattered. I think I will just go to bed. Will you be staying up long?" she yawned.

"No, I will be up as soon as I drink my tea. I'll lock up. Don't worry too much about Clodagh. She is one tough lady and she has been there before. She will be okay." He kissed her on the cheek.

"Hopefully. See you soon. Night."

Gill fell asleep hoping that Joe was right about Clodagh.

Gill's thoughts were interrupted by the ringing of the doorbell.

"Hi Matt, Joe is in the shower. Want a coffee while you wait for him?"

"No thanks, Gill. I am okay. How have you been? Joe tells me that you are very busy with lots of new interests."

"My life has changed completely in the past nine months. Brandon Lodge has been very good to me. I have made lots of new friends and am even teaching children how to knit. It's great. I can't believe that it is December already. Joe tells me that you will be joining us for Christmas," said Gill.

"Thanks for the invitation, Gill. I appreciate it. Christmas is a lonely bloody time. I will do my signature cheesecake." Matt sat on the couch.

"I love that cheesecake. Looking forward to it. Thanks again for the fabulous weekend away. The hotel was unreal. I could learn to live like that. Joe must be washing himself away. I'll put the kettle on." Gill put her knitting on the cushion beside her.

"He must be putting his glad rags on! We were thinking of going to that new tapas bar. Would you like to join us?"

"Thanks, Matt. I have this batch of teddies to finish. I'm actually dreaming of red and white bears!"

Matt picked one up. "This is really beautiful. Could I buy it? My niece, Peggy, would love it. You can put the money in the school kitty. I will give it to Joe. I must drop the car home. Joe insists that we walk from my place into town. That man is obsessed with exercise! Speak of the devil, here he is now."

"Evening Matt. I heard that last comment. If you threw a stone from your gate it would land in the middle of Patrick Street so stop complaining. I will be ready in five minutes." Joe grabbed his phone and headed back upstairs.

"How is Caroline these days? I heard that her old man bought her a wreck of the hotel out in the sticks for her birthday."

"Actually she is doing a great job with it. She has amazing plans for it and she is very happy. I don't know why you don't seem to like her." Gill glared at Matt.

"Sorry, Gill. I'm delighted for her. Oh here is the man of the moment." Matt was saved any further explanation as Joe walked into the room.

"See you later, love. Don't work too hard." Joe bent down and kissed her on the lips.

Matt waved.

She was still knitting when Joe arrived back home.

"Matt asked me to give you this. It's for the teddy he wants," Joe sat down beside her.

"That's great. I charged him twenty euros. I feel a bit guilty but it is for a good cause. He didn't have to put it in an envelope." She tore it open.

"Oh my God! It is a cheque for a thousand euros."

Margaret Kelleher

Chapter Nineteen

Clodagh

Clodagh couldn't believe that so much had happened in a few weeks. It was almost Christmas and her whole world had gone pear-shaped.

She could have lived with Beth falling for Danny Murray if things had worked out between them.

After her encounter with James and his family, she had tried to keep it together for Beth's sake. If Danny Murray was the one that Beth wanted to spend her life with, then Clodagh, James and his wife would just have to lump it. Only things hadn't worked out quite like that. For starters it was a shock to discover that James and Kate were not actually married. She had found this out when Beth told her that Danny's mother was getting married to the farm manager.

Clodagh had just about digested this information when she had a visit from the girl that Danny was seeing when he found Beth again. She said Danny had dumped her because she was pregnant. Clodagh could not take it in. It was like a rerun of what had happened thirty years previously! Whoever said that the apple doesn't fall far from the tree certainly knew what he was talking about. To be fair to Danny, he had told Beth about the pregnancy as soon as Pamela had told him. Danny didn't deny that the baby was his. He was not going to shirk his responsibilities but he didn't see any reason why he and Beth could not continue to be a couple. Beth decided that she needed some time to decide what to do and had gone back to their house in London.

Clodagh hoped that once Beth had a few days to think about things, that she would come home and deal with the situation. It was not as if times had not changed. The family unit had changed completely in the past thirty years. Danny could still be a hands on father without marrying Pamela.

Beth was struggling to come to terms with the whole thing. She had known that Danny had been seeing Pamela. She was confused. She knew that her feelings were unreasonable. Danny was a free agent when he had fathered that child. She had decided that she would give him some space in order to make the right decision. She was due to go to London to meet with some new designers that the shop was considering stocking. So Beth was back in Aunt Lizzie's house in London. David and Mike had promised to keep an eye on her. She had asked Danny not to contact her. She needed time to sort things out in her head. She decided to ring Clodagh as she had promised to keep in touch.

"Hi Mom, how are you?"

"Hi Beth, I am doing okay. How does it feel to be back in Aunt Lizzie's house?"

"It is just as it was. The agency is doing a great job of taking care of it and David or Mike inspect it every week. I'm sorry I scared you with my talk about going to Australia. I might come back here though. Mike is opening another three boutiques in London. I can manage them if I want the job. What do you think?" Beth asked.

"I want you to be happy. I will support you in whatever decision you make. Will you be coming home for Christmas? That party in the hotel had been organised so I will have to attend," Clodagh told her.

"I am not sure. I don't want you to spend Christmas alone so you might come over for a few days. We could have Christmas here in the house. David and Mike said that they would come. I want you to be happy too. It's okay with me if you and James get together. I mean that."

"Thanks, Beth. I don't think we are meant to be together but I am fine with that. Gill is calling later. We are going to get a takeaway and have a few drinks. She is staying over so it should be a good laugh. We will go to work together in the morning. I will talk to you again tomorrow. Love you."

"Love you too, Mom. Talk soon."

Thank God she was not rostered to work today. Clodagh knew that Gill and Ann were worried about her and Beth. Poor Gill would never make a poker player; she couldn't bluff to save her life! It had happened a few days before in the shop. Clodagh had received another message from James. She had asked Gill for her opinion.

"He looked like a nice enough man when Caroline pointed him out to me." She stopped talking and went tomato red.

"I didn't know that you had met him. What has Caroline got to do with James?" Clodagh was curious.

"I never actually met him but she had bumped into him at the Farmer's Market. They met a few times." Gill was mortified.

"And?" Clodagh prompted.

"They became friends." She looked away.

"Friends?" Clodagh echoed.

"Yes. They dated for a while. It is over now though. Caroline is back with Dylan, as you know."

"So what you are trying not to say is that Caroline and James were sleeping together."

Gill could only nod. Clodagh burst out laughing.

Gill looked at her for a few seconds, then joined in. Both women laughed and laughed until tears ran down their faces.

"This whole soap opera just gets weirder by the day." Clodagh began to tidy the baskets and sort the patterns. Both women worked side by side, each lost in her own thoughts.

Clodagh shook herself. It was almost seven o'clock. Gill would be here soon and she had lots to do.

Much later, when Gill had gone to bed, Clodagh tried to sort things out in her mind. The events of the past few weeks refused to leave her thoughts. When Gill had told her about James and her friend Caroline, she had reacted by laughing. In the dark of her bedroom, it didn't seem quite so funny. On a practical level, she had to admit that James was entitled to see anyone he wanted to. Up to a few weeks ago they hadn't seen each other in thirty years. Yet the thoughts of him wrapped around some other woman brought back memories that she didn't want to revisit. Then there was Kate Cashman. What had she been playing at back in April? She had definitely known who Clodagh was. She could have said, especially when Clodagh had invited her to lunch. She had declined the invitation. She had brought Beth safely back to the hotel and for that alone, Clodagh would be forever grateful to her. Beth had wandered into an area of The National Park that was only known to locals. It would have been ages before she would have been found.

Then there was Danny who was the image of his father. Beth had only taken a few minutes to fall for his charms and had been convinced that Aunt Lizzie had sent him to her, using her jewellery as a way of getting them together. The old woman was still trying to match make from the grave. What Clodagh didn't get was that the man Lizzie had chosen for Beth was a Murray. Lizzie had never hurt a soul while she was alive. Why would she do this to Clodagh now? She was always one to think outside the box, but this made no sense.

Then came Robert with the kiss. Poor man. She had gotten over any notions she had harboured about him and her becoming a couple. Maria was much more his type. Thankfully they had resolved their differences. The kiss had been explained, Robert's wife had passed away suddenly and when he had seen Clodagh on the floor, for a split second he had seen his wife. Poor Robert.

Last of all, James. She so wished that she could say that his reappearance into her life meant nothing to her. It meant everything. She had never stopped loving him. A few days after the opening, she discovered that he was not married and that Kate was going to marry her farm manager. Her hopes had soared, Beth and Danny, Kate and Pat and Clodagh and James. All living happily ever after. That dream lasted until the girl that Danny had been seeing announced that she was pregnant and the dream shattered.

Clodagh looked at the clock, two am. She needed some sleep. She had a group of students coming in tomorrow for a class in wool felting and Gill was due to go to the local school to see how the teddies were coming along. It would be a busy day. Just before she dropped off to sleep, Aunt Lizzie crept into her thoughts.

"Outside the box, Clodagh. Go for it, lass. You are not getting any younger!" she chuckled.

Straight to the point as usual.

Pamela

Pamela couldn't believe her luck.

She might actually be able to pull this off after all. If Angela agreed to help her then she would have the proof that Danny had demanded.

"You always said that you would stick pins in your own eyes rather than ruin your figure by getting pregnant. You have your phone programmed to beep the time to take your pill and you always insisted on condoms. It's pretty damned convenient that you suddenly find yourself pregnant a few days after we break up. Quite frankly Pamela, I don't believe you. If it is true, then prove it. I want to see the pregnancy test result." Danny had stormed out of her apartment and slammed the door.

That had happened three days ago. He had called her bluff. That might have the end of it if she hadn't remembered meeting Angela lurking outside the chemist shop earlier in the week. She was waiting for her neighbour to leave before she went in to buy a pregnancy test.

"You okay, Ange? You look like you are casing the place! Are you planning to come back later to rob it?" she joked.

"You are not far wrong there. I need to buy a pregnancy test and I'm waiting for Mollie Harrington to come out. She is the biggest gossip in Kerry. You work here, I don't suppose you would go in there and get me a few? I need to know if my wedding dress will still fit me. If you do this this, I will definitely owe you one. Anything you want, just ask." She pleaded with Pamela.

"No problem. How many do you want?" Pamela replied.

Ten minutes later the two women were in Pamela's bathroom. The first and second tests were both positive.

"Congratulations!" Pamela hugged her.

Angela was delighted.

"I'm getting married on New Year's Eve so I will get away with the dress as long as I don't stuff my face in the meantime. Shane will be delighted but keep it to yourself until after the wedding. Thanks so much for buying the tests. Remember, I owe you one." Angela said.

Danny

Danny decided to confide in his father. James listened to his son and his heart fell. It was a carbon copy of his own life thirty years before.

"When did she first suspect that she was pregnant?" James asked.

"Just after we broke up. I thought she was making it up so I asked for proof. I haven't heard anything from her since so I presume that it was a false alarm. I wanted you to know just in case you heard it from anyone else. You know what this place is like for gossip and Gertie is close to Pamela's family," Danny said.

"I presume that you have told your mother. Gertie calls over most days," James replied.

"I did. She gave me a lecture but since Pamela is not pregnant…"

"Hopefully not. If you do not love her then staying together is not a good idea." James signalled for another round of drinks.

"Well, I asked her to prove it and thankfully I haven't heard from her since. She was bluffing. I had to tell Beth. I couldn't keep something like this from her. I love Beth. If Pamela is pregnant then I will be there for my child as well."

James put his arm around his only son.

"Whatever happens, it will sort itself out. It is not like the old days when shotguns were produced by irate fathers. If Pamela is pregnant then let her know that you will be there for her but that you love someone else. After all, Beth knew that you were seeing Pamela," James assured Danny.

"Thanks, Dad. You know that I think that she actually knew that I was after buying Hillside Manor. Probably heard it from

Barney's daughter Angela. Those two are as thick as thieves. The fact that Pamela won't be living there with me probably pissed her off and sparked the whole pregnancy thing," Danny said.

"She will get over it. Try not to worry," James reassured his son.

"Thanks again, Dad. It's good to know that you are always there for me."

"I always will be, son."

James

James hadn't mentioned to Danny that he had arranged to meet Clodagh the following day. It might not turn out well considering his drunken state at the Quayside Hotel. He had told her that he was due to do a routine check in Brandon Lodge and they had agreed to meet in the wool shop. They needed to discuss the fact that Danny and Beth had declared undying love for each other. He wondered how that latest twist would affect things.

Pamela

"Jesus, Pamela. I can't do that. It would be so wrong. Even if I said yes, how do you suppose that you could get away with it? You are not pregnant." Angela was shocked.

"It doesn't matter. I know that there is no chance of getting back with Danny but if I can't have him then neither can she. It will be months before I have to think about that. Hopefully by then Beth Kenny will have legged it back to London and their relationship will be history." Pamela could see that Angela was not convinced.

"I don't want to do this, Pamela. It is wrong. You will destroy lots of lives. Why not just give up? Remember what happened last time? You don't want to go back into that place again!" Angela pleaded.

"You owe me one, Angela. Now I am collecting. I will not end up in that hospital again. I am perfectly sane. This is different." She raised her voice.

"Pamela, please think about this!"

"I will ring him in the morning. I'll let you know what time. I have the test. All you have to do is show up. This time tomorrow you won't owe me anything." Pamela's tone scared Angela.

Danny & Pamela

Danny was having a good day. He had managed to sell two properties and had earned a nice commission for himself. Beth had phoned to say that she was coming home in a few days and she promised to meet him. Hopefully by then Pamela would have come clean about the fake pregnancy and leave him alone. He hadn't heard from her since he had looked for proof.

"Shit. Speak of the devil!"

Pamela strode into the office.

"Hi Danny, you wanted proof. Come over to the apartment later and I will give you the results of this test. You can hold on to it until then, just in case you accuse me of cheating." She handed him one of two identical pregnancy tests that she had just purchased. The second one was safely stored at the bottom of her new Orla Kiely bag.

"See you later, Daddy. Doesn't that have a nice ring to it? Seven sharp." She turned on her heel and left.

Back in her apartment Pamela rang Angela.

"I have told Danny to be here at seven. You come over at a quarter to so that we can go over our story. I will even cook you a curry, even though cooking is against my religion." Pamela attempted to put Angela at ease as she knew she had freaked the other girl out the evening before. She needed Angela to make her plan work.

When Danny rang the doorbell he was surprised when Angela answered the door.

"Pamela is feeling sick. She is in the bathroom. I'll just go and see if she is okay." Angela looked very uneasy.

Danny sat on the couch and waited. Angela reappeared.

"She wants to know if you want to be in the bathroom when she takes the test."

"God, no. You stay with her." Danny handed her the box.

Angela felt terrible. Shane would kill her if he ever found out.
"Danny, look…" Angela started.
Pamela appeared at the bathroom door.
"Ready, Angela?"
It was a good five minutes before they came out of the bathroom. Angela looked like she was about to cry but Pamela looked triumphant.
"There you go. This is the test that you brought here. It says here that I am definitely pregnant. We need to talk. Angela would you mind if Danny and I could be alone? We will catch up for dinner soon." Pamela couldn't wait to get rid of the other girl.
Angela went to get her coat.
"Goodnight. See you soon."
Pamela waited until the door closed.
"Look at that Danny. She didn't even congratulate us. Must be jealous. Well, Daddy, what do we do now?"

Outside the apartment, Angela leaned against the wall. She wanted to throw up. Danny Murray was a decent guy and he and Beth looked good together. They looked good together. Pamela was unstable and had spent almost a year in a hospital. Danny was not the first man she had flipped over. Angela had only found out by accident when she had visited her cousin who was a nurse at the hospital. She hoped that Pamela would realise that she could not carry out this deception for too long. Angela should never have told her about Danny buying Hillside Manor. It was the final straw.

"You can't be serious, Danny. You want me to raise a child in this kip while you swan around Hillside Manor with the designer's daughter. I knew that bitch was trouble the minute I saw her. I am carrying your child and a baby needs two parents and a decent house. You will have to do better than that. We will have to make a go of it. I am sure Miss 'My bag got caught on your seat' will find some other fool to latch onto." Pamela was shouting.

"I am not a fool, Pamela and you need to calm down. I'm sure stress is bad for a baby. This child will have two parents, just not in the same house. My parents haven't lived together for years and Kathryn and I turned out alright. We will make it work. I will find you another place to live. I need to think about this. I am going for a drink in the hotel."

"Typical man. You want to leave me here sipping water while you waste our child's inheritance on alcohol." Pamela sank down on the couch.

"Don't be so melodramatic. I will talk to you in a few days. Goodnight, Pamela."

"No kiss then. You could stay here tonight. I have lots of drink here. I can't drink it, so you might as well."

"No, thanks. I need to be alone. I'll be in touch."

Pamela waited twenty minutes before pouring herself a very large gin and tonic. She had almost lost it and she needed to keep him onside. She would have to make a proper plan. She intended to break up Danny and that woman. Information was the key. She knew that there was another connection between the Murray family and Clodagh Kenny. She had a secret weapon to help her in her search. Kate Cashman's next door neighbour. Gertie knew everything about the Murrays. Pamela would pay her a visit early next morning. Twenty cigarettes and a bottle of vodka should get her all the information that she needed. She also needed to deal with Angela, who could ruin everything. She would sleep on it. She had an early start the next morning.

Kate

Kate pulled in as close as she could to the ditch to let the other car pass. She didn't want to scratch the car that she was driving since it was on loan from the garage while her own one was being serviced. The other car was going way too fast. She noted that the driver was a young girl. The only other house on the lane was Gertie's. She didn't receive many visitors. Kate felt guilty that she hadn't seen her neighbour in a few days. She would pick up some nice wool and go over later. After all, since Kate was on her way to Brandon Lodge to meet Clodagh Kenny, she would have no problem sourcing wool!

Pamela

Pamela parked her car, got out and hammered on the door.

"Jesus child, you trying to raise the dead? I know I'm old but I'm not quite a corpse yet. Come on in. It's a damn cold morning. What are you doing here at this hour? You haven't visited in about two years; you could have waited a few more minutes!" Gertie shuffled back into the dark kitchen.

"Can't I call on an old friend without getting the third degree?" Pamela followed the old woman inside.

Gertie gathered her shawl more closely around her shoulders and tucked a stray grey hair into her knitted beanie.

"The tea is on the range. It should be drawn by now. Pull that chair up to the fire and tell me as to what I owe the pleasure of your company, and don't bother sugar coating it. Just spit it out. You didn't drive out here at eight o'clock on a freezing cold December morning just to bring me an early Christmas present, or did you?"

Pamela laughed. "That's what I like about you Gertie, straight to the point. I did bring you something to keep the cold out but it is still in the car. I'm sure you will remind me about it before I leave." Pamela moved the wool and needles from the chair before moving it closer to the range. Gertie poured the tar black tea into two mugs and filled a plate with biscuits from a tin of Afternoon Tea.

"Another early present," she indicated to the tin.

"See, you are not the only visitor I get. Meals on wheels call as well, only more often. Now drink your tea. It will put hair on your chest." Sarcasm always became Gertie.

"Hopefully not. Things are bad enough without that happening." She tasted the brew and almost gagged.

"Jesus Gertie. What is in this? Hair of dog and eye of newt!" She stirred two more spoons of sugar into it. It still tasted awful.

"How are you doing now? No more relapses I hope. You behaving yourself girlie?" Gertie moved closer to Pamela.

"Of course I am. That was a mistake. That Jack totally overreacted. He should not have reported me to the guards. That hospital was horrible. I am never going back to that place." Pamela shuddered.

"I'm glad to hear it. Now, why are you here?"

"I was coming to see you anyway. Mam will call before Christmas. I wanted to ask you something." Pamela grimaced as she sipped the tea.

"Ah, I see. So would you tell me or I will be dead by the time you get to the point?" Gertie picked up her knitting.

"I want you to tell me all about Kate Cashman, James Murray and Clodagh Kenny."

"Why would you want to know that for? I heard that you and young Danny were dating, or whatever you young ones call it these days. I had hoped that it wasn't true."

"Thanks for the vote of confidence. I told you, I am cured. I love him and he loves me. I just need to know a bit about them, before I join the family," Pamela said.

"Sorry girlie. You have had a wasted journey. Kate Cashman is my friend and neighbour. Anyway, from what I hear, Danny has found someone else. You should not lie to your old babysitter," Gertie said crossly.

"That is not true, Gertie. Danny loves me, not that bitch." Pamela was practically screaming.

"Calm down now, girlie. I'm sure you are right. Why don't I make us some breakfast? Remember how you loved my sausage and black pudding sandwiches? Then we will talk about things." Gertie knew that she had to play along.

Kate, James & Clodagh

Brandon Lodge was not as Kate had imagined it to be. For starters it was much bigger. The hotel was as impressive as she remembered it. She would have loved to have had time to wander around inside the hotel. The front door was open and she could see the spiral staircase. It brought back memories of the nights spent dancing in the ballroom. It reminded her of James and of how much she had loved him. She had waited for her chance to get him away from Clodagh Kenny. Now she wanted them back together again. Life can be strange.

She took a deep breath and walked through the gateway and followed the signs to Beth's Knits. It didn't appear to be open so she decided to have a coffee. She could see a few people inside the huge window so she knew that it was open for business.

James was nervous. He had finally managed to persuade Clodagh to meet with him. He would have preferred if they were meeting at some other place, but she had insisted on Brandon Lodge. She had changed the venue to the Tearoom. He pulled into the car park.

Clodagh wasn't sure if she was doing the right thing. If Beth was prepared to listen to Danny, then Clodagh could do likewise with James.

When Clodagh arrived, she recognised the car that she had almost crashed into back in March.

"Damn. Ships that pass in the night."

He got out of the car and waited for her to do the same. He hoped that this meeting would break the ice between them. Ann and Gary had been told that Clodagh and James were having a business meeting. Gill knew the truth and was running the shop by herself.

"Morning!" Clodagh and James spoke together.

Through the Tearoom window, Kate could see that the wool shop was being unlocked by an attractive woman with beautiful blonde hair who was not Clodagh Kenny. Kate had presumed that she would be there herself. It had taken a lot of courage, as well as persuasion from Pat, to get Kate to this point. She wasn't sure if she could do it again on another day.

She still had to meet James and try to tell him how sorry she was for reading his letter. She didn't know if she would be able to admit to making a copy of it. He might never speak to her again. Still, one bridge at a time. Today it was Clodagh that she had to see.

"Fancy a top up?" Ann waved the coffee pot.

"No, thank you. I was wondering if Ms Kenny will be here today. I just saw another lady opening the shop."

"That was Gill. She is the manager. Clodagh will be in, though she will be out of the shop for a while. She has a meeting through there." Ann pointed towards the alcove.

"I might wander into the shop for a while. I need to get some yarn for my neighbour, she is a knitaholic!"

"You have come to the right place then. Ah, here is Clodagh now."

Kate stood up in order to prepare herself to deliver her speech. She was horrified when she saw that James was there as well.

Clodagh stopped dead and looked from Kate to James.

"Is this some kind of set up?"

"I'm sorry." Kate picked up her gloves that she had placed on the table. "I wanted to speak to you but I didn't know that James was going to be here. I would like a few moments of your time. Please?"

Clodagh looked at the other woman and sensed that she needed to have this conversation.

"We can use the office in the hotel itself. Maybe Gary would show you the way. I need to speak to James for a few minutes. I will be there as soon as I can." Clodagh attempted to smile.

James still hadn't spoken. As Kate followed Gary out, she stopped and touched James on the arm. "I would like to speak to you as well. Hopefully you will give me the chance," she whispered.

"I don't know if I can, Kate. Why are you here? Haven't you done enough to me?" He walked away from her and sat at the table that she had just vacated.

Ann had watched this exchange with interest. She knew that Clodagh was worried about Beth and that the whole thing was connected to James Murray and his family. She hoped that everything would be okay. She would slip out and tell Gill what was going on, just in case Clodagh needed some extra support.

Gill was piling yarn into baskets when Ann walked in.

"Hi Ann, you okay? You look very serious."

"Clodagh had a visitor this morning, a woman called Kate. She waited in the Tearoom for her. When Clodagh arrived she was not alone."

"James Murray was with her," Gill finished.

"Yeah. Now she and James are talking in the alcove and this Kate woman is waiting for her in the hotel. Gary took her over there. I hope everything will be alright. I'm a bit worried about her, she had been so down lately," Ann said.

"Hopefully. There is nothing we can do for the moment. She knows where we are. Thanks for telling me," Gill said

"No problem. I have made the sandwiches for the knitting group. Just shout when you need them."

"Will do. Thanks." Gill resumed sorting the baskets. She hoped that this woman was not going to complicate things further. If her name was Kate, then she was probably Danny's mother.

"I swear Clodagh, I have no idea why Kate is here. I haven't spoken to her since the night in the hotel. She did something that I find hard to forgive her for," he paused.

"What did she do?"

"She read the letter that I had written to you, the one that you didn't answer." He watched for a reaction.

"I see. Look, maybe this is not such a good idea. With everything that is going on between Danny and Beth and now Kate showing up here. It is all too weird. I must go and see what she has to say. I don't know what will happen then." Her voice shook.

"I will be around for a while. I have to see Eamonn," he said hopefully.

Clodagh shrugged and walked past him.

Gary was showing Kate around the hotel while they waited for Clodagh.

"This is going to be a restaurant. It was the original kitchen for the hotel. Ann is very excited. David McGovern has appointed her as chief designer." He heard footsteps on the stairs above their heads.

"That will be Clodagh." He led Kate up to the office. Clodagh was already standing by the window.

"Thanks, Gary. I'm sorry if I kept you."

"That's okay, Clodagh. Anytime. Nice meeting you Kate." He left two very nervous women together.

"Why are you here? You never told me who you were when we met in April. Don't get me wrong, I'm very grateful to you, but you should have said," Clodagh blurted out.

"I know. I'm sorry about that. I wasn't sure that it was you until we got back to the hotel. Beth was very upset and I just wanted to get her back safely. After all it could have been my own daughter lost in an unfamiliar place and I would hope that someone would have helped her. I am not here to cause trouble for you or your family. Do you mind if I sit down?"

"Oh God, I'm sorry. Please do. I am finding all this very strange. Perhaps I should sit down as well." Clodagh moved from beside the window and sat opposite Kate.

Kate cleared her throat and continued.

"I came here today for two reasons. The first is to tell you how sorry I am for all the trouble and heartache that I caused you and James. I know what I did was wrong. James loved you and only you. I set out to get him and I lied to him. He was, and still is, a very nice man. He spent so many years alone. For some reason your paths have crossed again. Please give him a chance. Listen to him. I cannot give you back the years together that I stole from you but maybe you could still have lots of time together." She twisted her gloves.

"I don't think that is a good idea. Too much water and all that. What is the second reason that brings you here?" Clodagh asked.

"It's about Danny and your daughter Beth. As you know they met back in April, on the same weekend that you and I met. Danny couldn't stop talking about her. I knew from his description that she was the same girl that I had met in the park. We had quite a chat and I discovered that she was around the same age as Danny. When he mentioned her I was horrified. You see I thought that James might have been her father. You had gone to London…" She looked at Clodagh.

"I know. Beth told me that you had explained that to Danny. I suppose it was easy to think that. I started raising Beth when she was barely three so she has always called me Mom. Elizabeth, her mother encouraged it. She always told Beth that she had a mammy, a Mom and a nana Lizzie. I have always considered her to be my daughter." Clodagh stood up, took a tray from the antique sideboard and placed in on the table. She opened a bottle of still water and filled two glasses.

"Thanks." Kate picked up the glass and sipped the chilled water.

"I know how you felt when you discovered that Danny and Beth were a couple. I felt the same way. I had just about accepted it until this pregnancy came to light. It was just too close to the bone," Clodagh paused.

"I understand. Danny thinks that Pamela is making up the whole thing. Even if she isn't, times have changed. Danny and Beth can still be together," Kate stood up.

"That will have to be their decision. As I am sure you know, Beth is in London. She will be home in a few days. We will just have to wait and see what happens. I do appreciate the courage it took for you to come here today. Thank you for that," Clodagh smiled.

"I changed the path of lives and I had no right to do that. I had a lot going on in my life back then. I've been holding grudges for so long that they became part of me. Pat has been standing on the side-lines waiting for me to notice him. Years have been wasted all round so I hope that things work out for everyone.

Give James a chance. He is one of life's good people." Kate was just about to leave when Clodagh spoke.

"You shouldn't be so hard on yourself. No lives have been ruined here. The paths may have changed but we all have lots to be grateful for. Hopefully our children will have better luck. Best of luck to you and Pat. He sounds like a wise man."

"Goodbye, Clodagh. I had better face the music with James. I should never have read that bloody letter. It was meant for your eyes only."

"Wait! What did it... No, forget it." Clodagh said.

"You never read it, did you?" Kate was shocked.

"No. I often wondered if I should have. It's too late now anyway."

"It's never too late. I did something unforgivable, not only did I read it but I copied it. I was going to return it to James." She took the envelope from her bag and placed it on the table.

"Good luck, Clodagh." She closed the door quietly behind her.

James was wandering aimlessly around the complex. This day wasn't turning out as planned. Why the hell was Kate here? What could they possibly have to talk about? He had only just found out about their meeting in April. He might as well go back to the Tearoom and wait for Kate. He wasn't going to get any work done anyway.

"Can I get you something with that?" Ann placed the coffee in front of James.

"I'll have the biggest slice of apple tart that you have please. I need the sugar rush."

"Ah, living dangerously I see. I'll be right back."

As he walked to his car, James wondered about Danny. He had just received a phone call from his son. It looked like Pamela was pregnant after all. She was not going to make things easy for Danny and Beth. He was just about to get into his car when he spotted Kate coming out of the wool shop. She was carrying two large bags bearing the shop logo. There was no sign of Clodagh.

Kate walked towards him. She could still see how attractive and sexy he was. He had this Elvis vibe. As she got closer to him she noticed that he looked troubled.

"Kate, I have just had a call from Danny. It appears that we are about to become grandparents after all. I have told him that I will meet him today. He is a bit shell-shocked."

"I will ring him later. You and he can chat first. It will work out. James, I am so sorry about everything." Kate touched his arm.

"We will talk about it some other time. I must get going. See you soon." He hugged her.

Clodagh watched this exchange from the hotel window. Her phone rang.

"Hi Beth, are you okay?"

"Danny just rang me. Pamela is pregnant. She took a test the other night. He was in the apartment at the time so there is no way that she could have faked it. I don't know what to do. If I stay here, then they might have a chance. I'd hate to think that an innocent child might suffer. What do you think?" Beth sounded unsure.

"I can't answer that Beth. You need to talk to Danny. Decide together. I hope it works out, pet. I'll be here if you need me, or I can go over there if you want." Clodagh's heart was breaking. She didn't want Beth to suffer as she had years ago.

"Thanks, Mom. I will ring again later." Beth hung up.

Clodagh wrapped her shawl around her shoulders and sat on the wishing chair. She held the envelope in her hand. It had been a bizarre morning.

"You okay, Clodagh?" Gill came and sat beside her.

Clodagh shrugged her shoulders. Eventually she spoke.

"You know Gill, life is sometimes a bitch. When you think that things were looking up, it all blows up in your face again. Beth is about to suffer the same fate that I did and there is nothing I can do about it. I wish that I had never come back here. If I had stayed in London, then none of this would have happened. Beth would not have met Danny Murray and my past would not be staring me in the face." Clodagh squashed the paper between her fingers.

"Do you want to talk about it? I can leave you alone if you prefer. I'm so glad that you did come here. You and Beth have changed my life for the better and I would hate to lose our friendship now." Gill put her arms around Clodagh and hugged her.

"I would hate that too. As you know, Kate Cashman turned up here this morning. She wanted to tell me how sorry she was for her part in the break up between me and James. She wants me to give him another chance. You know how I told you about the letter that James gave to my mother, well here it is." She passed the envelope to Gill.

"But how?" Gill asked.

"Kate made a copy. Now I am again faced with the choice of reading it or not!" Clodagh said.

"What will you do?" Gill asked her.

"I don't know. Last time I decided not to. What if that was the right thing to do? Maybe I should read it. God, I don't know."

"You don't have to make up your mind right now. Sleep on it."

"I know. Thanks, Gill. I just wish that I could make things right for Beth." She looked at her friend.

"Look Clodagh, you can't stop the world and get off when things go wrong. Joe and I wanted to when we lost our beautiful little boy, but you have to keep on going. Beth will have to deal with her setbacks herself. That's life. As tough as it sounds, that's how it works. You can sit here and wish as much as you like but it won't change anything. You have to play the cards that you have been dealt. You need to believe that you have equipped Beth with the tools to deal with whatever life doles out. Give yourself a break. Beth is a sensible girl and Danny seems like a nice lad. Trust in them to sort this out. Come on back in now. It is beginning to snow." Gill stood up.

"Thanks, Gill. I will be there in a minute." Clodagh picked up the envelope and removed the letter. She rubbed the wishing chair for inspiration.

"What's meant for you won't pass you by."

She turned around suddenly. There was nobody there.

She smiled. Maybe there was magic in the seat after all!

"Thanks, Aunt Lizzie. I'm on it. The 'shiver' to the rescue again." She unfolded the pages and began to read.

Dear Clodagh,

Remember the time I bought you that enormous box of lavender stuff for Valentine's Day? I suppose you are wondering why I am mentioning that now. Well, it makes me think of how you always wanted letters to pass on to our children and you said that the box that stuff came in would be the perfect place to keep the letters. (I suspect that the contents of the box got a more timely death.) You were going to tie the letters up in a red ribbon and keep them safe. Every year, as we grew older and happier together, we would read them and congratulate ourselves on how our love and marriage survived.

I used to laugh and say that I would rather walk barefoot over hot coals before I put my feelings down on paper. You would have me so you wouldn't need letters. I promised you that I would simply tell our family how much I loved you.

I do love you and I will always love you but I have destroyed everything. I slept with someone else. I should have been strong enough to resist the temptation. I am not going to blame anyone else. It was down to me.

When Kate Cashman told me that she was pregnant, my first reaction was to run as far away as I could with you. I soon realised that you would never allow such a thing to happen. You would have told me to face up to my responsibilities. It broke my heart to see the look on your face the night that I told you. You looked so broken and I did that to you. I am so sorry about everything. If I had one wish, it would be to have the power to turn back time and to take away the pain that I caused.

When you left for London, I wished you all the luck in the world, what else could I do? I wanted to run after you. I was at the airport the day you left. Claire felt that I should try and stop you from leaving. I wanted to, I really

Chips in a Bag, Classy Mr Murray

did. I was torn between my heart and my head. I wanted to drink myself into a stupor but the last time that I had done that it had cost me my future.

When I left the airport I vowed to make all this right someday. I would be a good father to my child, but I could not marry Kate I didn't love her and marrying would only complicate things further. I suppose, deep down, I felt that if I was still single, I somehow had a chance with you.

Kate wasn't expecting me to come back to her that day. She had just left her father who was spitting fire and demanding a wedding. Apparently, he was even prepared to produce the shotgun and chase me up the aisle. I told her that I could not marry her but she begged me not to leave her to face her father as a single mother. We went away for a short holiday and came back 'married.' It satisfied her old man and shut the gossips up. I was pleased for Kate. She is a lovely person, just not my love. When I met you, I gave you my heart and you will always have it. A few weeks after we came back, Kate's father died and she moved into the farm house. I stayed in the apartment. I knew nothing about farming and she had Pat, the farm manager, to help her.

A few days ago Kate came to my office. She was very upset. She told me that she thought that she had always loved me but that she had deliberately set out to trap me (her words not mine). She had convinced herself that she was pregnant and the man didn't want to know. She discovered that she was not about a week after we had first slept together. She liked what we had so she kept it to herself.

She said that I now had a way out of the fiasco of our pretend marriage. I could go and find you and make everything right. I wanted to but there was still a baby to consider. I wanted to be part of my child's life but I wanted you as well.

I went to see your mother, though I wasn't sure of what type of reception I would get. Thankfully your neighbour was pretending to clean her windows (in the rain) so I got invited in. She refused to give me your address, but agreed to send this on to you. She was a bit surprised when I asked her for the lavender box that was on the sideboard. As it was empty, she gave it to me. She asked what I wanted it for. I told her that I wanted to keep it for memories. I think she thought that I had lost all reason! She could be right!

I know that this is not the type of letter that you had envisaged for the box so I am going to put something into it every year until we get together *again. We will be together again. I gave you my heart and someday I will come and claim it back. Hopefully you will give me yours along with it. I would give anything to have you in my life. You are my life. All my love. James*

Chapter Twenty

Beth

David was upset. He and Mike had gone to the house to check up on Beth and had found her crying.

"You are like a daughter to me, Beth, and this is all my fault," he said. "I should never have bought that place. If we had all stayed in London, then none of this would have happened. Maybe I could buy James Murray out of this contract."

He paced the floor, whirled around and grabbed the startled Beth in a bear hug.

"Oh my poor darling. I'm so very sorry. His son is treating you just as he treated Clodagh. I promised her that I would always be there for you and I have failed you both. Not to mind what Lizzie would say if she were still alive! She will probably appear in my bedroom tonight and beat me with her walking stick."

Beth struggled to free herself.

"It is not that bad. You can let me go now." She spoke through a mouthful of crombie.

"I am so sorry." He released his grip and collapsed into an armchair. Mike handed him a large brandy which he downed in one go.

"Good Lord, man. Calm down. This is not about you. Let the poor girl speak. Getting rid of James Murray and his family will not change anything. We must look to the future." Mike held up his hand to still any more rants from David.

"He is right you know. Leave the contract alone. That company is doing a good job. I still hope that Mom and James will get back together again. I like him. I rang Mom today and told her that I would be home in a few days. I will talk to Danny. I was upset because Pamela is pregnant and I had hoped that she was making it up. Danny thought so as well. I don't know what I will do. I keep thinking that maybe, if I wasn't in the picture, then Danny and Pamela would be able to make a go of things. The baby would have a proper family. I didn't know my father and sometimes I miss that," Beth sighed.

"You are in the picture. Danny can't just wipe you away. Go and talk to him, and to Clodagh. You can come back here and manage the boutiques any time you like but be sure that it is what you really want," Mike told her.

"Thanks, Mike. I am really glad that you are here. I can always rely on you to give sensible advice." Beth hugged him.

"Well someone must be the voice of reason here!" He indicated David who was fanning himself with a tea towel.

"I wouldn't change anything about him. He is perfect just as he is, and so are you." Beth hugged him.

"I have a meeting at three so I will leave you two alone for a while. I will pick you up at seven for dinner. Do you want me to book your flight home?" Mike turned to Beth.

"Thanks, Mike. That would be great."

"See you both later." Mike closed the door quietly behind him.

"David, will you tell me about my mother? I remember some things about her, especially when she had no hair. She used to wear these lovely colourful knitted scarves. At night when she used to take it off, she would put it in that lovely wooden box that she had brought over from Ireland with her. Then she would sit me on the side of the bed and ask me to choose the scarf that she would wear the next day.

'What colour of the rainbow will we be tomorrow?'

I would choose the scarf and she would pick my clothes to match. I often wondered where those scarves went to or even where they came from." Beth said.

"Clodagh made them all. My mother used to take her to the wool shop and they would get the most beautiful yarns. I didn't know anything about knitting at the time but certain types of yarns had irritated your mother's skin, so they had to be careful about what they bought. She kept them all for you. She knew that you might need to see them someday. She said that I would know when to give you that box that you mentioned. It has more than just the scarves in it. She was a very wise young woman. She left us much too soon. I will get the box for you if you want me to." David stood up.

"Thank you. I would like that."

The box was just as she had remembered it down to the broken hinge. It stood on the kitchen table where she had placed it and she had been looking at it now for thirty-nine minutes. David had suddenly discovered that he had to be somewhere else and she was alone in the dark room. The only light came from the street lights and the passing cars. Her phone beeped. It was a message from Danny.

The house seemed to echo with voices from the past, but they comforted rather than frightened her. She made two decisions simultaneously. She typed a message to Danny. *Will talk tomorrow, promise x*

She opened the box.

The colours almost jumped from the box. She was transported back in time. She picked up the purple scarf and held it to her face. It smelled of her mother and Beth was a child again, warm and loved. She knew what she had to do. Her tears soaked her mother's scarf.

Danny
Danny had four missed calls from a private number. They were probably all from the same person but why would that person not leave a voicemail. He had a separate phone line for work related calls so whoever had tried to contact him had access to his personal number. It had to be someone that knew him. He had left his phone on the hall table at lunchtime. The message from Beth cheered him up so he put the missed calls to the back of his mind.

Angela
Angela was torn between her fear of Pamela and her need to put things right. She had blocked her number in case Pamela might

answer the phone. She knew that Pamela would not be a happy bunny if she knew what Angela intended to do. Indeed, a bunny-boiler would be more Pamela's style as her last boyfriend had found out. Angela's aunt had assured her that the stay in the hospital had sorted Pamela out. Angela was not convinced, but her aunt had always been good to her so she had agreed to help Pamela make new friends. Unfortunately, Angela had introduced Pamela into her circle of friends and to Danny Murray. He was really Shane's friend and when she had confessed her part in Pamela's deception to him, he had gone ballistic.

"I don't believe that you could be so evil. I wanted nothing more than to have a baby with you and marry you but this is a side of you that I do not like. You have twenty-four hours to make this right. Ring me when you have done it. Just think how you would feel if someone did that to me. That shrew is totally unhinged. I don't know why you would do such a thing!" He had slammed the door on his way out.

Tomorrow she would go and see Danny. She would explain and apologise. Hopefully Shane would forgive her or she would be facing life as a single mother.

Kate

It was about five o'clock when Kate arrived back in Killarney. She decided to visit Gertie. She had picked up some lovely yarn and a pattern for a vintage inspired shawl. It would be perfect for her wedding to Pat. Gertie had been knitting for Kate and for her children for as long as Kate could remember. She had also bought yarn for Gertie herself. She was surprised to see the car that passed her that morning parked in the driveway.

She knocked on the door but when she didn't get an answer, she let herself in with the key that she had. She held her phone in her hand.

"Gertie. Are you here?" she called out.

She walked along the hall that led to the kitchen. The door was ajar and the lights on. She pushed the door and looked inside.

She could see Gertie on the chair. She tightened her grip on the phone and prayed hard.

"Gertie? Are you alright?" To her relief the older woman stirred.

"Thank God!"

"Oh hi Kate. What are you thanking Him for?"

"You didn't answer my knock so I thought something had happened to you. You feeling okay?" Kate noticed the almost empty gin bottle on the table.

"Yes, I am fine. I had a visitor today. We indulged in a little Christmas spirits!" Gertie rubbed her throbbing head.

"Is your guest still here? I noticed the car outside." Kate put on the kettle and popped some bread in the toaster.

"No, she went home by taxi hours ago. How are things with you? Any date set yet?" Gertie went to the cupboard and took out some painkillers.

"Not yet. You will be the first to know. Nothing will be done until the New Year. Danny is in a bit of a fix with his love life. I need to sort that out first."

"What is wrong with him? That boy was always too soft for his own good. He wouldn't hurt a fly."

"He thinks that he has met the girl that he wants to spend the rest of his life with." Kate buttered the toast and poured the tea.

"Surely that is a good thing." Gertie sipped the tea and hope that her head would stop pounding.

"It should be, but he was involved with this other girl, Pamela. She says that she is pregnant. Danny was convinced that she was lying but she did a test while he was in the apartment. It's so complicated, my brain is fried trying to process it, so let's change the subject. On a lighter note, I got you some new yarn today. I also got a lovely pattern for a vintage shawl that I am hoping you will make for me for the wedding. I will leave the bag here and you can look at the stuff tomorrow." Kate could see that Gertie was feeling unwell.

"Thanks, Kate. I think I need an early night. I will walk over to your place tomorrow. Thanks for the tea and toast."

Kate locked the door behind her. As she climbed into her car she could not shake the feeling that Gertie couldn't wait to be rid of her.

Gertie

After Kate's car had pulled out of the driveway, Gertie poured the last of the tea and sat by the dying fire. She tried to process what she had just been told. Danny Murray was a good lad, he had always been kind and helpful to Gertie and she didn't want to see him wronged. Pamela was not pregnant.

After she had calmed Pamela down with the food, she had listened to the girl describe how she and Danny were going to get married and live in Hillside Manor. They were meant to be together, and she would see to it that they were married as soon as possible. She had even asked Gertie to make her a wrap as it would be a Christmas wedding.

"God, girlie. What's the rush? Your mother likes nothing better than to throw a big party. She won't be happy if her only daughter rushes up the aisle! Are you pregnant? Is that why you can't wait a while longer? There is an old proverb that says marry in haste, repent at leisure. You don't want that to happen to you."

"I have my reasons. I need to make an honest man of him before things change." Pamela could not meet the old woman's eyes.

"You are up to something, Pamela. Remember, I know you better than anyone else. I reared you and I know when you are not being truthful. Please don't hurt anyone again. If you and Danny are meant to be together, then you will be. If not…"

"Don't say that, Gertie. We will be together and that bitch will not spoil it for me. There will be no need for me to hurt anyone." She eyed the poker by the fire. Gertie noticed.

"Well then, girlie, let's celebrate your good news. Would you like a nip of gin? It is a cold morning and it will warm us. Just the one."

"Yes, that is a very good idea. We can drink to my future with Danny and to long life for all of us."

"I'll just throw a few sods on the fire and give it a poke." Gertie picked up the turf bucket and emptied it into the fire. After she had used the poker she put it outside in the scullery.

"Here you go, Pamela, health and happiness to you both." Gertie sipped her drink which was heavy on the tonic and light on the gin. She handed Pamela a glass three quarters full of gin. She felt mean trying to get the girl drunk but she needed to get the real story and alcohol was a great tongue loosener.

"Thanks, Gertie. This is a bit strong, almost as strong as the tea." Pamela sipped it slowly.

"It isn't every day that a child I helped to raise gets engaged. I like everything strong. You can take your time with it. I will do us a nice stew for lunch. That will coat your insides and you will be grand. Cheers."

A few hours later Gertie was putting the finishing touches to the dinner in the kitchen, while Pamela enjoyed her third large gin and listened to music in the front room.

Gertie shook herself and picked up the bag of yarn that Kate had left for her. She felt guilty about the way that she had acted with Kate earlier. She had practically pushed her friend out the door but she had needed time to decide how best to sort this out. Pamela had eventually come clean but Gertie knew that she had to tread carefully. She would have to visit Pamela's mother in the morning and then see Kate later in the evening. Hopefully Pamela would be back in the care of her therapist before long and Danny would be able to get on with his life.

Kate

After Kate left Gertie, she drove back into Killarney. She had asked James to meet her in his office. They were going to talk properly before Danny would join them. He was already there when she arrived. His expression had not softened much since morning. She straightened her shoulders and plastered a smile on her face.

"I am so sorry, James. I know that you are very angry with me and I don't blame you. I should never have read it, but I did and there is no changing that fact. I always hoped that someone would love me that much, and now someone does. Now you need to go and get the woman you still love." Kate held her breath.

"I am glad you think so. Pity Clodagh didn't feel the same way about it. She never replied so I would be wasting my time. I don't blame her really. Anyway, we have more important matters to discuss, Danny," James sighed.

"She never read the letter."

"What do you mean? How would you know that?" James asked.

"She told me today, though I think she may have read it by now," Kate almost whispered.

"It's been a long week Kate, so please explain that." James looked exhausted.

"You better sit down. I didn't just read your letter, I made a copy. I felt so guilty about how I had lied to you and I wanted to remind myself that you didn't love me. It was a form of self-persecution. I was going to tell you and give it back. I had it in my bag today and when Clodagh said that she never read it, I gave it to her instead."

"Jesus, Kate. I can't believe you did any of this." He was about to say something else when he spotted Danny coming up the steps.

"Hi son," Kate hugged Danny and went to put on the kettle.

"It will take more than tea to sort this one out, Mam." Danny attempted a joke. James still hadn't spoken.

"Well we need to start somewhere." Kate glanced at James.

"Are you sure that she is actually pregnant?" James was clinging to the slim chance that history was not about to repeat itself.

"I mean did you see her take the test?" he continued.

"Of course not. The bathroom was crowded enough with Angela in there as well. Anyway it involves piddling on a stick. That's private stuff," Danny shuddered.

"It's a bit late in the day to be shy." James took the cup that Kate handed him.

"I know this is a mess. I will be a good father to this baby, but Pamela wants the whole nine yards, big wedding and happy ever after. She says that it is all or nothing. She is threatening to have an abortion. I don't want that to happen but I love Beth. I don't want to live a lie."

Kate and James exchanged a look that spoke volumes.

"Look Danny, you need to give Pamela time to digest all of this. Hopefully she will come around. Having a baby is scary. What about Beth? Is she back from London yet?" Kate asked.

"She will be back tomorrow. Thankfully she is going to meet me in the Airport Hotel in Cork. I hope we can sort this out. It has been a shock for her as well. The whole thing is such a mess. What if she decides to finish with me?" Danny was worried.

"It will all work out," Kate assured him.

Beth

Beth felt better after a good night's sleep. She had woken up surrounded by the contents of her mother's treasure box. The previous evening, she had spent over an hour going through the things that she had found inside the box.

Her mother had been a very smart woman. The notes that she had left gave Beth hope. She had replaced everything in the chest, except for one sheet of paper which she had put in her handbag.

David and Mike had returned to a much happier young woman. They had gone to dinner and had spent a very pleasant evening together. They had returned to Aunt Lizzie's house. David and Mike had stayed over and gone to bed. Beth had taken the treasure box to her room and had spent ages going through it before falling asleep.

Pamela

Pamela was in the horrors. She could barely remember coming home and had slept fully clothed. That was not a good sign. She tried to remember what she had told Gertie but her head was full of cotton wool. Everything was muffled and painful. Bringing that bottle of gin was a bad idea. Pamela had wanted to make

Gertie drunk enough to spill her guts, but the old wagon had outsmarted her. That was a mistake that Pamela would have to fix. Another visit was called for.

Gertie may have been Pamela's childminder since she was two but she was also very close to Kate Cashman. They were neighbours and good friends. If Gertie had managed to get the whole story from Pamela, then she would know that the pregnancy story was a lie. If she passed this on to Kate, then Pamela would be history in Danny's life and that bitch with the English accent would have won. As well as that Gertie knew all about Pamela's past. She was a loose cannon.

Angela was also a problem. She was turning out to be such a Virgin Mary. This whole thing would have to be sorted as soon as possible. The threat of abortion had been a good move on her part. Danny had been horrified and it would be a get out of jail card for her if she needed one.

Gill

Gill was tired. She had stayed up late trying to get the bears finished for the fundraiser. Her earlier conversation with Clodagh played on her mind.

Beth was in love with Danny Murray but didn't know if she could stay with him and Clodagh was still in love with his father and felt that she could not see him again.

"You okay, love? You seem miles away. You should go to bed. You have made plenty of money already. Matt loves his bear. He keeps it on his desk. I'm not sure what kind of message that will send to his clients!" Joe smiled and put his arms around her.

She promptly burst into tears.

Joe held her tightly and let her cry. Eventually she stopped.

"Want to talk about it?" He asked gently. He handed her his hankie.

"Don't worry. It's a clean one! Now, blow. You can hold onto that," he added jokingly.

"Thanks, Joe. I was just thinking about the problems that Clodagh and Beth are having. Yet I would give anything to be in

Clodagh's shoes. Having a child to worry about would be a dream come true. Why did it have to happen to us? We would have been good parents. I know it. Maybe if I had changed my diet or rested more."

"We have been through this over and over again. It was not anyone's fault." Joe hugged her tightly.

"Look Gill, you have been working very hard lately. You are not working tomorrow and we are going away for the weekend. Clodagh will be fine. Beth will be home by then and I'm sure that they will sort out their problems."

"Where will we go?" she asked.

"Mystery tour. Now go to bed and get some sleep. I will lock up."

After Gill had gone upstairs, Joe rang Matt.

"I need a favour."

Danny & Beth
Danny waited for Beth to get in touch. He wanted to ring her but he felt that needed to let her set the pace. He had plenty to keep his mind occupied. He had a property viewing in an hour. It was on the edge of town and priced to sell. He gathered all the relevant documents together and put them into his briefcase. His phone pinged.

Flight due in at six. Meet me in hotel lobby at seven.

"Thank you, God."

Just as he was leaving the office he got another message.

Meet me in the morning at eleven. I need to talk to you xxx.

At least he would have a chance to speak to Beth first.

Thankfully the plane took off on time. Beth fastened her seat belt, sat back and closed her eyes. She still was not certain of what she was going to say to Danny. She loved him but maybe she could forget about him. They hadn't been together very long. She could go back to London and make a life there again. She knew the city so well and had loved living there. She had the house and a brand new exciting career was hers for the taking. She had lost count of the number of exclusive boutiques that Mike had opened all over Europe in the past few years. Going through her mother's things had brought back memories of her childhood. Even though she had been well cared for, she often wondered what it would have been like to have both parents in her life. At the age of three, she'd had neither. Beth didn't want to be responsible for something like that happening to some other child. Maybe it would be best if she left Danny and Pamela to work things out between them.

After she had stowed her luggage in her car Beth waited for Danny in the hotel lobby.

Danny had closed the deal on the house and whistled as he drove to Cork. He had packed an overnight bag – just in case.

Gertie
Gertie was on her way to meet Pamela's mother. Hopefully between them they would be able to persuade Pamela to come clean to Danny and maybe to agree to go back to her doctor. Though to be honest she had gotten the impression that Martine would prefer not to have to deal with her daughter's problems anymore.

Pat & Kate
Pat put the tickets into the biggest envelope that he could find. He had Kathryn to thank for helping him to organise the surprise trip to Paris. He needed Kate's passport and so he had enlisted the help of her daughter. His first choice would have been Danny, but that young fellow had enough to deal with already. He hoped that everything would work out for him and that lovely girl that he was in love with.

Chapter Twenty-One

Kate

As soon as Pat had left, Kate rang James and told him about the surprise trip.

"I know this is not a good time to be leaving. Kathryn helped him with the arrangements. The flight is tomorrow morning at six. I will be back on Monday. Do you think Danny will be okay?"

"Well, well. Good old, Pat. I didn't think that he had a romantic bone in his body and here he is organising trips to the love capital of the world. You go and enjoy yourself. Send me a picture from the top of the Eiffel Tower," James told her.

"It is just bad timing with this situation. It's so unfair and I feel so guilty. I should have told Danny back in April that I knew that Beth was the girl he was looking for. If only I had told him then. He would have found her sooner and none of this would have happened. I should stay here and help him. I'm sure Pat won't mind. We can go to Paris anytime. I will ring him now."

"You will do nothing of the sort. I will be here if Danny needs support. He is thirty, not ten and maybe it is time we let him sort out his own problems. Someone else is trying to get through to me. I will be in touch," James hung up.

About half an hour later James rang back.

"All okay, James? Is it Danny or Kathryn?" Kate asked worriedly.

"No. They are fine. I just got a call from Barney's sister. Debbie collapsed today. Angela found her on the floor at lunchtime. She is on her way to Dublin. It is not looking good. I know that you two are friends and I didn't want you hearing it from someone else," he answered.

"Oh God, I am so sorry to hear that. I haven't seen her for a while. I have been meaning to call over. She was completely taken up with Angela's wedding. I hope she will be okay," Kate was shocked.

"I will ring Barney in the morning. I hope that you have a great weekend. You deserve the love of a good man," James told her.

"You are a good man, James, just not mine. Please go and see Clodagh. You deserve happiness too, and I'm going to risk your wrath here, but maybe your wish is about to come true… go and turn back time." Kate hoped that her reference to his letter to Clodagh would be taken in the spirit that she meant it.

"What are we like? You might be right but, as you pointed out, Clodagh never read that letter. Anyway, it is getting late. I will leave you to it. I will check on the house tomorrow. I presume that Pat has sorted out the farm."

"He has. Thanks, James. See you on Monday."

Angela

Angela was inconsolable. She was waiting for Shane to drive her to Dublin. She kept seeing her mother lying on the floor. The ambulance had arrived at the same time as her father. The doctors thought that it might have been a brain haemorrhage but couldn't be sure until all the tests were done. Now they had sent her to Dublin. Oh God, please don't let her die. She didn't even know about the baby. Then it struck her. She had done a terrible thing by lying for Pamela and now God was punishing her by taking her mother. She had to put it right. She saw Shane and burst into tears.

Gertie

Gertie arrived back home around eight in the evening. Her visit to Martine had not gone according to plan. The other woman had changed since Gertie had seen her over two years ago.

"Look Gertie, I am delighted that you are still concerned about Pamela but there is no need. She is happy and in love. She is even talking about getting married. I have spent the past twenty-eight years taking care of her. I have met someone that I could be happy with. I need a break. You know how I spent all my time with her after her Dad died. His suicide really affected her, she was only seven. She never got over finding his body. Doesn't she deserve a little happiness? We all do." Martine pleaded.

"She is living a lie. Danny is not in love with her. She is pretending to be pregnant and I think that she could turn violent again. We can't allow that to happen. Please talk to her. She will listen to you," Gertie begged.

"She won't this time. She really loves this Danny. She said that they would be moving into that beautiful house that he just bought. Please leave her be. I am so tired of not having a life of my own. I am going to sell this place and move to Galway with Charles. I can't do any of that if Pamela is sick again. She didn't mean to hurt anyone, she just lost her temper and picked up the hurley. She was so sorry. She is fine now. You are over-reacting. I will talk to her about the pregnancy thing. That's not right." She promised Gertie.

As Gertie locked up for the night, she knew that Pamela's mother would not keep her promise. She could hardly blame her. She was young when she had married Gertie's cousin and had to bring up Pamela by herself when he took his own life. Martine deserved a break as well. Gertie would just have to sort this one out by herself. First thing in the morning she would call over to see Kate. Danny did not deserve this. He had often trimmed her hedges and cut her grass as well as many other little jobs around the house.

Pamela

Pamela was soaking in the bath in preparation for her meeting with Danny the following morning. She would soon have him all to herself. She had heard from Kathryn Murray's friend, Jane, that the English bitch had hightailed it back to London and was even planning on going to Australia. That was the best news that she had heard all week. All Pamela had to do was ensure that she didn't lose the baby until the coast was clear. If she played her cards right, then she and Danny might even be engaged by then.

She would have to hurry up if she was going to get her Christmas wish. It was now the tenth of December with barely two weeks to Christmas Eve. The deposit that she had put on the diamond solitaire in Browne's Jewellers might not have been such a bad idea. She and Danny would laugh about it later.

Everything was going according to plan. Well almost. She was a bit worried about Angela having an attack of conscience but now that her mother was sick, well it was an ill wind and all that!

Gertie was another matter. Pamela would just have to play that one by ear.

James

James toyed with the idea of ringing Danny to tell him about Barney's wife. Danny didn't know her well but he was very friendly with Barney and he knew Angela as well. James knew that Danny was meeting Beth in Cork so he decided to wait until morning. On impulse he decided to send Clodagh a message. He wanted to ring her but he was afraid that she would hang up on him.

Can we talk?

Beth

Beth wished that she could have a drink but she didn't want to leave her car at the airport overnight. She was going to Brandon Lodge early next morning to speak to Clodagh.

She saw Danny before he saw her. He was so sexy and handsome. How she wanted to spend the rest of her life with him. She almost weakened. He spotted her and waved.

"Hi Beth, I am so glad that you are here." She allowed herself to be hugged.

"Hello Danny, how are things with everyone?" He noticed the serious look in her eyes.

"Do you want to have something to eat or a drink?" he asked.

"Maybe a sandwich and a coffee. We can go into the bar here. It has lots of secluded areas and we will be able to talk." Danny felt cold dread grasp his heart.

"Beth, I am not going to like this conversation, am I?" he asked.

"It is not that simple. Let's find a quiet corner. Please." She touched his arm.

"Can we get a room? We don't have to sleep together but if you are going to break up with me, I would like to hold you close all night long, enough to last a lifetime." She could see tears glisten in his beautiful sad eyes.

She couldn't trust herself to speak, so she just nodded.

While Danny checked in, Beth collected her case from the car. Her heart was breaking but she knew that she had to give him a chance to make a go of it with Pamela, for the baby's sake. She knew that he loved her. That look in his eyes told her that. She almost wished that he would try to get her to change her mind.

Gertie

'Saturday December eleventh, only fourteen more sleeps to Christmas.' The chirpy radio presenter beamed into Gertie's kitchen.

"Glad someone is looking forward to it," Gertie told Harry who was waiting patiently to be let out. He wagged his tail.

After she had unlocked and let the dog out, Gertie bustled around the kitchen and thought about what she had to do that morning. As soon as she had eaten breakfast, she would head across the fields to Kate's place. After that she intended to see Pamela. She owed it to the girl to tell her what she had done. Hopefully she would be able to persuade her that it was all for the best.

James

James woke early and checked his messages. He still hadn't heard from Barney. Hopefully that was a good sign. He would give it another hour and then he would ring Barney's sister. Clodagh had agreed to meet him at two o'clock on Sunday in Brandon Lodge. He still didn't know if she had read that bloody letter or not. Pouring his heart out on paper had probably been a mistake. He thought about those advertisements on the radio. 'Dear thirty-year-old me, that pension was a great idea, but the letter was the misguided action of a bloody idiot. The fact that that self-same idiot had a box with almost thirty more soppy notes in it is beyond comprehension.'

He made a strong coffee and looked out the window where the scene was breath-taking. The hedges glinted with the early morning frost and the bare trees stood to attention. It was so quiet and peaceful, not a creature stirred. It was as near to paradise as someone could get and James had been grateful for the sanctuary it offered him over the years. When he had realised that he and Kate could not live together he had bought this house with its large gardens. It had a spectacular views of the mountains. It was falling down when he first saw it, but he had had plenty of time to fix it up. He had been living in the apartment that Danny now lived in so he was able to do the place up bit by bit. It had taken him almost five years. He had poured all his emotions into the bricks and mortar that made up his home.

The ringing of his phone jolted him back to reality.

"Hello Barney, how is she?" James held his breath.

"Not as bad as they first thought. The MRI scan was clear so they are a bit baffled. They are running a few more tests. She is groggy and not making much sense. Hopefully I will know more by Monday. You know what weekends are like in hospitals. I was talking to Danny. He is going to show a client around for me on Monday. Is the lad okay? He sounded a bit down. Must go James, Angela is calling me. Talk soon." Barney hung up.

James decided to call into town to see if Danny was home. He would ring Kate later and update her and he had to check on the farmhouse before dark.

Gertie

Gertie was surprised to find Kate's place locked up. As far as she could recall Kate had intended to spend Saturday icing the Christmas cakes that she had made. After knocking a few times, she decided to walk around to the barn, maybe Pat could throw some light on Kate's whereabouts. As she rounded the corner she came face to face with a young man that she knew worked as farm relief.

"Hello. What are you doing here?"

"I am looking after the farm. Pat and Kate are gone away for the weekend. They will be back on Monday," he replied.

"Oh, she never mentioned that to me," Gertie told him.

"It was a surprise. Who would have thought that old Uncle Pat would have it in him! Paris, I believe. They left early this morning," he said.

"Oh I see. That's very nice. Sure I will see her when she gets back. I will let you get on with your work. Bye now."

"Bye." Kieran walked away from her.

"I suppose another few days won't make much difference!" Harry wagged his tail in agreement.

Beth

Beth arrived at her Mom's house just before eleven. She had not slept much the previous night. Danny had left the hotel for Killarney without having any breakfast. Beth had left shortly afterwards. There was no more to be said. It was better this way.

Clodagh heard the car pull into the driveway and opened the door. One look told her all she needed to know. She opened her arms.

When they had settled in the kitchen with tea and toast, Beth told Clodagh about her plans.

"Are you sure about this Beth. I really don't want you to go but I did the same thing myself so I am in no position to try and stop you." Clodagh paced the kitchen floor. She turned and looked at the unhappy girl.

"Do you really want to go back to London? Can't you both find some way around this? Things have moved on. Family structures have changed. You obviously love Danny, take your chance with him. I ran away and now I know that there was another way," she pleaded.

Beth shook her head.

"I can't do this to an innocent baby. I didn't say that I would never see him again. I am going to stay away for a few months. Smithfield's have a shop in London. I will work there for three months. Danny and I have agreed to meet on the first anniversary of Brandon Lodge. It gives us both time to decide if we really want to spend our lives together. It's not forever." Beth assured her.

"You are so much stronger than I was back then. I don't regret the way my life turned out but now." Clodagh shrugged.

"You need to speak to James. He is not married and neither are you. Give it a go, Mom. You both deserve the chance to see this through. I will not allow you to use Danny and I as an excuse. You became my mother when I needed one. I am all grown up now. Go and get yourself a life," Beth said.

James

Paddy placed two pints on the counter
"Any news, James? Your family sagas are very interesting these days. You planning on drinking for two tonight? I hear that the lovebirds have taken themselves off to Paris to buy the ring. It's far from French cities that pair were reared. No wonder you are drinking doubles!" Danny's arrival prevented James from replying to Paddy.

James picked up the drinks and indicated to Danny to follow him.

They sat at the very back of the bar.

"We will be able to see him from here. That nosey bastard has enough fodder on our family as it is without giving him anymore," James told his son. "You okay Danny?"

"I won't lie to you, Dad. Beth has decided that we need to spend three months apart. She thinks that it will give both of us the chance to see if we really want to be together. I love her, Dad and I want to spend my life with her but the thought of my child having a life without me is upsetting. I won't lie to you. I am trying not to cry. Imagine what Paddy would make of that." Danny sipped his pint.

Chips in a Bag, Classy Mr Murray

"Look son, things have changed for the best in the past thirty years. Pamela is hurting. Hopefully she will put the needs of the baby before her own wishes. She will come around. After all, that baby will have grandparents that will love him or her. Don't give up on Beth yet." James saw Paddy approach and decide to use the local grapevine to get the latest news.

"Any updates on Debbie? You usually have the latest." James appealed to the other man's vanity. He wasn't disappointed.

"She is a bit better. Not as bad as they first thought. She should be back in Cork in the next few days. Apparently, it had something to do with her medication," Paddy confirmed.

"Thanks, Paddy. This place would be lost if we didn't have you to keep us updated." James almost choked on the words.

"Wonder you didn't know that yourself James, what with you and Barney being so tight! Didn't you and Danny there get a great deal on that mansion out in Hillside? Sure it's big enough to house more than one woman, if you get my drift!" Paddy added maliciously.

"Easy now Paddy, your horns are showing. We will have the same again." James deflected any confrontation as he could feel Danny stiffen beside him.

Danny waited until the barman had retreated.

"He is some prick, Dad. How is he still serving behind the bar? He hasn't the manners of a pig." Danny checked his phone in the vain hope that Beth had been in touch.

"He is part of the furniture. Take no notice of him. He is pissed off because he doesn't know as much as he would like. Here he comes now."

"Thanks Paddy." The other man grunted and placed the drinks on the table.

"Thanks, Dad. I wanted to clock him but he would probably have made a news story about it. Mam texted me earlier. She got some whopper of a ring by all accounts. You okay with that?" Danny asked his Dad.

"I'm fine, son. Your mother deserves a second chance. She has spent her whole life worrying about other people, it's time she put herself first." James sipped his pint.

"What about you and Clodagh? You both need a second chance too. Go for it, Dad." Danny raised his glass.

"Thanks, son."

Clodagh

After tossing and turning for hours Clodagh finally gave up on sleep at five am. She pulled back the duvet and padded across the carpeted floor to the window. It was pitch black outside, and rain lashed the glass.

"At least I can always rely on the weather to sympathise!" She threw on her dressing gown and made her way to the kitchen. A strong coffee was called for.

As she sipped her drink, she pondered on how things had turned out. She thought about the letter that she had read thirty years too late. She wondered if her decisions would have been different if she had known that he and Kate had never married. One phrase kept circling in her head… turning back time. If she could do that right this minute, would she change anything? She knew the answer to that. Her life in London had been great and she had loved every minute of it. The people in her life were all important to her. David and Mike were like parents and brothers all rolled into one. Aunt Lizzie had influenced every business decision that Clodagh had made and had provided the capital to make her dreams come true. She may not have given birth to Beth, but she had become a mother to her after Elizabeth had died. They both had travelled all over the world with David and Mike and all their boutiques stocked her designs. Dates had come and gone. She had enjoyed their company but had never found anyone to live up to James. Yet she had been happy. Her mind cleared and she knew what she was going to tell James.

As she rinsed her cup in the sink, she realised that she had been sitting there for hours. Tiny shards of daylight were piercing the night sky and she realised that the rain had stopped. It might be a good day after all.

As it was still early, she decided that she would visit her parent's grave and then do something that she had not done for years. She would go to mass in the church that she had been frogmarched to every Sunday until she left for London. She was not entirely sure why she was going to do this, the graveyard where her parents were buried was miles in another direction.

As she showered, she wondered what exactly was in the lavender box. When James had presented it to her she had been amazed at the number of items that it contained. Soaps, bath salts, perfume, hand cream, body lotion and God knows how many more products, all smelling the same! Jesus, how she still hated the smell of lavender. She had seen the box taking centre stage in the local chemist's window display and it had not come cheap. The only problem was that The Walton's would have been hard pushed to get through it in a year! The shop assistant had definitely seen him coming.

She pulled in to Brandon Lodge just before two. Thankfully James had not arrived yet. She waved at Eamonn, who was doing a routine security check. Having parked her car, she pulled on her jacket and wound the red scarf around her neck. She walked purposely to her destination. She had sent James a message telling him where to find her.

Clodagh sat on the wishing chair and waited for James. They had made quite a few wishes here when they were younger. It was a different world and another time. They were not those two people anymore.

The sound of a twig breaking startled her from her daydream. James came and sat next to her.

"Thank you for meeting me and I like your scarf by the way. Bit retro though."

"Wow, when did you become an expert on fashion eras?" Clodagh was impressed. She unwound the scarf and stretched it out along both their legs.

"See here. It has a hole in it and it has started to unravel. What does that tell you?" she looked at him.

"Is this some kind of test? Am I supposed to say something deep and meaningful?" he asked.

"No, I just want you to tell me what you think it means." She waited for him to answer.

"Maybe it means that it is only a small hole and that once it is repaired it will be as good as new." He looked at her hopefully.

"But it was made years ago so even if I find some yarn to match, it will still be noticeable because that particular dye lot can never be gotten again. It will be still a red scarf, but not a perfect one." She began to pick at the scarf and it started to unravel more.

"What are you doing, Clodagh? Are you going to destroy it? Are you trying to tell me that you are destroying any chance of us taking up our relationship again?" James dreaded her answer.

"No, that is not what I am saying at all. This scarf was important to me when I made it and it was important to you when you kept it. For some reason Danny felt the need to wear it to Brandon Lodge when he met Beth again. Now it has a hole in it, probably caused by me when I pulled it off him. I am not destroying it. I will use the yarn to remake it into something modern. A new life for the yarn and maybe a new life for us. Wanting to turn back time is futile and I don't think either of us would want to change our lives that much. We need to take the good from the past and make it into something new." She paused and looked at the confused but happy man beside her.

"Are you saying that we can try again?" he asked hopefully.

"Not try again, James. Start again, only not yet."

"What do you mean by that?"

"Beth is going to London for three months and she and Danny are not going to see one another until the first anniversary of Brandon Lodge. I am going with her. Gill is perfectly capable of running the shop here. You and I can take the time to see how we feel about everything. What happens in their lives may impact on ours. I am not saying that if they decide not to see one another again that we should do the same. They are adults and can work things out for themselves. I hope Pamela will come to realise that she can still have her baby with Danny's support."

"Will be get to see one another at all until then?" he asked.

"Well, I have one favour to ask you," she hesitated.

"Will I like it?"

"I want you to send me one of the notes that you put in the lavender box, every week."

"Right. That might not be as informative as you might like," he said sheepishly.

"You mean you didn't write something every year and put it into the box." She pretended to be shocked.

"Actually, I did, but not always a note. Sometimes I put in something that reminded me of you."

"Such as?" she was not going to let him off lightly.

"You will have to wait and see. Where would you like me to send them to?" he searched his pockets looking for a pen to write with.

"I will give you the address before we leave here. Let's make a wish before we go back." She reached out and entwined her fingers in his.

Chapter Twenty-Two

Brandon Lodge

Gertie waited until Tuesday before she braved the cold to visit Kate. Thankfully there was light in the kitchen and she could see Pat further down the field. He waved at her and she waved back. She had heard from Paddy that Danny was drowning his sorrows because the English girl was staying in London. On top of that Pamela's mother had been in touch to say that Pamela was happy, sane and pregnant. She was telling anyone that would listen that Pamela and Danny were moving into Hillside Manor.

"Hi Gertie, come on in. I've the kettle on. It's very cold this morning. You must have smelled the scones. They are piping hot, just right for eating." Kate filled a plate and put out some butter and strawberry jam. Gertie got stuck in immediately.

"I have come to see the ring that the whole town is talking about. Rumour has it that it is the biggest rock ever seen hereabouts. Give me a look. If I make a wish, then Paddy might finally realise just how much he loves me!" she joked.

Kate opened the drawer under the table and passed the ring to Gertie.

"I was afraid that it would end up in the scones so I took it off," she explained.

"It is beautiful, but not as big as people would have us believe. Still you can't believe everything you hear around here. That's kind of why I am really here." Gertie paused while Kate poured the tea.

Kate caught the serious note in her neighbour's voice.

"What is it, Gertie? Spit it out. It's not like you to beat around the bush."

"Okay, I know about Danny and Pamela. I have known that girl all her life and she is not pregnant," she blurted out. "She called to see me because she wanted information on you, James and the designer woman that he used to date. I didn't tell her anything. I can't say too much here but that girl saw something that no child should see and it affected her. She has had a few mental health issues in the past. I plied her with gin and she told me everything."

"What are you telling me, Gertie? Is my son in danger?" Kate stood up.

"No, she loves him. The other girl has left the country so hopefully there is no one in danger."

"I don't understand it. Danny said that she took the test while he was in the apartment. She showed it to him."

"It was the other one who took the test. You know, Barney's daughter. Look where that got her! Her mother nearly died. Flying in the face of God is never a good idea. I'm telling you the truth. I came over to tell you last week but you weren't here. I called to see Pamela's mother but she was no help. I can't blame her but that is no help to young Danny." Gertie sliced into another scone.

"I don't think Beth is in London yet. She is not due to go for another few days. We will have to handle this carefully. James and Danny are gone to Manchester with Conor. They flew out this morning and won't be back until late tonight. Can you find out if Pamela is working today?" Kate began to pace the floor.

"She works in the chemist shop. I will give Maurice a ring."

After she had made the call, Gertie told Kate that Pamela had taken a day's holidays.

"Do you really think that she would hurt someone, Gertie?" Kate asked.

"Well, she did once before. Please don't ask me to tell you anymore," Gertie replied.

"We could be all wrong here but I think we should take a trip ourselves to Brandon Lodge," Kate decided.

"I am ready and waiting," Gertie stood up.

Gill and Ann were discussing Gill's surprise trip to the Christmas markets in Belfast.

"I felt like royalty. A helicopter ride of all things! That Matt has connections everywhere."

Gill recognised Kate immediately.

"You go and warn Clodagh. I'll stall her and her friend." Gill stood just inside the door of the wool shop and pretended to tidy the baskets of yarn. Ann went to the bookshop as she had seen Clodagh go in there a few minutes before.

"Welcome back. You can't have used up all that yarn already," she joked.

"Hello Gill, nice to meet you again. This is my friend Gertie, the knitaholic. I would like to speak to Clodagh if that is possible." She correctly read Gill's expression. "I assure you that I am not here to cause trouble."

Clodagh came out of the bookshop closely followed by Ann and Robert.

"I need to tell you something. It won't take long. Please. It could help Danny and Beth," Kate blurted out.

"I think that they have already decided on their plans. What could possibly change that? It is too late," Clodagh said sadly.

Gertie stepped forward. "Come on, woman. Be sensible. She risked our necks driving here. She only touched the road in patches. Get in there and listen to what she has to say. I'm freezing my bits off out here. There's a grand smell of baking from somewhere." Gertie shivered to prove her point.

"You don't happen to be related to anyone called Lizzie, do you?" Clodagh felt herself smile.

"Who knows? I hear that you are the famous designer that James is so taken with! Famous for your hospitality as well, I hope!"

Seated in the Tearoom, Gertie tucked into more scones and a slice of tart. Clodagh and Kate sat in the alcove. Kate told Clodagh what Gertie had told her.

"Do you think that Pamela will come back here looking for Beth? Is that why you came? To warn her?" Clodagh was sceptical.

"I may have overreacted. I must be watching too much Criminal Minds. It seemed like a good idea at the time." Kate felt stupid.

Chips in a Bag, Classy Mr Murray

"The shop was busy this morning but I didn't see Pamela and Beth is in Dublin today looking at some new designer that Smithfield's is considering. Are you sure that your friend has the right story? I would hate to get Beth's hopes up. She really loves your son. A turn up for the books."

"I know. Who would have guessed? What are we going to do?" Kate asked.

"I don't know. We will have to think about this," Clodagh sighed.

Danny

Danny had a busy day planned so he was not impressed when Pamela rang and asked her to meet him in the station at eight o'clock. She was in Dublin on a shopping spree. She was becoming clingier by the day. He kept hoping that she would see sense and decide to raise the child between them. By four o'clock his head was pounding so his heart sank when he saw his mother and neighbour hurrying up the steps to his office.

"Evening ladies, to what do I owe the pleasure?" he forced a smile.

"Hi son, sorry to barge in on you like this but this is too important to discuss over the phone. I'm not sure that Clodagh took me seriously but Gertie says that Pamela could be a bit dangerous so we went."

"Slow down Mam, you are not making any sense. Pamela is not dangerous. She's just a bit all over the place at the moment. She's pregnant after all." Danny was baffled.

"That's just it, Danny, she's not pregnant. Angela is!"

"For feck sake! Am I supposed to be responsible for that as well? Have you two been hitting the gin?" he laughed.

Gertie caught him by the arm and led him over to the couch.

"Sit and listen. I have something to tell you and I am sorry for waiting so long. The truth is that Pamela was never pregnant. She somehow got Angela to take the test for her. You saw her results. Pamela thinks that she loves you and will do anything to keep you.

That is why your mother and I went to meet Clodagh Kenny this morning," she told him.

"What do you mean when you say that she would do anything? Would she harm Beth?" he asked in disbelief.

"She might. She did harm someone a while back. She can become a bit obsessed with people. We had thought that she might have gone to Brandon Lodge but she wasn't there. Beth is in Dublin, hopefully far enough away from any harm," Gertie reassured him.

"Sweet Jesus! Pamela is in Dublin as well. Surely you don't think that she followed Beth there?" He rang Beth's phone but it went straight to voicemail.

"Ring Pamela and find out where she is now," Kate dialled Clodagh's number.

Pamela answered almost immediately.

"Hi darling, are you missing me?"

"Of course, I am. I was just wondering what time your train is arriving in at? I will meet you at the station. I can't wait to see you," he lied.

"I am on the train now. Should be there around seven. I got some brochures in Arnott's. I can't wait to start decorating our new home. I love you, Danny."

"Love you too. See you soon." He hung up. "She is on the train. Did you get on to Clodagh?" he turned to his mother.

"Yes. She spoke to Beth about half an hour ago. She is in a hotel outside Dublin and is fine. Clodagh did not tell her anything about Pamela. She said that it was your place to sort that one out."

James

James could not believe what Kate had told him. He felt a mixture of anger and relief. If Pamela was not pregnant then Danny and Beth could have their happy ever after. He and Clodagh could explore their relationship with a little less guilt. He had never met Pamela but he could not imagine that she would pose a physical danger to anyone. Hopefully as soon as she realised that she had been rumbled, she would just give up and find someone else to pester.

"You alright, James? You look like you have seen a ghost." Conor came into the hotel room.

"More drama at home. I will fill you in later. We had better be going or we will be late for the meeting." He grabbed his coat.

Danny & Pamela

Danny texted Pamela and told her that his car had broken down and that he could not collect her after all. He arranged to meet her at the Quayside Hotel later.

"Why can't we meet in town? I hate that place," she answered.

"I have to meet some people there. It won't take long," he answered.

"Okay. I will see you there. I love you."

"You too," he lied.

Having arrived early, Danny ordered a pint. Frank, the barman, chatted easily about the weather and the scandals of the day. He told Danny all about his impending hip replacement and his worries about returning to work in the hotel.

When Frank went to serve the only other customer in the bar, Danny spotted Pamela.

"Hi, Danny? Why don't we go back to mine and we can talk about the baby?" She rubbed her stomach.

"I already told you that I was meeting someone here. Ah, here they are," Danny waved.

Pamela stiffened when she saw Shane and Angela walk towards them.

"Shit. I thought that they were still in Dublin."

"What was that, Pamela? Did you say something?" Danny noted the look on her face.

Shane pulled out the stool next to Danny and sat down. Angela lagged behind.

"Evening all. How are you Danny? Have a drink on us. The usual, Pamela? A litre of gin and a pack of lies?"

Shane nodded to the barman. "Two coffees and a pint."

Pamela turned to go.

"Hang on there. You are surely not heading off yet, Pamela. Angela has something that she needs to say to you. Do stay a while." He grabbed her arm.

Angela walked over to Pamela and slapped her across the face.

"You are a complete psycho. You are not pregnant. You never have been. Go back to stirring your cauldron," Angela said – she was shaking.

Pamela was shocked into silence. She picked up her jacket and made to leave.

"Danny, she is lying… you know me…"

"Get lost, Pamela. I never want to see you again."

Three Months Later

David made his way to the microphone.

"Good evening to you all. I would like to welcome you all here tonight to this beautiful hotel. It has been an eventful year but Brandon Lodge Enterprise Park is one year old and thriving. In the twelve months since I last stood here, the lives of many people have changed for the better. Tonight is a time for celebration and a toasting of success. The people responsible for bringing us back together tonight are all here." He looked around the crowded hall.

"Brandon Lodge not only continues to succeed but will grow. I am pleased to announce that the last remaining units have been renovated and leases have been signed. Our little community is about to expand, but more about that later. Waiters are circulating among you with champagne to toast our present success and our success in the future. As soon as you all have a drink, I will propose a toast." He stepped back and waited for a few minutes.

"To Brandon Lodge!"

"I wonder who the other leaseholders are?" Gill turned to Ann.

"I heard that there is a boutique and a chemist. Other than that... What do you think of Clodagh inviting the whole Murray clan here tonight?" Ann pointed to the table by the door.

"I am just glad that she and Beth have come home. It appears that both Danny and James spent quite a few weekends in London. I just hope that everything works out for them. I guess it is a bit strange that Kate, her husband and that neighbour, Gertie are here as well." Gill sipped her drink.

"You are right. It is great to see them back. I don't care if they brought the whole population of county Kerry with them. I missed Clodagh and Beth while they were away," Ann agreed.

"I think that our better halves are speculating again," Gary nudged Joe.

"Nothing new there then!" Joe joked.

Just as coffee was served, David returned to the podium.

"Ladies and gentlemen, I have one more, very pleasant duty to perform here tonight. I am not sure if all of you are aware of the more romantic side of Brandon Lodge."

"What is he on about?" Clodagh whispered to Beth.

"I don't know," she lied.

"I could spend a long time sharing the romantic liaisons that have occurred since last year, but there is a man quaking in his boots, so I am going to put him out of his misery. Please welcome, James Murray." David began to clap.

"What are you doing?" Clodagh asked as James stood up.

James walked to the top of the room and took the microphone from David, who then sat down.

"Ladies and gentlemen, I am not used to making speeches. I am not even a great letter writer, but tonight I am going to step outside of my comfort zone and will, hopefully, impress the one person who means the world to me," James paused.

"Jesus wept, what's going on?" Clodagh looked at Beth.

"A long time ago, in this very hotel, I met a very beautiful girl. At the time, she was not mine to love, but when we finally became a couple, I was over the moon. Unfortunately, things did not go as planned and our paths diverted. I know that she was happy and so was I. Yet there was always a missing link in my life and when I met Clodagh again, my life became complete. A few months ago, Clodagh pointed out that we could never turn back time. She was right. She said that we should take the experiences of the past and make new dreams. Tonight, I am going to do just that." He walked back towards the table.

"Jesus!" Clodagh whispered, watching his approach.

"Shhh, Mom! This is the romantic bit." Beth tightened her grip on Danny's arm.

James reached her table and took her hand. The room held its breath.

"Many years ago, we talked about our dream of spending our lives together. We even chose a ring. It was…"

"…a sapphire surrounded by diamonds," Clodagh finished his sentence.

"Go for it, Dad." Danny handed James a box.

"I hope it is still what you want. It has been waiting a long time, and so have I. Please say yes." He opened the box and the stones glinted in the lights of the chandeliers.

Clodagh looked at James, at the ring and at Beth. In the corner of the room she almost swore that she could see Aunt Lizzie smiling.

"Clodagh, marry me please? I love you so much," he said.

Clodagh stood up. "You took your time, Mr Murray. Yes, I will marry you." The ballroom exploded with applause.

James placed the ring on Clodagh's finger.

"It's cold outside so you will need this," Beth hugged her Mom and placed her shawl around her shoulders.

"Outside?" Clodagh repeated.

James took her by the arm and led her outside. They walked down the steps and Clodagh spotted a chip van. She burst out laughing. "Well, well, chips in a bag. Very classy, Mr Murray."

The End

Chips in a Bag, Classy Mr Murray

Gill's Scarf

Gill's Scarf

Size: 6 x 39 inches / 15 x100 cm.
Materials: 150 grammes of any Dk /Cotton yarn.
1 pair of 4mm. (UK.8) needles.
Cable needle. (cn)
Pompom maker. (Optional)
Brooch. (Optional)

Tension: 24 stitches (sts) and 32 rows (10cm) over stocking stitch using 4mm. needles.
Use larger or smaller needles to obtain correct tension.

Special abbreviations.
C4B. = Slip 2sts onto cn (cable needle) and hold at back of work, Knit 2, then K2 from cn.
C4F= Slip 2 sts onto cn and hold at front of work, K2, then K2 from cn.
Double Seed Stitch worked over 4 rows and over odd number of stitches.
Row 1. (Right side) K1, *(p1, k1). Repeat from * to end.
Row 2. * P1, K1. Repeat from * to end.
Row 3. * P1, K1. Repeat from * to end.
Row 4. * K1, p1. Repeat from * to end.
Repeat rows 1-4 for double seed stitch.
Scarf Pattern.
Cast on 46 stitches.

Row 1.
K1. (P1, k1) until 19 sts. have been worked. (C4b, C4f) K1, (p1, k1) to end.
Row 2.
(P1, k1) until 19 sts. have been worked, purl 8, (P1, k1) to end.
Row 3.
(P1, k1) for 19 sts. K8. (P1, k1) to end.

Row 4.
K1, P1 for 19 sts., p8, (K1, p1) to end.
Repeat rows 1 to 4 until 20 rows have been worked.
Row 21.
Seed st. 11 sts. (C4b, C4f) 3 times, Seed st. 11.
Row 22.
Seed st. 11, P24, Seed st. 11.
Row 23.
Seed st. 11, K24, Seed st. 11.
Row 24.
Seed st. 11, p24, seed st. 11.
Repeat rows 21 to 24 until 20 rows have been worked. (40 rows worked in total)

Row 41.
Seed st 3, (C4b, C4f) 5 times, Seed st. 3.
Row 42.
Seed st 3, p 40, seed st. 3.
Row 43.
Seed st. 3, k 40, seed st. 3.
Row 44.
Sed st. 3, p 40, seed st. 3.
Repeat until 20 rows have worked. (Total rows worked 60)
Row 61 to 80. (Repeat rows 21 to 40.)
Repeat rows 1 to 80 twice more, then rows 1 to 20 once more. Cast off.
Make 8 x 4" pompoms and attach 4 to each end of scarf.
Brooch optional.

Message from the Author

Dear Reader

Thank you so much for purchasing my book. I hope you enjoyed reading it. I would appreciate some feedback. Please leave a review on whatever site you used to buy the book from. Cover design by my son Chris Kelleher who can be contacted at chriskellcsn@gmail.com.

Many thanks,
Margaret.

www.ingramcontent.com/pod-product-compliance
Lightning Source LLC
Chambersburg PA
CBHW021118300426
44113CB00006B/198